The Scramble *for the* Teenage Dollar

The Scramble for the Teenage Dollar

CREATING THE YOUTH MARKET IN MID-CENTURY CANADA

Katharine Rollwagen

UBC Press

© UBC Press 2025

All rights reserved. No part of this publication may be reproduced, stored in a retrieval system, or transmitted, in any form or by any means, without prior written permission of the publisher, or, in Canada, in the case of photocopying or other reprographic copying, a licence from Access Copyright, www.accesscopyright.ca.

Printed in Canada on FSC-certified ancient-forest-free paper (100% post-consumer recycled) that is processed chlorine- and acid-free.

UBC Press is a Benetech Global Certified Accessible™ publisher. The epub version of this book meets stringent accessibility standards, ensuring it is available to people with diverse needs.

Library and Archives Canada Cataloguing in Publication

Title: The scramble for the teenage dollar : creating the youth market in mid-century Canada / Katharine Rollwagen.
Names: Rollwagen, Katharine, author.
Description: Includes bibliographical references and index.
Identifiers: Canadiana (print) 20250127571 | Canadiana (ebook) 20250127660 | ISBN 9780774869881 (hardcover) | ISBN 9780774869911 (EPUB) | ISBN 9780774869904 (PDF)
Subjects: LCSH: Teenage consumers—Canada—History—20th century. | LCSH: Eaton's (Department store)—History—20th century. | LCSH: Consumer behavior—Canada—History—20th century. | LCSH: Consumption (Economics)—Canada—History—20th century. | LCSH: Marketing—Canada—History—20th century.
Classification: LCC HF5415.33.C3 R65 2025 | DDC 339.4/708350971—dc23

UBC Press gratefully acknowledges the financial support for our publishing program of the Government of Canada, the Canada Council for the Arts, and the British Columbia Arts Council.

This book has been published with the help of a grant from the Canadian Federation for the Humanities and Social Sciences, through the Scholarly Book Awards, using funds provided by the Social Sciences and Humanities Research Council of Canada.

UBC Press is situated on the traditional, ancestral, and unceded territory of the xʷməθkʷəy̓əm (Musqueam) people. This land has always been a place of learning for the xʷməθkʷəy̓əm, who have passed on their culture, history, and traditions for millennia, from one generation to the next.

UBC Press
The University of British Columbia

www.ubcpress.ca

Contents

List of Figures vii
Acknowledgments ix

Introduction 3

1. **Calling All Co-eds!**
   The Teenager Appears in Canadian Women's Magazines 23

2. **Act Your Age**
   Authority and the Meanings of Teenage Consumption 52

3. **Students in the Store**
   Making Space for Teenagers at Eaton's 82

4. **Tailored for Teens**
   Selling Age, Gender, and Sophistication 103

5. **Eaton's Goes to School**
   Commodifying Students and Educating Consumers 130

Conclusion 154

Notes 159
Selected Bibliography 189
Image Credits 201
Index 203

Figures

1.1 Kotex advertisement featuring an Irving Nurick drawing, *Chatelaine*, May 1943   24

1.2 Teenaged cover girl on the *Canadian Home Journal* back-to-school issue, September 1946   45

1.3 Window display at the Eaton's Winnipeg store announcing the selection of *Canadian Home Journal* cover girl, 1948   47

2.1 Junior Executive member Don Beauprie with an unidentified female member of the Junior Council in a photo taken for use in an advertisement for Eaton's Montreal store   60

3.1 Members of the Toronto Junior Council watching Rusty Fellows, from the display department of the Eaton's College Street store, adjust a veil as an unnamed fellow councillor models a wedding dress, 1958   87

3.2 The Montreal Junior Executive, 1947   87

3.3 Members of the Junior Executive practising their selling techniques in the Winnipeg store, 1959   89

3.4 Program for a Junior Council Fashion Show, March 1950   92

3.5 Eaton's employee Paul Johnson in the Hi-Spot with American actors Cora Sue Collins and Rosemary Rice, as customers await autographs, 1943   98

3.6 Canadian Cover Girl promotional display in the College Toggery department at Eaton's Queen Street store, 1949   100

4.1 Senior Girls' sizes, with longer skirt lengths than Girls' dresses, Eaton's Fall and Winter 1935–36 Catalogue   112

4.2 "Fashion Keeps Tabs on Teensters" dress style demonstrating the idea of an in-between style, Eaton's Spring and Summer 1941 Catalogue   117

— Figures —

4.3 Teen dresses illustrated in the Eaton's Spring and Summer 1948 Catalogue 127

4.4 Grad suits from the Eaton's Fall and Winter 1948–49 Catalogue 128

5.1 Members of the Montreal Junior Executive selling tickets to the Red Feather Frolic, 1947 136

5.2 A dance at Montreal West High School in full swing, with members of the Eaton's Junior Executive operating the Band Box, 1947 or 1948 137

5.3 Don Beauprie and other members of the Montreal Junior Executive operating the Band Box 137

5.4 Commercial High School principal Mr. F.N. Stephen speaking with Mr. J. Clifford, Eaton's advertising supervisor, at an event organized for school principals at the Toronto store, October 18, 1947 143

Acknowledgments

THINKING ABOUT all the colleagues and friends who helped bring this book into your hands has filled me with gratitude and awe that so many people – besides me – thought it a worthwhile endeavour. Words seem insufficient to express my thanks.

At UBC Press, James MacNevin has been my able champion, with production editor Katrina Petrik providing welcome support and guidance. Camilla Blakeley worked meticulous magic with the manuscript, improving it in so many ways. Many thanks go to the anonymous reviewers who I hope will see some of their thoughtful suggestions in the pages that follow. Any errors remain my own.

I would also like to thank the editorial teams at both *Histoire Sociale/Social History* and *Historical Studies in Education*. Parts of chapters 3 and 5 appeared previously in my article "Eaton's Goes to School: Youth Councils and the Commodification of the Teenaged Consumer at Canada's Largest Department Store, 1940–1960," *Histoire Sociale/Social History* 47, 95 (2014): 683–705. Another part of chapter 5 was previously published in "Classrooms for Consumer Society: Practical Education and Secondary School Reform in Post-Second World War Canada," *Historical Studies in Education* 28, 1 (2016): 32–52. Many thanks to the editors for shepherding these pieces into print the first time and allowing me to revisit and expand on them here.

The development of this book was made possible by the Vancouver Island University Faculty Association's (VIUFA) Assisted Leave program. Thank you to my VIUFA colleagues who served on the leave committee in 2019 and saw merit in my application. The Vancouver Island University Research Activity Committee awarded me a Publish Grant to cover the cost of reproducing images, for which I am grateful. The research for this book was also initially funded by a Canada Graduate Scholarship from

— Acknowledgments —

the Social Sciences and Humanities Research Council of Canada, as well as by the Wilson Institute for Canadian History at McMaster University.

Countless librarians and archivists have contributed to this book, many of them out of my sight. Living in Ottawa for nine years, I was a sometimes-daily occupant of the Library and Archives Canada reading room and made multiple trips to the Archives of Ontario. I want to thank the staff at both institutions for being so helpful and patient. I am especially grateful to Chloe Montpetit at the Archives of Ontario for helping to track down images in the T. Eaton Company fonds. Thanks also to Chris Hebda, for recovering files when I thought all hope was lost.

Some historians are more likely to encounter their material in the flesh than others. I'm so glad that Rod Beauprie got in touch and shared his father's photographs from the Montreal Junior Executive (some of which are included here). Andrée Paradis Dell telephoned me out of the blue one day, and later shared photos from her time as an Eaton's Junior Councillor in Montreal. I hope others will also get in touch!

The best part of working in academia remains, for me, the ever-expanding and enriching network of mentors and colleagues from whom I am always learning. A complete list of the people I've met who shaped my thinking would be long, but I can't miss the opportunity to express my gratitude to Ian MacPherson, Lynne Marks, Chad Gaffield, Timothy Stanley, Corinne Gaudin, Viv Nelles, Mona Gleason, and Marni Stanley for being exceptional mentors.

I am privileged to work at the intersection of histories of consumer culture, childhood and youth, and education, and to learn from exceptional scholars in all three areas. Thanks to the members of the Society for the History of Children and Youth, the Canadian History of Education Association, the Canadian Historical Association's Histories of Children and Youth Group, and Child and Teen Consumption folks for listening and questioning at numerous conferences over the years. Special thanks to Ben Bradley, Natalie Coulter, Jason Ellis, and Helle Jensen for their consistent encouragement and kind words.

Writing can be an isolating activity, but thankfully I have colleagues who make it less so. The history department at Vancouver Island University is such a generous crew. Thanks Tim Lewis, John Hinde,

— Acknowledgments —

Kenneth Duggan, Murat Inan, Stephen Davies, Whitney Wood, Cheryl Warsh, and Cathryn Spence for steering our little ship through calm and rough seas. Chelsea Horton and Camie Augustus read early drafts of every chapter, providing valuable comments, and asking probing questions that helped to clarify my arguments. Especially during the first year of the COVID-19 pandemic, when they were both teaching online full time, their generosity was astonishing. Without their invaluable assistance and companionship, I believe this book would not exist.

Finally, I am grateful to come from a family whose members value teaching, research, and learning. My parents and sisters remain my biggest cheerleaders in life. To Darrell – my partner in everything – thank you, my love.

To Felix and Annika, who were stardust when I began thinking about the history of the teenager and are now teenagers themselves, I dedicate this book.

The Scramble *for the* Teenage Dollar

Introduction

IN SEPTEMBER 1957, *Maclean's* writer John Clare reported on the rising influence of a new group of consumers. In an article entitled "The Scramble for the Teen-Age Dollar," Clare explained that the economic impact of young people in their teen years amounted to "$100 million a year – or more" in purchases. They were keen clothes shoppers and avid cosmetics buyers who could even influence the type and colour of their parents' next car. Businesses from typewriter manufacturers to cosmetic companies were targeting these younger customers with advertising campaigns, special products, contests, and fan clubs. And teenagers were buying: spending wages, allowances, and their parents' money on clothing, beauty products, and entertainment. "Young people are loaded," Clare noted, claiming, "Today's teenagers are spending their new wealth in a way that makes them important customers." What consequences would this rash of spending have on family life, parental authority, and the well-being of Canada's next generation of adults? Clare associated consumer status with adulthood, noting that the time to become "serious shoppers" had arrived ahead of schedule for many young people. He concluded that teenagers were "coming to economic maturity a few years younger than they ever did before," as retailers and advertisers were "out-hustling each other to cash in on the market that just grew up."[1]

Clare's article illustrates neatly what this book is about: when and how Canadian retailers and advertisers singled out and idealized people in their teen years as a new and powerful group of consumers in the middle decades of the twentieth century. Not only did the desire to appeal to teenagers as a specific type of consumer alter retailing and advertising practices in Canada (as elsewhere), but segmentation of the consumer marketplace by age – and related intersecting identities – connected teenage identity more closely to consumer capitalism. Serious shoppers –

those deemed capable of making independent and informed purchases – were adults. Consumption was an increasingly important marker of full citizenship, and cheaper and more available consumer goods promised greater levels of democracy and inclusion in many capitalist countries. How did the market actors of this period – the retailers, advertisers, and consumer magazines of the 1930s, '40s, and '50s – make consumption and consumerism a central tenet of teenage identity in Canada?

Clare's article in *Maclean's* heralded growing teenage purchasing power in the late 1950s, a decade often associated with rising wages and spending among Canadians. As James Onusko notes in his history of childhood and youth in postwar Calgary, the first two decades that followed the Second World War are often viewed as "an idyllic period when great hopes and relative prosperity went hand in hand for people of all ages."[2] Because of the ongoing cultural and social influence of the baby boom generation, there is a persistent belief among Canadians that these young people were the first teenagers. The first of the 8 million babies born in Canada between 1943 and 1964 (as well as the million immigrant children who arrived during the same period) began to reach their teens in the mid-1950s, and certainly altered the structure and meaning of adolescence in the same way that they had influenced the culture and politics of early childhood.[3] In *Born at the Right Time*, Doug Owram points to the 1960s as the years when teenagers – the boomers – became a market force in Canada. Prior to then, he argues, "adolescents were unable to exert much cultural presence."[4]

Canadians in their teens garnered an increasing amount of media attention in the late 1950s. Headlines in *Maclean's* in 1959 asked, "Going Steady: Is It Ruining Our Teen-Agers?" and "Is 'Car Craziness' a Menace to Our Teenagers?"[5] These articles assumed readers understood what a "teenager" was – not just a person in their teen years but a high school student with enough disposable income to go on dates and buy an automobile, or at least to buy gasoline for the family car. By the time John Clare wrote about the so-called discovery of the teenaged consumer in 1957, the teenager was already well understood by manufacturers, retailers, and advertisers as a customer with distinct purchasing power and spending habits. While their increasing numbers made them even more

(4)

— Introduction —

attractive to retailers and advertisers by the late 1950s, historian Bettina Liverant notes that "the rise of consumer society was not simply the result of economic changes in productivity and affluence; it involved and required changes to the way people think."[6] Canadian retailers and advertisers worked to construct an image of the teenager that would appeal to young people and encourage them to associate consumer goods with their stage of life.

The teenaged consumer emerged at a time when consumer consciousness was on the rise among Canadians. Following the First World War, ambivalence and anxiety about the pace of change often connected the physical, mental, and spiritual health of children and adolescents to the health of the country as a whole. Those labelled "youth" in the 1920s were the focus of a mounting number of experts, with growing authority. In her history of adolescence, Cynthia Comacchio reveals the ways in which young people were increasingly talked about as if they shared common experiences, including the upheaval caused by the Great War, the lengthening amount of time spent at school, and their attraction to dance halls and movie theatres. Anxieties about young people's behaviour intersected with the greater availability and diversity of standardized goods advertised nationally in print and, later, on the radio. These goods – sold in urban department stores built as "palaces of consumption," through widely distributed mail-order catalogues, or in expanding chain stores – altered people's perceptions of themselves and others. In advertisements and on the screen, young women were encouraged to absorb fashion and beauty ideals that reshaped white settler femininity into a focus on youthfulness and novelty. And as a growing number of young women worked for wages, more had the means to participate, to varying degrees, in a burgeoning consumer culture. Their purchasing power granted them status and autonomy in the eyes of retailers. At the same time, access to goods and the status they conveyed was gendered, classed, and racialized, privileging white and wealthy Canadians above Indigenous, Black, immigrant, and working-class people.[7]

Beginning in the mid-1930s and continuing into the decades that followed, access to and participation in the consumer economy became an important marker of citizenship, presented as both a right and a civic

(5)

duty. Per capita spending increased drastically during the Second World War, even as purchasing (and not purchasing) acquired patriotic meaning. Following the war, relative economic stability further solidified consumerism both in Canadian policy and in Canadians' everyday practices. As Bettina Liverant notes, "responsible spending, debt management, and the use of goods to fashion personal identity displaced older themes of thrift, self-denial, and character" by the 1950s.[8] These economic, social, and cultural shifts were not uncontested, as many Canadians debated who should be able to access goods, and how. Canada was a consumer society – a society in which one's relationship to the market was an increasingly essential element of one's identity and experience.[9] Building on the important work of numerous historians who have examined youth culture and/or consumer culture in Canada, this book explores how consumer culture altered Canadians' perceptions of people in their teen years, helping to shape a distinct teenage culture that was always and already implicated in consumer society.

But is this really a Canadian story, or just part of an American one? As anyone living in Canada today knows, consumer culture and media move easily over national boundaries. American magazines, broadcast signals, films, products, brands, and retailers tend to move north, making it tempting to assume that the evolution of a commercialized teenage culture in Canada matched that in the United States.[10] Popular culture may blur geographic and historical differences, but historians need to point out and interrogate the extent to which national contexts matter. As members of the Modern Girl Around the World Research Group have demonstrated, similarities in advertising imagery and messaging do not lessen the importance of exploring the ambitions, anxieties, and economies of places where cultural artifacts are produced and consumed. The image of the modern girl – a type characterized by her freedom from traditionally dutiful female roles and often associated with American consumer culture – resonated in China, India, Australia, and parts of Africa in the 1920s and 1930s.[11] Historians have noted that Canadians generally consumed in different ways than their southern neighbours did in the postwar period. Smaller per capita incomes, higher prices, and different regulatory regimes resulted in more modest visions of abundance than Americans

— Introduction —

had.[12] Nevertheless, corporate interests, academics, policy makers, and politicians all sought to improve Canadians' access to goods and with it their ability to consume, and it is worth asking how the teenage market segment emerged from the set of circumstances particular to Canada.

Focusing specifically on the corporate rhetorical and visual strategies of market actors – employees working for Canada's retailers, advertisers, and consumer magazines – the chapters that follow demonstrate how cultural understandings of the teenager evolved in step with the rise of consumer culture in the mid-twentieth century. From the late 1930s into the 1950s, retailers and advertisers argued that teenagers were "old enough" and "ready" to make informed purchasing decisions, yet "young enough" to require distinct products and inexperienced enough to necessitate the guidance of experts. Teenagers' active participation in the retail marketplace, they suggested, marked a rite of passage to adulthood. Specifically, by imagining an ideal teenaged consumer, and marketing directly to teenagers, Canadian market actors were influencing at what age young people could be expected to make their own consumer choices and achieve a measure of economic autonomy – heralding teenagers as the market that just grew up.

LOCATING THE TEENAGER

The idealized vision of a teenaged consumer that retailers and advertisers discussed, studied, and appealed to in these decades – a white, middle-class, typically urban student with spending money and a keen eye for quality merchandise – did not in fact reflect the experiences of most Canadian teens. As Cynthia Comacchio notes, "The socio-cultural meanings assigned to adolescence – what it is seen to typify at particular moments – not infrequently reveal more about the pressing concerns of 'society' (or at least of a sector that has political and economic influence) than about what the young were actually doing."[13] Many people in their teen years were already avid consumers by the 1930s, and there is ample evidence to show that young people in industrialized countries often contributed to the family income, purchased items for themselves and family members, and spent money on commercial leisure pursuits.[14] What changed over the middle decades of the twentieth century was the tendency to talk about these customers as a cohesive group. Market actors fashioned commercial discourses of the teenager: the words, images, and associations generated and circulated by those working in department stores, advertising agencies, magazines, and newspapers that fostered the idea that high school students constituted a special group of consumers, and that participating actively in the consumer marketplace was an integral part of growing up.

The term *teenager* itself was novel in this period; Canadians would have been more familiar with *adolescent*. In the early twentieth century, adolescence was a relatively new idea used to describe – and problematize – the changes experienced during puberty. American psychologist and child studies expert G. Stanley Hall is best known for his multi-volume study of adolescence, published in 1904, in which he described the physical and social changes inherent to this newly defined stage of life. Hall believed in an essential adolescent period of life, a natural biological process experienced by young people regardless of culture, economics, or geography. Adolescence was a period of "storm and stress," in Hall's words, when young people experienced unusually rapid physical and mental growth – a "new birth" when young bodies and minds were more plastic than they would be as adults.[15] As a result, adolescence was a crucial period of character formation. Children were supposed to abandon the selfish and inward focus of their early years and adopt an altruistic frame of mind, to cultivate thoughts and emotions – such as love, religious fervour, and appreciation of nature and art – that were beyond those Hall believed children were capable of forming. Hall was not without his critics, but his ideas legitimized the adolescent as a study subject and were used increasingly in medical, educational, and legal circles to justify young people's behaviour and different treatment by medical professionals, schools, and courts. His description of adolescence as a crucial period of identity formation and a time of personal trial exemplifies the shift in thinking about childhood and adolescence taking place at the turn of the twentieth century.

The term *teenager* is more directly linked to age than *adolescent* and at the same time more disconnected from the physical changes of puberty.

— Introduction —

The adjective *teenage* and noun *teenager* can be found in the occasional newspaper article from the 1910s, used to describe young people and their activities. Initially, both the noun and the adjective were hyphenated and often appeared in quotation marks, implying that they were unfamiliar or slang terms.[16] The now-familiar compound *teenager* began to appear regularly in print only in the late 1950s. Like all age categories, *teenager* is a construct; the term emerged from a particular set of historical circumstances, created and sustained because it suited prevailing economic and cultural systems, including capitalism and patriarchy.

Words such as *adolescent* and *teenager* are often used interchangeably and can have overlapping connotations. As Mary Louise Adams notes in her history of postwar youth sexuality in Canada, however, the words applied to young people can carry gendered, classed, and racialized assumptions. *Youth*, for example, is often used to describe younger males in trouble, often working class and sometimes racialized as non-white boys and young men whose appearance or behaviour threatens the social order.[17] *Teenager*, on the other hand, is arguably more often associated with commercialized leisure, passive consumption (and thus femininity), and a level of economic stability. Mid-twentieth-century market actors were never completely consistent when categorizing young consumers as teenagers, youth, or students, but it is telling that they never described their target market as adolescent.

To explore the teenager's emergence as a distinct market segment, this book relies on corporate archives, mail-order catalogues, and consumer magazines, and to a lesser extent on national daily newspapers. Corporate marketing strategies, merchandise displays, advertising campaigns, editorial decisions, and newspaper coverage of young people all illuminate the ways in which age-based and economic identities converged and shaped each other. In the service of their industry, department store employees, advertising workers, and magazine columnists together developed a commercial construct of the teenager based on an amalgam of imagined and genuine characteristics. In his study of American children's clothing manufacturers and retailers in the early twentieth century, Daniel Thomas Cook coined the term *commercial personae*, demonstrating how this industry discussed, debated, and designed products for "the toddler" and

(9)

used this persona to sell middle-class mothers on their young children's specific clothing needs. Commercial personae serve the corporate interest of sustaining and expanding markets, while also becoming commodities; since consumer personae helped advertisers sell and retailers profit, they acquired a value that could be exchanged.[18] I am interested in how Canadian retailers and consumer magazines spoke about and to their customers, both behind closed doors and publicly.

As Canada's largest retailer in the middle decades of the twentieth century, the T. Eaton Company Limited was well positioned to influence and expand a commercialized teenage culture. Eaton's was iconic. No other retail company in Canada matched its commercial or cultural reach, which by the 1930s extended to forty-seven stores in Canadian cities and a far-reaching mail-order business with a hundred separate offices. Families patronized the retailer from all corners of the country. Its founders were sometimes treated like royalty and were equally famous for their philanthropic work and infamous for their paternalist employment policies. To many Canadians, Eaton's was much more than a retail store; it was a major employer, a public institution, a sign of Canadian greatness, and a symbol of national identity.[19] As Steve Penfold notes in his history of the company's long-running annual Santa Claus Parade, Eaton's was "a powerful department store at a time when the form was the dominant expression of North American consumer capitalism."[20] By the 1930s, Canada had several department store companies that operated nationally, and others, such as Spencer's in British Columbia and Holman's in the Maritime provinces, serving regional markets.[21] All advertised themselves as agents of economic and social progress, naturalizing consumerism while reinforcing colonial images of Canada as a white settler state where middle-class shopping was the privilege of a "civilized" population.[22] Eaton's, however, "dominated its markets to an almost unmatched degree," shaping not only Canadians' shopping habits but also its competitors' practices. Despite increasing competition from specialty shops and discount retailers, at the end of the 1960s, Eaton's maintained forty-eight department stores and was the fourth-largest employer in Canada.[23]

— Introduction —

At the heart of Eaton's efforts to know and attract young customers were the company's Junior Councils and Junior Executives, groups of hand-picked high school students from urban and suburban centres who were invited to weekly meetings with company employees. There they offered their opinions of store merchandise, heard from guest speakers, learned about the retail industry, and participated in a range of advertising and public relations events. The program began in 1939 at the Toronto store, and by 1950 Eaton's stores in Montreal, Winnipeg, Hamilton, Calgary, and Edmonton were recruiting hundreds of senior high school students each year. From window displays and contests to fashion shows and high school dances, Eaton's relied on these teenagers to legitimize its claim to be "the Store for Young Canada." The Junior Councils (for girls) and Junior Executives (for boys) granted Eaton's unprecedented access to a large and growing market segment in urban high schools.

Eaton's employees led the councils and executives in each city, and some kept records of their weekly and monthly interactions with the student representatives. In surviving records, employees often speak candidly of their intention to foster loyalty among teenaged customers, sharing with each other their successes and failures about what "worked" with the groups. The picture is fragmented, as most of the records still available were generated by two Eaton's employees who led meetings, corresponded with high school officials, promoted the students' opinions among their co-workers, and selected students to serve in their respective stores in the 1940s and early 1950s. In Winnipeg, Tom Miller was a sales manager; in Toronto, Jack Brockie was the merchandise display manager. Brockie started the program in 1939, led the groups throughout the 1940s, and continued to keep tabs on the students when he later became the head of Eaton's public relations office. Brockie was, in Steve Penfold's words, "perfectly suited to the corporatization of wonder," as he also led the team that designed and executed the company's annual Santa Claus Parade for more than three decades, beginning in 1928.[24] He was experienced in building spectacle and appealing to the young. The memos, meeting minutes, budgets, and other documents created by Miller and Brockie offer a glimpse into the "backstage of social encounters – a space

(11)

— The Scramble for the Teenage Dollar —

away from the scrutinizing gaze of the general public where the work of erecting a façade gets accomplished."[25]

Eaton's catalogues are another avenue through which to explore the company's depictions of and appeals to teenagers during these decades. Produced semi-annually and delivered free (for previous customers) to urban and rural households across the country, the catalogues offered a wide variety of goods but featured clothing above all. As historian Wendy Mitchinson notes, the catalogues can tell us only what was sold, not what was purchased. Nevertheless, the clothing displayed and described is a rich source of information about the size and gendering of body image over time.[26] The catalogues also hint at who Eaton's believed was holding the purse strings when purchasing clothing. Before 1930, clothing for younger customers was often sold to "mother," with retailers highlighting its durability, practical construction, and ease of laundering, but this focus began to shift in subsequent decades.[27] Sampling men's and women's clothing in all sizes sold in the Eaton's catalogues from 1930 to 1960, and paying close attention to the visual and textual information offered, reveals the company's efforts to tailor their merchandise to teenaged girls and boys and to speak to them directly as customers.

Eaton's corporate archives, catalogues, and advertising provide ample evidence of the company's creation of the ideal consuming teenager. At the same time, my decision to focus primarily on one department store shapes and limits the scope of this book. The T. Eaton Company fonds, from where I drew on the source materials, includes records generated by Eaton's executives and employees across Canada but tends to overrepresent the company's flagship Queen Street and College Street locations in Toronto, and to a lesser extent its Winnipeg and Montreal operations. What we know about the Council program in Calgary and Edmonton, for example, is limited to information gathered through Eaton's head office in Toronto. And although the catalogues reached many rural customers, young and old, the images contained in them projected urban fashions from the cities outward. Consumer culture in all forms tended to associate cities with modernity – novelty, mobility, and opportunity – in contrast to a pre-modern countryside. While histories of rural consumers point out that people outside cities

— Introduction —

participated in various ways in Canada's burgeoning consumer economy, the commercialized ideal consumer continued to be associated with city life.[28] During this period, as Mary Louise Adams notes, "Toronto was the centre of English-language publishing, broadcasting, and cultural production, a position that contributed to the publicizing of urban issues and Toronto-based perspectives across the country."[29] Although focusing on Eaton's precludes adequate representation of the distinctive regional histories and economies of Canada, this approach has merit because my arguments are about the commercial *persona* of the teenager: a persona that flattened many geographic and other distinctions between young people in its effort to present a typical Canadian teenager.

Eaton's was also not the only company appealing to teenagers as notionally new customers in these decades. Other large retailers, such as the Hudson's Bay Company, also used advertising and promotions to appeal to children and youth in different ways. The Robert Simpson Company organized a club for high school students at its Toronto store, called the Collegiate Club. The Quebec retailer Dupuis Frères included clothing items for "l'adolescente" and the "jeune fille" in its catalogues.[30] And many smaller local and regional retailers, such as Ogilvy's in Ottawa, placed advertisements in high school yearbooks and local newspapers to curry favour with younger customers. Department stores' approaches to organization and marketing "grew from emulation as much as innovation," and borrowing was common: the Eaton's catalogues copied techniques from American stores such as Montgomery Ward and Marshall Fields; representatives from Macy's visited Eaton's in 1924 to learn about its Santa Claus Parade; and in Canada, rival stores kept close tabs on each other.[31]

Eaton's is the focus here because the scope, duration, and intensity of its youth marketing efforts were unrivalled in this period. No other retailer focused as many resources on creating and circulating industry knowledge about "the teenager" and appealing to white, middle-class, urban high school students as ideal young customers. Other companies copied Eaton's example on a smaller scale. Dupuis Frères exerted considerable influence but only in Quebec. Simpson's had a mail-order catalogue but of a modest size compared to Eaton's (prior to being purchased by Sears Roebuck in 1951). Furthermore, Eaton's efforts to define who the Canadian teenager was and what the teenager liked to wear, do, and buy are documented in greater detail than other corporate efforts, and readily accessible in the company's substantial fonds at the Archives of Ontario. Future research may illuminate distinctions between department store youth promotions and their reception in different cities or regions. As Michael Dawson's work on shopping regulations in Vancouver and Victoria in the decades following the Second World War suggests, smaller and independent businesses and local bylaws certainly matter in the history of consumer culture in Canada, and deserve further study.[32] This book focuses on Eaton's, however, because the company "forged a national retail space" and was, by the 1930s, "geographically ubiquitous."[33] Decisions made in its Toronto offices about when, how, and why to advertise to teenagers reverberated through its branches and competitors, and made a larger cultural impact on Canadians' understanding of young people's relationship to consumer markets than those of other retailers.

If corporate records represent the backstage thoughts and actions of market actors, consumer magazines and newspapers demonstrate the increasing coverage and commentary about young people that shaped shifting public discourses of youth. Close reading of *Chatelaine*, *Canadian Home Journal*, and *Mayfair*, alongside searches of the *Globe and Mail* and *Toronto Daily Star* newspapers, helps to illustrate adults' shifting impressions of and concerns about teenage appearance and spending habits, and what both might indicate about Canada's future. These publications' feature articles, regular columns, advertisements, and images produced, reinforced, and sometimes challenged Canadians' understanding and expectations of young people. As cultural theorist Stuart Hall argues, representation is one of the key practices that produces culture: "We give things meaning by how we *represent* them – the words we use about them, the stories we tell about them, the images of them we produce, the emotions we associate with them, the ways we classify and conceptualize them, the values we place on them."[34] While historians have used consumer magazines such as *Chatelaine* to explore gendered middle-class consumer culture and portrayals of women, representations of younger people in Canadian publications have not been explored to date.[35]

— Introduction —

I have chosen to focus on mass-market periodicals that had a largely adult audience, rather than on gender-specific girls' and boys' publications, or on the teen magazines that began to appear on newsstands in North America and Britain in the 1930s and 1940s. Some Canadian teenagers may have read publications like *Seventeen*, but Canada did not have its own domestic teen magazine until 1964, when *Miss Chatelaine* was launched to respond to a teenage market segment that was by then established and large enough to attract the advertising needed to support a separate publication. *Miss Chatelaine* – and young Canadians' consumer culture in the 1960s and beyond – awaits further study. Locating the emerging teenaged consumer requires a focus on earlier, adult-focused periodicals.

CHILDHOOD IN TWENTIETH-CENTURY CANADA

Young people are among the more vulnerable and powerless members of any society, and yet historians since the 1970s have demonstrated that children and concerns about childhood have driven historical change in Canada in significant ways. The twentieth century was, in the words of Swedish thinker Ellen Key in 1900, the century of the child. In numerous industrial societies, including Canada, age consciousness and assumptions about what childhood was – and what children were supposed to be doing – changed drastically between the 1890s and the 1930s. Middle-class reformers advanced the notion that children should be nurtured, that their environment shaped their adult character, and that they needed to be both sheltered from and prepared for the influence of the world outside the home.[36] As attitudes toward childhood and child rearing changed (particularly among those with higher class status and influence), new laws set age restrictions for employment, school leaving, and marriage.[37] From juvenile courts to the Canadian Council on Child Welfare, new institutions regulated the process of growing up. These were based on the belief that allowing children to engage in activities that might compromise their presumed innocence was dangerous not only for the children but for society generally. As Neil Sutherland points out, concerns about child welfare greatly influenced the development of Canadian social policy.[38] School grades, sports teams, service groups, and summer camps also became more peer

(15)

based as the twentieth century progressed, reflecting a growing belief that children developed best alongside other children of the same age.[39]

Throughout the twentieth century, then, children acquired their own spaces, organizations, and material objects that shaped their experiences and set them apart from adults. Historians Marta Gutman and Ning de Coninck-Smith argue that this "islanding" of childhood from adulthood is part of an ongoing process – driven by medical science, socio-economic conditions, and cultural practices – to define a "good childhood," safe from the potentially corrupting influence of activities and responsibilities deemed too mature for children to handle.[40] This process separates the lifespan into distinct periods with different expectations and experiences. It also differentiates periods of childhood, so that parents and caregivers today refer to their offspring as toddlers, kids, tweens, and teens, and understand that each phase has its own set of developmental goals, activities, and social expectations.[41] Children's lives did not – and still do not – fit neatly into these categories, and their experiences depend greatly on their parents' incomes and skills, their own gender and sexuality, their ethnic or racialized identities, their health, their access to schooling, and their geographic location, among other factors.[42]

Even though individual children have diverse experiences that belie easy categorization, children are often deployed collectively and rhetorically to signal any number of promising or problematic social issues throughout history.[43] Adults in North America's settler societies have consistently pointed to young people's appearance, health, or behaviour as an indication of a society's future, idealizing white, able-bodied, and economically secure children as the nation's best hope for the future. As Laura Ishiguro asserts, "Young people were central to, rather than distractions from, the settler colonial project." In colonial British Columbia, members of the Corps of Royal Engineers were sent to survey land and build infrastructure, bringing their families with them. Their children were physical manifestations of the future, expanding white settler society by growing up to do the physical, cultural, and reproductive work of the burgeoning settler state. Their young, white bodies may have represented a drain on the Engineers' resources, but they were central to the plan to "create an ongoing white familial settler future."[44]

(16)

— Introduction —

The argument that young people were "important to a collective politics of aspiration" applies as much to mid-twentieth century teenagers as it does to the children of British settlers.[45] In the context of both the Great Depression and the Second World War, adults imagined the future of Canada through the potential and real futures of their children. Concerns about the consequences of unemployment and idleness fuelled the creation of federal–provincial training schemes in the late 1930s and the Canadian Youth Commission in the early 1940s. Adults feared that youth – young men in particular – had limited prospects. Without work they were less likely to marry, have children, and head households, threatening national economic and social stability. Experts decided that occupational training would ensure young people grew into productive, independent citizens.[46] It was white settler children who mattered in these discourses; Indigenous, immigrant, and other racialized children only threatened Canadians' vision of the future settler state.

Similarly, market actors' persistent portrayal of the teenaged consumer as white reinforced the idea that only white settler teenagers mattered, or could be autonomous agents, in the marketplace. Kristine Alexander notes the centrality of Indigenous young people to the aspirations of the settler state, but to Canada's retailers and advertisers, Indigenous people were anti-modern symbols of a romanticized pioneer past, used to sell vacations and travel.[47] In other words, they were content rather than customers. Indigenous youth and young people of colour were excluded from the status of full economic maturity and independence that participating in consumer culture increasingly signified in the 1940s and '50s. As the islanding of childhood created distinct, age-appropriate spaces and experiences for some children throughout the twentieth century, it also left many marginalized children outside the shifting definition of a good childhood. Indigenous children, who remained legally dependent wards of the state under the federal Indian Act, were infantilized regardless of their age. Much work needs to be done to tell the stories of racialized young people in Canada. By focusing on corporate archives and mass magazines that cultivated an ideal image of the teenager, this book overlooks the ways in which Indigenous, Black, and other racialized young Canadians participated in the burgeoning consumer culture, engaged with products, worked in the retail industry, or perceived of themselves as consumers. I hope, however, that by drawing attention to the ways in which market actors perpetuated white supremacy, I will motivate future study in these areas.

GROWING UP IN A CONSUMER SOCIETY

Capitalism has not only contributed to the islanding of childhood but benefited from it. After the First World War, children were more and more widely excluded from the paid workforce, where many had laboured out of necessity since a young age, and at the same time they were more and more often the subject of marketing campaigns. Parents, especially middle-class parents, were encouraged to spend money on their offspring, indulge their children's consumer desires, and give them allowances.[48] Children moved from occupying an economically useful position within families to serving a more emotional, even sacred role, but historian Viviana Zelizer argues that this shift did not prevent their increasing participation in the consumer marketplace.[49] They functioned both as motivation for parental spending and as consumers in their own right. Growing up in consumer culture meant that childhood itself was framed by consumerism.

The image of the child consumer provoked strong reactions from adults for whom commercialized leisure and a desire for material goods symbolized peril for the rising generation. If children were more vulnerable, more innocent, and in need of protection from the adult world, they might be more easily corrupted by commercialized messages that threatened to undermine parents' moral authority.[50] Concerns about the content of movies, popular radio programs, and comic books reflected these anxieties, as did the increasing availability of television in Canada beginning in the 1950s.[51] In 1957, the same year that Clare drew attention to Canadian retailers' scramble for the teenage dollar, American journalist Vance Packard published a critique of the advertising industry, *The Hidden Persuaders*, in which he argued that advertising agencies were studying consumers' motivation in order to manipulate them for corporate profits. To make his point, Packard focused special attention on

— Introduction —

what he called "the psycho-seduction of children," raising fears about advertising campaigns that preyed on young girls' insecurities over their appearance and made cigarette smoking appear glamourous and fun.[52] Like Packard, scholars, parents, and other child advocates then and now have often assumed that children are "incomplete" people – potential adults – who are not intelligent or experienced enough to assert themselves in the marketplace.

In many ways, concerns that young people were being duped by advertising echo feminist debates about women's consumption. To what extent are female consumers liberated or manipulated by their interactions with the marketplace? In the 1970s and '80s, scholars began to explore the ways in which consumer goods offered some women – particularly white settler women – access to economic and political power. By linking women's consumption to their domestic labour, historians drew attention to the value and significance of women's work within Canadian households. Their analyses reveal how women embraced consumption and consumer culture for a variety of reasons and, in the process, both challenged and reinforced gendered and racialized social norms.[53] Similar arguments about the liberating effects of consumer culture for children shaped a new sociology of childhood beginning in the 1980s.[54] These approaches emphasize that children are not merely potential adults but social actors who know and choose, whose individuality and agency are affirmed by marketplace participation. Through consumption they discover and express their individuality, not simply absorbing messages but making their own, often creative meanings from advertising and consumer goods.

Despite the value of acknowledging that young people have not been powerless in the face of mass consumer culture, approaches focused on the emancipatory power of the marketplace in children's lives fail to acknowledge the ways in which market actors have worked for their own ends to present children as rational subjects. Manufacturers, retailers, and advertisers began incorporating the supposedly liberating and individualizing power of material goods into sales messages from the 1920s onward, such as by using images of stylish, attractive, and independent women to sell cigarettes.[55] If the child is an individual who chooses products and uses them to express individuality and achieve social success in various

(19)

contexts, market actors have argued, to accuse them of manipulation is to deny the child's agency.

For historians, this can make it difficult to find evidence of and analyze children's relationship to advertising, shopping, and consumer goods. Historians have increasingly grappled with the concept of agency, questioning its utility as a framework for understanding children's significance to historical change.[56] Rather than seeking evidence of young people's everyday encounters with consumer culture, I argue that market actors like Eaton's sought to make those encounters seem natural, expected, and commonplace. The concept of agency was deployed to convince Canadians that young people could – and should – make consumer choices. As Daniel Cook notes, "The uncertainty of children's agency renders defensible all sorts of claims and counterclaims about who children 'are' and what children 'want,' allowing most anyone to frame the child in any number of ways – for example as a competent social actor, deserving of rights, as needing protection and guidance, and so on."[57] Just as experts attempted throughout the twentieth century to shape and maintain the boundaries of a "good" childhood defined by school attendance, organized recreation, and child-specific social services, market actors worked to include the consumer marketplace in a broader understanding of good childhood, in which it was important to recognize young people's ability to make rational choices. It was in their interest to present the teenager as a capable consumer, an autonomous figure with economic and cultural power who demanded recognition. Market actors' rhetorical and visual depictions of their teenaged customers framed teenage experiences in the marketplace.

This construction of the commercial persona of the teenager is the focus of the chapters that follow, which can be divided into two parts. Chapters 1 and 2 explore representations of and debates about young people as consumers in mass-market print publications from the 1930s to the 1950s. Chapter 1 outlines the increasing volume of magazine content that focused on Canadian high school students over this period, examining *Chatelaine*, *Canadian Home Journal*, and *Mayfair* in particular. The prevailing image of young women in these magazines was that of the co-ed: a poised college or high school student easily identified by her

— Introduction —

style and her proficient use of commodities. The chapter argues that the co-ed persona both reflected and reinforced white settler femininity in Canada by presenting the so-called typical teenager as a white, middle-class, cisgendered, heterosexual student, an image that excluded many Canadian youth.

Market actors were keen to normalize teenagers' consumption, to make spending and shopping a natural part of acting one's age. However, the argument that young people could make wise consumer choices was not uncontested, and Chapter 2 demonstrates some of the ways in which adults remade the meaning of young people's consumption in this period. Consumer magazines and newspapers show that both age and gender shaped adults' expectations, linking consumer behaviour to maturity. Examples from the Second World War, when certain commodities were rationed and consumption was reframed as a patriotic duty, illustrate how adults criticized young people's participation in fashion trends as irrational and immature. At the same time, ideas about the importance of personality and peer influence to adolescent development and mental health muted many concerns about fads and helped to normalize the purchase and use of consumer goods to fashion an age-appropriate identity.

The final three chapters narrow the focus of analysis in order to detail Eaton's imagining of the teenaged commercial persona in three locales: its stores, its catalogues, and Canadian urban high schools. The Junior Council and Junior Executive program invited urban teenagers into stores, granting the company unprecedented access to these high school students. Chapter 3 outlines the company's various marketing strategies to make space for teenagers in their stores, including weekly Junior Council and Executive activities, fashion shows, and specialized clothing departments. Chapter 4 uses an extensive and systematic sampling of the popular Eaton's catalogues published out of the Toronto office from 1930 to 1960 to explore how the company imagined teenaged bodies and appealed to teenaged customers through clothing styles and sizes, demonstrating how in-between sizes and styles emerged and proliferated. Finally, Chapter 5 examines Eaton's relationship to high schools through the Council program, which allowed the company to educate and commodify the teenager in distinctly gendered ways in the

1940s and 1950s. The program was a valuable public relations tool for the department store at a time when practical education was gaining traction among Canadian educators.

As you read this book, I urge you to keep in mind the broader questions that motivated its writing. Where do young people fit in the history of Canada's consumer culture? How did ideas about who should consume, and how, match Canadians' understanding of childhood and growing up? The words and deeds of retailers and advertisers both historicize and complicate what John Clare presented in 1957 as a straightforward scramble for the teenage dollar, revealing the ways in which market actors brought the teenaged consumer to life.

1

Calling All Co-eds!

The Teenager Appears in Canadian Women's Magazines

MARY PEATE was an avid magazine consumer as a young woman in Montreal in the early 1940s. In her memoir, *Girl in a Sloppy Joe Sweater*, she writes that after school she often joined a friend running errands for her mother and they always stopped to buy a magazine, reading it from cover to cover together when they got home. Mary and her friend Cath read everything "from the ads to the stories and illustrations."[1] Peate remembered reading articles aloud, collecting advertisements they admired, consulting advice columns, and even regularly returning magazines, if they could, and using the same money to buy a different magazine. Magazines were valuable commodities in these young women's lives: a source of advice, curiosity, inspiration, and pleasure. Much of the content was directed at women older than themselves: wage-earning women, wives, and mothers. As late as 1935, women's magazines rarely addressed or represented young women in their teen years as a distinct group whose needs and desires might differ from women who were working either for wages or in running their households.

— The Scramble for the Teenage Dollar —

1.1 Kotex advertisement featuring an Irving Nurick drawing, *Chatelaine*, May 1943, 43.

After 1935, however, girls in their teens appeared with regularity as fashionable co-eds who relied on magazine editors' advice to guide their purchases. Mary and Cath, two white, fifteen-year-old high school students, increasingly saw themselves reflected in the magazines' pages. In the early 1940s, representations of the teenaged girl, such as those drawn by American commercial artist Irving Nurick in a campaign for Kotex sanitary pads, were becoming both more numerous and more familiar. Mary and Cath admired Nurick, whose "drawings of teenage girls were so accurate that we had the feeling he was following us around, sketching us."[2] Nurick's drawings outlined the visual characteristics of the idealized middle-class North American teenaged girl; she was the co-ed (a high school, college, or university student) with a slender figure, loose, shoulder-length hair affixed with a bow, wearing a knee-length skirt, a sweater, and loafers (see Figure 1.1). White, middle-class, heterosexual, and cisgendered, she navigated the potential pitfalls of puberty, friendships, family life, and romance with the help of the commodities advertised and advice procured in popular magazines.

Mass-market Canadian magazines gave shape to the co-ed identity in the 1930s, '40s, and '50s. In *Chatelaine, Canadian Home Journal*, and *Mayfair*, editors, writers, and advertisers coached young readers on how to achieve an ideal feminine appearance during their studies to ensure their success as adult women. Over these decades, representations of the co-ed increased and also shifted from a college or university student in the 1930s to a high school student by the late 1940s. As a growing number of teenaged girls occupied the halls of schools and university campuses, the co-ed embodied many adults' hopes and fears for the future of Canada as a white settler nation. The co-ed was a type – a variation on the modern girl that emerged in the 1920s – available to those with the socio-economic status and racialized ability to perform the fresh-faced and exuberant persona that so resonated with Mary and Cath as they pored over magazines after school.

By the time popular Canadian magazines turned their attention to younger female readers in the mid-1930s, magazines were already a well-established source of advice, entertainment, and advertising in North America. From the turn of the twentieth century, American and Canadian periodicals such as *McCall's Magazine, Ladies' Home Journal*, and *Saturday Night* were encouraging women, in particular, to fashion their identities from a widening number of consumer products.[3] The magazine was "a crucible of modern consumer culture," connecting readers to national advertising campaigns and advice from a growing number of "experts" in beauty, fashion, household management, psychology, and child rearing.[4] Homemakers and young working women – those presumed to make purchases for their households, families, and themselves – were the target audience.

Mass-market magazines were, first and foremost, a means of advertising products. As Ellen Gruber Garvey notes, while some magazines were more prescriptive than others, "all wanted their readers to buy goods from the advertisers on whom their revenues depended."[5] In the first half of the twentieth century many publishers owned both popular and trade magazines. *Chatelaine* and *Mayfair* publisher J.B. Maclean founded several of Canada's earliest and most widely read trade papers, including *Canadian Grocer* and the *Dry Goods Review*. James Acton, who first published *Canadian Home Journal*, published a shoe and leather goods journal and advertisements for footwear featured prominently in the first issues of the *Journal*.[6] The magazine and advertising industries grew alongside and depended upon each other; advertisers needed magazines to publish ads and publishers needed advertisers to purchase space. Publishers and editors wanted readers to use their magazines to guide them in consumer purchases. Editors and columnists positioned themselves as "honest brokers" who tested and recommended clothing fabrics and styles, cosmetics, household cleaners, cookware, and appliances.[7] At the same time, publishers used their circulation figures and subscription lists to sell their readers' attention to manufacturers and advertisers. A recent content analysis of *Canadian Home Journal* noted that by the 1920s, half of the magazine's content was advertising.[8]

The *Canadian Home Journal*, *Chatelaine*, and *Mayfair* were widely read in Canada in the 1930s, '40s, and '50s. The *Canadian Home Journal* appeared monthly from 1905 until 1958 and directed much of its content to white, middle-class homemakers, wives, and mothers. It was the first women's magazine published in Canada with a national scope, and the most widely read prior to the appearance of *Chatelaine*. Perhaps Canada's best known and most studied women's magazine, *Chatelaine* first appeared on newsstands in 1928 and sought to appeal to young white working women and housewives. By 1930, *Chatelaine* and the *Journal* together reached more than 250,000 households each month. *Chatelaine*'s circulation increased from 378,866 in 1950 to 745,589 in 1960, purportedly reaching nearly one-quarter of Canada's adult population.[9] The third and smallest publication of the trio, *Mayfair*, began publication in 1927. *Mayfair* aspired to an upper-class female readership, reflected in its focus on Paris fashions, country houses, and reports on Junior League charity events, balls, and similar events of the social season in Toronto and Montreal. In its thirty-four years of publication, circulation reached twenty thousand readers monthly.[10] As mass-market magazines began to lose advertising revenues to television in the 1950s, *Mayfair* tried to carve out a niche as a travel magazine before ceasing publication in 1961. Valerie Korinek demonstrates that *Chatelaine* remained a commercial success in part due to its editors' willingness to address contemporary issues and spark debate among readers.[11] In 1964, Maclean Hunter expanded on its success with the publication of *Miss Chatelaine*, Canada's first magazine dedicated exclusively to teenaged girls.

Of course, other periodicals were available to young readers besides these mass-market publications. From the turn of the twentieth century, a growing number of magazines and papers catered to a broad audience of girls who were single, young, and either in school or working for wages. Commercial publishers produced some of these, and others, like the popular *Girls' Own Paper*, were published by missionary societies and focused on spreading Christian values. After the First World War, numerous periodicals in England began targeting the growing number of unmarried, wage-earning young women in their teen years with purchasing power, often specifically by occupation.[12] In the 1930s, magazines like *Miss Modern* "gave colourful expression to the possibilities afforded by being young, female, and modern" and targeted an expanding working- and middle-class readership who saw themselves as neither schoolgirls nor grown women but old enough to be working full time.[13] In the United States, both *Calling All Girls* and *Seventeen* began publication in the 1940s and were marketed to teenaged girls specifically.[14] While some of these publications were no doubt available and read in Canada, teenaged girls did not have a dedicated domestic magazine until *Miss Chatelaine* appeared on newsstands.

Magazines intended for a broader adult female audience uncover the emerging signs of the teenager in Canada. *Chatelaine, Mayfair,* and the *Canadian Home Journal* talked both *about* and *to* girls in their teen years, addressing and idealizing a teenaged consumer before the advent of teen-specific magazines. Although their contents reflect the priorities and expectations of their adult writers, editors, advertisers, and publishers more than the opinions and desires of younger readers, these magazines were key cultural producers. As sociologist Stuart Hall has argued, mass media plays an important cultural role in modern societies; consumer magazines produce "social knowledge, or social imagery, through which we perceive the 'worlds,' the 'lived realities' of others."[15] Magazine content shaped and disseminated the characteristics of an idealized co-ed for young readers to embrace or reject, but their efforts were visible to readers of all ages. In feature articles, beauty columns, fashion spreads,

(27)

and advertisements, magazines connected the physical, social, and psychological dimensions of growing up to commodities, brands, and styles.

Mass-market magazines propagated a new visual culture in the first half of the twentieth century, presenting readers with images of ideal femininity that also appeared in motion pictures and beauty pageants, and on city streets. Illustrated magazines encouraged Canadians to see themselves and others in new ways, offering consumers stylized personae for emulation, and products to help them look the part and presumably gain the associated social status. Perhaps no image captures this increasingly commodified femininity better than that of the modern girl. Appearing in industrializing cities across the world in the 1920s and 1930s, "adorned in provocative fashions, [and] in pursuit of romantic love, Modern girls appeared to disregard the roles of dutiful daughter, wife, and mother."[16] They smoked and drank, they wore makeup and leg-revealing dresses. Crucially, they were seen to do so – seen in the factory or office and in the streets, seen in films and in magazines. They challenged convention and embraced novelty, but as Jane Nicholas and others have argued, the modern girl was produced and performed through commodities that shaped her body and made her "a spectacular object for visual consumption."[17] Visual media, including magazines, disseminated the image of the modern girl globally, making her an icon as well as the face of growing multinational cosmetic companies.

At the same time that the modern girl spoke of young women's sexuality, independence, and mobility, textual and photographic representations of young women reinforced classed and racialized assumptions. In Canada and other settler nations such as Australia and New Zealand, as Liz Conor notes, "practices of appearing were circumscribed by colonial visions." In Australia, Aboriginal and Islander women were "cast as inassimilable to the cosmopolitan consumerism which was integral to the modernist ideology of nation-building"; the modern woman was white or, through the use of skin-whitening creams, should endeavour to appear white.[18] Similarly, Indigenous, Black, and other racialized women – as well as working-class white women – were not present as embodiments of beauty, charm, poise, or respectability on the pages of Canadian women's magazines. This does not mean that there was no Black beauty culture in Canada. As Cheryl Thompson demonstrates in *Beauty in a Box,* this culture thrived in African Canadian newspapers and in the salons of enterprising beauty culturalists, including Viola Desmond. However, Black beauty and Black-focused topics were notably absent from *Chatelaine* until 1959, Thompson notes, at which point Black women appeared only in articles on interracial marriage and immigration "under the purview of 'diversifying' the breadth of the magazine's social awareness, not with regard to its beauty imagery," an area that continued to be "an exclusively white woman's domain until the 1970s."[19] In advertising, Black women were depicted as racialized stereotypes, such as the matronly, acquiescent, and eager-to-please mammy, Aunt Jemima.[20] When they excluded and othered Black women and associated ideal femininity with white women, magazines reinforced "the de facto racialization of white female bodies as sites of privilege, supremacy, and power."[21]

My reading of these magazines has been shaped by scholars of the modern girl and the commodified settler femininity she embodied. Inspired by their perspective, I argue that the co-ed represented in Canadian women's magazines from the mid-1930s into the 1950s is a variation – perhaps a younger sister? – of the modern girl. Unlike the modern girl of the 1920s, the co-ed didn't work for wages, smoke, or drink, although she was similarly young, mobile, and visible. She appeared always as a student – first on college campuses and in later iterations in high school hallways – who dressed to suit her campus social activities and used commodities to present her "natural" beauty. While she consumed transnational trends and products, she was lauded as a typical example of Canadian feminine youth. Magazines wanted young readers to believe that with the right commodities any girl could appear as the smart and popular co-ed.

REACHING YOUNGER READERS
The Shifting Focus of Women's Magazines

The term *co-ed* captured college or university students as well as those attending high schools, and Canadian editors and advertisers sometimes applied the term broadly to both. The number of articles and advertisements offering her advice and products in *Chatelaine,* the *Canadian Home*

Journal, and *Mayfair* swelled from the 1930s to the 1950s. While women in their teen years were barely mentioned or distinguished in women's magazines in the early 1930s, by the 1940s they were clearly a target readership, and by the 1950s, they commanded their own monthly content. A survey of content over these decades demonstrates that these mass-market magazines focused increasing attention on the high school girl as the ideal co-ed and young consumer.

In the early 1930s, Canadian women's magazines rarely included content for children or adolescents. Mothers were an important audience, and numerous articles advised them about children's clothing, health, or hygiene, or advertised clothing or sewing patterns in children's sizes, but whether married or unmarried, women were the largest and most lucrative audience. In contrast, references to female college students appeared in American magazines such as *Ladies' Home Journal* and *Good Housekeeping* in the early 1900s. By the 1920s, these publications printed regular advice and advertisements for the college co-ed.[22] Building off the increasing number of Americans attending postsecondary institutions, as well as the popularity of all things youthful after the First World War, the co-ed was a marketing phenomenon south of the border. It is likely that many Canadians associated certain styles and products with college campuses and student life, given that the *Ladies' Home Journal* enjoyed wide readership in Canada. Yet no Canadian magazine paid similar attention to female college students until the mid-1930s.

Marking a shift to focusing on younger readers, in 1936 *Mayfair* began targeting college students specifically in their fall fashion spreads.[23] The following year, the *Canadian Home Journal* also began addressing younger readers more directly, with a monthly 'Teens and Twenties column that included career advice, fashion, and etiquette. Columnist Grace Garner expected readers either to be or to aspire to be part of the middle class; she profiled women working in fashion design or studying medicine, for example, and offered tips on matters such as packing for a summer vacation and redecorating a bedroom.[24] In the September 1938 column, Garner extended a special welcome to the incoming high school students among readers: "You are *Miss* 'Teens and Twenties now – an individual – not just Mrs. So-and-So's little girl."[25] The start of high school was a new

(30)

chapter in a girl's life, with different activities and challenges to reflect her new status.

In the early 1940s, an increasing number of magazine articles began to refer to young women specifically as *teen-agers* (always hyphenated), part of a group with distinct fashion and beauty needs and leisure pursuits. Articles in *Chatelaine* explained "'Teens' Routines" and exclaimed, "Teen-Agers Love These!" A how-to article about bedroom decor was titled "The Teens Get Ideas."[26] Articles about teenagers' pastimes and beauty advice specifically for teenagers were featured in the *Journal* and *Mayfair*.[27] Advertisements addressing teenaged readers directly were less common, but an increasing number of products referred to teenagers in their advertising, including promotions for skin creams, breakfast cereals, sewing machines, and sanitary napkins.[28]

Teenagers began to garner their own special features and issues, beginning in 1942 with the *Journal*'s Toast-to-the-Teens, an annual August issue that continued until 1950. *Chatelaine* published a series of feature articles referred to as 'Teen-Age Specials in 1945 and 1946. The articles covered a variety of topics, such as etiquette, career counselling, and clothing, and appeared in issues that included fashion stories, beauty columns, and advertisements aimed at female students. In August 1945, *Mayfair* changed the name of its annual College Issue to the Junior Issue and dedicated it to "The 'Teenagers! ... Those modern young lads and lassies who are the essence of today's youth."[29] It seems more than coincidence that Canadian magazines began making these changes just as *Seventeen* magazine appeared on newsstands in the United States and published its survey of American high school girls called *Life with Teena* in 1945.[30]

Back-to-school content was rare in Canadian magazines before the mid-1930s but quickly became the primary focus of August and/or September issues. *Mayfair* began to include fashions specifically for college students in its September issues, and by 1941, both the *Journal* and *Chatelaine* focused substantial parts of their September issues on younger readers they assumed were heading back to school and needed "lessons in femininity," to borrow Penny Tinkler's phrase, in order to put their best foot forward.[31] From 1943 to 1950, the *Journal* devoted an entire issue to the co-ed, and offered fashion spreads, surveys of high school and college

(31)

students' favourite movies and music, etiquette advice, home decorating suggestions, and beauty tips. In the 1940s, most of the content targeted at teenagers appeared in the late summer and early fall, when the school term began.[32] Editors and advertisers viewed students as potentially lucrative consumers and saw the beginning of the school year as an opportune time to advise them on purchases to augment their appearance in the classroom. Fashion stories and advertisements helped to foster the link between school and shopping that has become so lucrative for today's clothing retailers.[33]

Teenage content increased again in the late 1940s and 1950s when both *Chatelaine* and the *Journal* began publishing regular columns for teenaged readers focused on beauty advice and etiquette tips. These columns allowed the magazines to promote products and practices directly to younger readers, emphasizing their significance as a group while also implying that their value lay primarily in their appearance. In September 1949, *Chatelaine* began a sporadic feature called Teen Page, dedicated "to you ... the teen-year old," who was "staking this space for Chatelaine's teen-age news each month." *Chatelaine* gave the impression that teenagers were taking "their" share of the magazine. The column offered assistance with "all sorts of things – your manners, your looks, your clothes, your dates, your future," so that its reader could be a "bright-eyed, bright-thinking young person, ready to take a vital part in tomorrow's world."[34] The *Journal* included two columns between 1954 and 1958, when it ceased publication: Teenager's Datebook and Teen Session. Whereas the Datebook offered fashion and beauty advice, Teen Session featured teenagers' own opinions on selected issues, asking a panel of "typical teen-age boys and girls," as the magazine called them, to discuss school discipline, dating, and etiquette, among other topics. The *Journal* claimed the column was "for, and by, teenagers (in which parents may eavesdrop!)," addressing younger readers directly. In September 1956, *Chatelaine* began a new page for younger readers called Teen Tempo, which ran almost monthly until 1963. The one-page column was "packed with ideas and advice on dating, etiquette, clothes, records, and the sayings and doings of teen-agers all across Canada."[35] As magazines dedicated space to teenage content, they also included more teen-focused advertisements, mainly for beauty and personal care products. By the early 1960s, publisher Maclean Hunter believed teenagers constituted a large enough market segment to attract significant advertising dollars and merit their own magazine. It hoped that with *Miss Chatelaine*, published four to six times a year, it could "wean Canadian girls off American teen magazines."[36]

TOP OF THE CLASS
School Attendance and Affluence

As representations of young women multiplied in Canadian magazines in the 1930s and '40s, girls in their teen years were increasingly portrayed within the context of educational institutions. On the surface, this shift appeared to make sense, as the number of young women (and men) attending Canadian universities, colleges, and high schools rose over these decades. Nevertheless, the co-ed represented only a small and affluent minority of young women.

The increasing coverage of the co-ed in Canadian magazines was not in response to surging numbers of students. Ontario's high school population quadrupled between 1918 and 1938, but less than 40 percent of those aged fifteen to nineteen were attending secondary schools in September 1939. For every hundred children in the province who entered Grade 1 in that year, thirty completed Grade 10, and only three entered university.[37] Even in the early 1950s, slightly less than half of Manitoba's children remained in school until Grade 10. Some provinces raised the compulsory age of school attendance to sixteen, but grade retardation was still common, meaning that some students reached sixteen before they completed Grade 9 successfully. In several provinces, mandatory schooling for older teenagers applied only in urban areas; children in more rural school districts could still leave school at fourteen – and many did.[38] Although the number of young people in Canadian universities was rising, with 36,300 full-time enrolments in 1940, they represented only a fraction of the population aged 20–24 – just 3.5 percent in 1941.[39] Further, there were a mere six to seven thousand female undergraduates across Canada at that time, and women constituted between a fifth and a quarter of full-time university students between 1925 and 1960.[40] By contrast, nearly three-quarters

(33)

of American teenagers attended secondary schools in 1940 and university enrolment topped 10 percent.[41]

Although they were less numerous than their American counterparts, Canadian high school and university students were typically more economically secure than peers who left school for the workforce at the first opportunity. Numerous factors influenced decisions to remain in school or find work, but family income was a crucial one. Faced with difficult decisions about their children's education, some families were able to give younger siblings educational opportunities denied to older children because their wages had been needed. Those who remained in school were more likely to have families with some form of secure income and no need to send (additional) teenaged children out to work. Some teenagers, like Mary Peate, expected to complete high school and attend college but had to change their plans in response to changing family circumstances.[42]

While young women in Canada were certainly working outside the home more than ever before in the 1930s and '40s, Canadian magazines rarely referred to single, working women as teenagers. The co-ed did not work for wages; she existed in high school halls and on university campuses. In her *Journal* column, Grace Garner often gave readers advice about preparing for a job, or highlighted older women working in notably feminine occupations such as fashion design, but she rarely included content about young women working. Once a woman left school to work, she was no longer a teenager, regardless of her age. She had grown up. Magazines were of course also keen to encourage consumption among young working women, but made clear distinctions between her lifestyle and that of the co-ed.

Magazine editors depicted the co-ed as affluent enough to spend money she did not earn herself on new clothing and other commodities essential to the student lifestyle. The potential sources of young readers' funds were only ever hinted at, with the intimation that the ideal co-ed came from an upper-middle class family that had presumably weathered the Great Depression and had sufficient funds to both pay tuition and purchase new clothing. The co-ed was the fortunate beneficiary of "money and clothes from dad and mother," suggesting that even though she selected her own garments she did not pay for them.[43] For example, one column from the

Journal in 1938 encouraged readers to spend their "birthday cheque" on dancing lessons so they could impress their male peers at campus events. The same column made a weak reference to budgeting, cautioning girls to "appreciate that father is doing his best," but also assumed readers received a regular sum from their parents, even if they had to "acknowledge the limits of an allowance."[44] In 1941, *Mayfair* writer Gertrude Stayner posed as a college student discussing a back-to-school shopping trip made at her father's expense. "Poor Daddy," she sighed after describing her decision to purchase two different suit jackets to accommodate different skirt styles. "I guess I'll have to have a heart to heart talk with him about the advantages and disadvantages of hips before he gets the bill."[45] Evidently fashion, rather than budget, sometimes had to dictate purchases.

Advertisements for fur coats in *Mayfair* illustrate and complicate the class position of the co-ed in the late 1930s. Furs were standard advertising fare in the magazine, which saw itself as dedicated to the pursuits of Canada's elite, including the debutante balls and charity fundraisers hosted by Montreal's Junior League.[46] Fur coats have long been seen as status symbols, being expensive and requiring care. Their owners' lives were "nocturnal, rather than organized in labour-filled daylight – the starlets, wives of notables, the cultured, and the classy individualists, or simply, the truly rich."[47] By the 1930s, however, new treatment processes and mass manufacturing had caused a proliferation of "industrialized furs" sold at lower prices. Offering the cheaper coats alongside more expensive ones, retailers were "reaching while separating out lower-income purchasers."[48] The fur coat had been democratized.

Nevertheless, furs remained costly for many female students. Those advertised in *Mayfair*'s fashion spreads were not imitations, and served to reinforce the elite status of the co-ed. The September 1937 College Issue of *Mayfair* featured a grey squirrel coat "good for those all-important rushing teas [at a sorority] and rugby week-ends."[49] *Mayfair* promoted squirrel, raccoon, and kangaroo as "budget furs" that still managed to "make some of the most dashing young styles."[50] Fur trim was also a less expensive option; one wool coat in 1940 was advertised as featuring a "massive collar of selected Canadian Raccoon" for $55.[51] Another from 1942 noted that kangaroo fur "suggests costly beaver, yet it is an inexpensive fur that fits into college clothing budgets."[52] Kangaroo might have been cheaper than other furs, but a fur coat still cost approximately four times as much as a wool one.[53] Retailers also sold *Mayfair* readers on the value of a durable and versatile fur coat. One spread in 1943 called a full-length muskrat a "Round-the-clock Coat – casual enough to wear over campus clothes, smooth enough to go to the most important off-campus party!"[54] If you could wear your fur coat everywhere and it lasted a long time, perhaps the cost was not as great. Given that undergraduate arts students could expect to spend approximately $500 a year on tuition, books, and residence, however, it seems unlikely that many college students had fur coats in their dorm closets.[55] The co-ed who graced magazine pages in her fur coat implied that advertisers understood and sought to profit from the middle- and upper-class status of most female students. As magazines shifted their focus more singly to high school students in the 1940s, fur coats were no longer advertised as part of the co-ed's wardrobe.

LOOKING THE PART
Feminine Appearance in the Campus Scene

Magazines linked female students' appearance and use of commodities to their success at school, encouraging readers to spend time studying magazines and spend money to make sure they made the most of their school experience. Book smarts or intellectual curiosity mattered much less than appearance, as fashion editor Gertrude Stayner reminded readers in 1942: "Don't get the idea that because you got a first in History you don't need any lipstick."[56] Magazines illustrated and described the co-ed look, setting her within a campus scene. From one perspective, the co-ed claimed feminine space for young women on university campuses, where women were still very much in the minority. But if the co-ed allowed teenaged girls to imagine graduating from high school and attending university, she also embodied the importance of appearance – of being visible – to feminine success on campus.

"When you look right you feel right ... When you feel right you have fun ... When you're having a bit of fun you work hard," *Chatelaine* fashion editor Evelyn Kelly explained when suggesting that students purchase a selection of back-to-school clothes.[57] In this case, achieving good grades depended on looking "right": following the recommendations of magazines, wearing the correct clothes for a particular social situation, and scrutinizing one's appearance carefully through a heteronormative gaze. The female college student was encouraged to "Go Back a Smarter Girl," not by brushing up on her studies but by using the beginning of term to reassess her wardrobe and purchase new clothes.[58] Another article in the *Journal* asked young women to take a "Prep Course in College Fashions" by studying the clothing displayed.[59] Fashion advertorials used headlines such as "Majoring in Classics" and "Extra Credits in a College Wardrobe" to underscore the value of a female college student's clothing; the "classics" they were supposed to be studying were plaid skirts, not Latin, and extra credit, in this case, was for choosing a dress that could be worn both to classes and to afternoon tea parties.[60] Such fashion features suggested that the real study for the co-ed was of herself.

While magazines encouraged young readers to scrutinize and augment their wardrobe before the beginning of each school year, the basic elements varied little. Specific types of clothing characterized the co-ed's appearance. By choosing these essential garments, young readers donned a uniform of sorts, one that magazines argued would signify their student status to peers and ensure their social success. Young readers eager to adopt the co-ed look were encouraged to think that their current clothing would not be acceptable on campus. "Perhaps for the first time in your young life, you are planning a completely new wardrobe – to take with you on this big adventure," *Journal* writer Margaret Thornton told readers.[61] Anyone wishing to be a co-ed needed a "college trousseau" of versatile garments befitting an active social calendar. In 1938, *Mayfair* recommended packing a suit, four sweaters or jersey blouses, two skirts, nine dresses (formal and informal), two coats and an evening wrap or cape, five pairs of shoes, six pairs of pyjamas, and a flannel coat – to say nothing of hats, gloves, purses, and other accessories.[62] *Chatelaine* and *Journal* editors were typically more selective in their recommendations for back-to-school clothes.

Magazines promoted a wide array of garments to young readers, and editors and advertisers made it clear that there was a distinct student style. *Mayfair* insisted that the fashion industry was working hard to provide the specific garments required for a successful student experience. In September 1938, the magazine chastised readers, "It is an innocent error on your part to think that the harvest of smart college-going clothes has fallen haphazard into the shops. Designers and stylists, through intensive research, have delved into the very mood of college life, its problems and demands."[63] The magazine did not provide any details about this research, but its reprimand served to remind young students that manufacturers and retailers were acting in their best interests. They could trust that the garments advertised for co-eds were best suited for school days.

Fashion editors took pains to describe in detail what the co-ed should wear in order to look the part, and most agreed that clothes for campus should be sensible and versatile. Many college students adopted casual styles out of practical need. Low-heeled Oxford shoes were easier for long walks between classes, and sweaters were necessary in drafty school buildings.[64] *Chatelaine* was quick to point out that good-quality skirts and blouses could be worn both to class and to casual social events. One photograph caption informed readers, "When we meet at the drugstore after four for cokes, we want school clothes that have held their shape and are simple and well-cut but soft."[65] Similarly, *Mayfair* advertised a dress from Eaton's that "doubles for academic lectures and a rushing tea."[66] The co-ed was active, mobile, and yet concerned to maintain her good appearance as she moved quickly from one activity to another. While the cut, colour, and fabric of garments changed over time, skirts, blouses, and sweaters appeared year after year. The skirts were pleated or A-line, at the knee or mid-calf, and worn with fitted blouses and knitted sweaters. Fashion editors pointed out that separates could be mixed and matched easily, giving young readers a more diverse wardrobe. Conservative colours and patterns were advised and could be "pepped up" with accessories purchased more regularly.[67]

Although magazines promoted practicality, they took every opportunity to remind readers that the co-ed was always on display for her peers and should never be too casual. Dormitories were often spaces where students "pioneered new standards of casual dress," with many preferring "loose-fitting clothes that allowed the student to put her feet up on

— Calling All Co-eds! —

the desk or crawl under her bed to fetch a runaway ping-pong ball."[68] Magazine columnists acknowledged that pyjamas, slippers, and dressing gowns, or housecoats, were essential items for dormitory living, "to slip into for study, beauty rites, or chinning with your roommate."[69] At the same time, the co-ed never forgot – even in her dorm room – that her appearance mattered. One outfit displayed in *Mayfair* included a tailored jacket and skirt for classes, with "matching slacks for studying in residence." The accompanying photograph was of a young woman studying from a folio of notes, semi-reclined in an armchair with her feet up. The co-ed could relax but still be ready for action, "a clever solution to the quick-change problem of the girl with the crowded timetable."[70] Housecoats and pyjamas were advertised as cozy and warm, but those modelling them were often posed standing, smiling, and fully conscious of the reader's gaze. The implicit message was that the co-ed's appearance would be scrutinized even within the semi-privacy of her dorm room.

Throughout the late 1930s and the 1940s, the co-ed was recognizable in magazines not only because of her appearance but also because of her surroundings. Models were situated within campus scenes and described as engaging in apparently typical student experiences. Most fashion spreads and advertisements placed the co-ed beside imposing brick buildings, some with Ionic columns, grand entrances, or ivy-covered walls. Some stood in front of stone archways or in rooms lined with full bookshelves. Others occupied the stands at athletic fields or strolled along walks lined with mature trees. Sometimes they carried books and binders, or held a scroll and mortar board. The trappings of a college dorm room occasionally appeared in advertisements, featuring models flanked by desks and with books piled on the floor, or standing in rooms decorated with sports banners and college crests.[71] Advertisers labelled dresses and housecoats as "Co-ed" and "Varsity Velvet."[72] While there might be nothing distinctive about the housecoat itself, the setting marked it as a garment particularly suited to college life. Similarly, some fashion spreads focused on the campus ritual of supporting the school team, such as a *Journal* feature by Grace Garner from October 1938: "On Saturday afternoon when you shout, 'Come on, team!', be appropriately enthusiastic – and turned out – in this gay plaid wool dress."[73]

(39)

Magazine fashion spreads and advertisements underlined that within the campus scene the co-ed was always potentially subject to the gaze of men around her: classmates, potential dates, and professors. Presenting a "consistently attractive appearance on Campus" was smart, according to Garner, because then "you are always prepared for chance encounters which so often result in those casual but pleasant and profitable investments of time at the local fountain of refreshment." This potential for romance depended on young women following Garner's advice. As a reminder of the heterosexual male gaze, fashion photographs and illustrations often positioned young men beside or below the female model as admirers, or walking in the near distance behind her to suggest a yet-to-occur encounter. Image and text combined to delineate the co-ed: the female student whose appearance was as important as her academic ability, or more so, and who achieved her feminine look by purchasing clothing recommended to her in consumer magazines.

NATURAL, YOUTHFUL
Beauty Advice for the Co-ed

Just as common clothing items and styles in the magazines helped to cultivate and popularize the ideal appearance of the co-ed, beauty advice set age-appropriate standards, instructing young readers on how to discipline their bodies and habits to present an ideal appearance. As Jane Nicholas describes in *The Modern Girl*, beauty advice and advertisements gave the impression that beauty aids possessed a magical power. A beauty regimen could be transformative, making women beautiful with seemingly little effort – provided they followed the advice. Cosmetics and personal care products were sold as an essential part of feminine visibility because the modern woman wished to be seen in public, to be admired and desired.

As numerous historians of women's beauty culture have made clear, appearing beautiful required both commodities and constant effort.[74] Although beauty aids were available at a wide range of prices – meaning that working-class women could, and did, participate in beauty culture – these aids and their advertisements privileged whiteness as the feminine ideal, making it difficult for racialized women to appear as beautiful and

— Calling All Co-eds! —

modern.[75] Age mattered, too. Youth itself was a hot commodity beginning in the 1920s. Beauty columnists and advertisers regularly reminded women of the need to appear youthful, and the term *youthful* became synonymous with other positive terms such as *vitality, health, beauty,* and *modernity.*[76] Magazines provided advice on how to appear young and outlined the techniques and commodities necessary to achieve youthfulness, regardless of age. Nonetheless, beneath the advice lay an implicit assumption that at some point in the life course, women could no longer meet the feminine beauty ideal. Older women had to work much harder to appear younger, to reverse what advertisers called "unnecessary neglect."[77]

Adult women were the primary audience for the beauty advice found in magazines, bearing "the brunt of this body-work that increasingly took the body to problematic pieces and provided 'solutions' in jars for purchase."[78] However, columnists and advertisers increasingly addressed younger readers in *Chatelaine, Mayfair,* and *Canadian Home Journal* in the 1940s, presenting them with beauty advice for the co-ed. On the one hand, teenagers were reminded that their youth bestowed an envious "natural" beauty that they had only to maintain; on the other hand, they read that puberty, though a natural biological process, presented obstacles to an ideal appearance. If youth signified beauty, it followed that younger people should be beautiful naturally. Nevertheless, oily skin and hair, "excess" fat, body odour, and the onset of menstruation might cloud their beauty. These "problems" could be overcome with discipline and the correct commodities. Yet despite their frequent discussion of how to shape awkward teenaged bodies and young habits to beauty, magazines depicted only the ideal result: a slender, active, and well-groomed white female student with clear skin, glossy hair, and shining eyes. This was the co-ed: a young white woman who surmounted the challenges of puberty with ease.

Beauty editors and advertisers never tired of reminding young readers that their young age gave them natural beauty. "We older folk all envy the peaches-and-cream complexions and shiny, silky hair of you 'teenagers," noted beauty editor Eva Nagel Wolf in one of *Canadian Home Journal*'s back-to-school issues. At the same time, those in their teen years were told to "profit by our experience and heed a note of warning." Wolf

(41)

reminded her readers, "If you would have a smooth complexion and lovely hair when you are twenty, thirty, forty, begin caring for them when you are in your 'teens! We promise that this is not going to be too arduous. It merely means a regular routine which, if observed faithfully, will ensure pleasing and satisfying results later on."[79]

Columnists like Wolf advised teenaged girls to develop habits and use specific products to either find, enhance, or maintain their natural beauty into adulthood. "'Well-groomed—and simple!' That's the slogan for the modern girl," Jean Alexander informed *Chatelaine* readers in 1942, urging them not to "neglect one single thing which will contribute to that good grooming" but simultaneously to avoid working "too hard at giving ourselves an elegant glaze."[80] Two types of products were considered particularly important to teenaged girls in this period: facial soaps and sanitary napkins. Advice regarding skin care and menstruation illustrate the tension between supposedly natural beauty and the expected challenges of puberty.

Beauty experts and advertisers paid a lot of attention to adolescent skin. The co-ed had a clear complexion, rosy with health and vitality, unblemished by pimples.[81] And yet imperfect skin was also an expected part of puberty, when hormonal changes could make skin oilier or drier. One Ivory soap campaign appealed to "Captivating Teens" by pointing out that "your fresh, youthful beauty is often marred by too-active oil glands" before advising them to wash with Ivory three times each day.[82] Beauty columnists and advertisers promoted face-washing routines to avoid "problem" skin and acne. *Chatelaine* urged girls heading back to school to "start now ... to train yourself to keep your face fresh and glowing and *clean*." If pimples persisted it was "time to look at your diet" to eliminate rich and greasy foods.[83] Young readers who did not succeed with soap and/or vegetables were out of luck, as *Mayfair* noted: "It is hopeless to try and achieve beauty results by covering up a poor complexion with makeup."[84] *Chatelaine* columnist Adele White concurred. "To try and conceal an outbreak of acne by slathering on a double dose of foundation cream and makeup is running the risk of infection, with serious trouble ahead," she cautioned young readers.[85] In *Canadian Home Journal*, Wolf recommended girls apply a powder foundation, but only if their skin was clear. A complexion as "petal-smooth as a dewy rose" could be had with the right soap and the right hygiene habits.[86] *Chatelaine* fashion and beauty editor Vivian Wilcox seconded the simple routine, arguing in 1958 that most sixteen-year-old girls' beauty aids should be "sensibly confined to a facecloth, hairbrush, powder, and lipstick."[87]

At the same time, magazines reinforced the idea that beauty required study, again drawing parallels between the co-ed's successful appearance and her academic pursuits. As an advertisement for Elizabeth Arden noted, beauty was not a "snap course," but "the college girl who applies herself to better looks as diligently as she applies herself to chemistry or athletics is going to have honors as long as she likes."[88] Helena Rubenstein offered a "Young Modern Kit" as a ready-to-go "Beauty Course" for students who were heading "Back to school – back to books – back to classmates' appraising looks!"[89] Without clear skin, teenaged girls risked social ostracization. Ads for Ponds Cold Cream focused attention on vivacious teenaged girls who claimed to have avoided skin problems because they used the product advertised. "What does a good complexion mean to a high school girl?" one of the models was asked, to which she responded, "Plenty! No inferiority complex – loads more fun! And it's so easy to help keep your skin in condition."[90] The co-eds who appeared alongside beauty columns and in advertisements already possessed the ideal complexion. They stood smiling and seemingly carefree, and attributed their beauty to the judicious use of quality soaps and simple but regular skincare routines.

The onset of menstruation for girls was also presented as a potential obstacle to social success because, like a poor complexion, it could negatively affect their appearance. Similarly, it required specific habits and products, careful attention, and self-scrutiny. The subject of menstruation was still somewhat taboo. Puberty was sometimes discussed in women's magazines, but advertisements for sanitary napkins did not typically display the product or make explicit reference to menstruation. Kotex advertisements referred to "difficult days," "problem days," or "'certain' times" and, while they promoted the superior qualities of their cotton napkins, said nothing about what they were for or how to use them.[91] Kotex's "Are You in the Know?" campaign in the 1940s and early '50s made it clear that menstruation was only a problem if girls let it affect their confidence. In several advertisements, adolescent girls are pictured looking despondent while wondering why other girls didn't let problem days slow them down. When girls felt "blue," they should rely on Kotex to make them "confident, comfortable, carefree."[92] Rather than acknowledging that menstruation might cause painful cramping, heightened emotions, or fatigue, Kotex claimed it was anxiety about awkward or ineffective sanitary napkins that kept girls from their typical activities.

The co-ed in Kotex advertisements occasionally wore a pained expression, but it was not menstrual discomfort that caused her dismay. She was preoccupied with the thought that she was missing the active social life of a teenaged girl and worried that her condition would be visible to others. Kotex reassured readers that its "flat, pressed ends fit your figure, keep your secret safe."[93] The ad always included an illustration of the confident and active co-ed, having overcome any potential awkwardness because she used Kotex, playing basketball or cheerleading, dancing or surrounded by male admirers.

Canadian magazines thus featured beauty advice that produced the clean, groomed, and confident co-ed. While she was often lauded as a natural beauty, implying that her appearance was effortless, the co-ed required a regime to maintain her look that involved diet, exercise, sleep, a schedule for washing skin and hair, and products tailored to the oily skin and problem days teenaged girls could expect.

A WORTHY REPRESENTATIVE OF THE COLLEGIATE CROWD
The Cover Girl

Every year from 1943 to 1950, the *Canadian Home Journal* selected one female high school student to feature on the cover of its September back-to-school issue. In many ways, the *Journal's* cover girl embodied the quintessential co-ed in her appearance, her student status, and the economic activity she generated as a consumer. Cover girls embodied settler femininity; they were invariably white, middle-class high school students who used consumer products to present a respectable, confident self. Although she won the contest by visually standing out from the

— Calling All Co-eds! —

1.2 Teenaged cover girl on the *Canadian Home Journal* back-to-school issue, September 1946.

competition, the *Journal* insisted that the cover girl was also a "worthy representative of the collegiate crowd," a typical example of Canadian youth. She was thus simultaneously outstanding and standard, lauded as the feminine ideal that other high school girls should emulate. As Patrizia Gentile notes in her study of Canadian beauty pageants, "finding the 'ideal Canadian girl' reinstated whiteness and class hierarchies at the centre of the making of national subjectivities."[94] The celebrated white middle-class co-ed was a future mother and homemaker of a Canadian nation in which racialized and working-class or impoverished teenaged girls appeared to have no part.

From a marketing perspective, the Cover Girl contest was a lucrative collaboration between the *Journal* and Eaton's department stores, part of what Gentile calls the "beauty industrial complex" that connected those working in media, fashion, cosmetics, entertainment, and advertising.[95] Eaton's provided the *Journal* with access to a ready pool of potential cover girls from the Junior Councils. To be eligible for the contest, teenaged girls had to be members of one of these groups, which operated in Toronto, Montreal, Winnipeg, Hamilton, Calgary, and Edmonton in the 1940s and early '50s. At each Eaton's store, staff worked with local high schools to recruit sixteen- to eighteen-year-old students who could provide store employees with a teenage perspective on merchandise and report on current trends among their peers. Students were also promised that they would learn about the operations of a large retailer. The activities of the Junior Council and the boys' equivalent, the Junior Executive, are discussed in detail in subsequent chapters. Eaton's sent portraits of the junior councillors from each store to the *Journal* each year. Runners-up often appeared in other parts of the back-to-school issues, sometimes modelling merchandise – much of which came from Eaton's. On several occasions, the *Journal* ran a parallel dress design contest for teenaged girls, and the cover girl wore the winning style. The magazine was also featured in Eaton's window displays and store departments. When one of the Winnipeg junior councillors was chosen as the cover girl in 1948, for example, Eaton's dressed a window with photos of junior councillors and executives and several copies of the *Journal* spread open to various fashion spreads featuring Eaton's merchandise (see Figure 1.3).

The competition process was described in the back-to-school issues. In the first stage of the contest, the girls' peers – boys who were part of Eaton's Junior Executive groups – selected those they deemed the best. These choices were forwarded to the *Journal* for judging. The final decision rested with one or more men with some claim to authority about

— Calling All Co-eds! —

1.3 Window display at the Eaton's Winnipeg store announcing the selection of the *Canadian Home Journal* cover girl, 1948.

female beauty, typically artists, illustrators, or members of the film industry, who examined the photographs and determined the winner. She was then flown to Toronto for a "whirl of posings and parties," photographed for the cover, and interviewed for the magazine.[96] In one or two instances, a *Journal* editor reconnected with the cover girl the following year to provide a chatty update on her life since graduating from high school.

Multiple aspects of the competition reinforced the idea that teenaged girls' appearance would be scrutinized. Judging the contest using photographs – and including some of them in the magazine for readers to see – encouraged teenaged girls to pay close attention to their appearance.

Studio portraits "magnified the importance of a flawless face and a body that correctly measured up," Liz Conor notes. In her examination of beauty contestants in 1920s Australia, she argues that the use of photographs meant "beauty had to be redefined as evident in visual and measurable qualities, such as facial proportions, bodily measurements, the shape of the head, and its placement on the shoulders."[97] When the managing director of a British film company picked the 1946 cover girl from his New York hotel based solely on photographs, he claimed to have selected "the most interesting and attractive young personality in the group."[98] His assertion rested on the idea that a girl's personality was discernible from her portrait; her attractiveness suggested other admirable qualities such as intelligence, health, and moral character. Young readers were invited to compare their own faces in the mirror to the portraits they saw in the magazine, to see if they measured up.

Nevertheless, the *Journal* consistently avoided calling the competition a beauty contest. The winners were typically described as "poised and charming," and the magazine emphasized that "being attractive is not only a matter of 'looks', but a deeper, richer one of intelligence and pleasing disposition illuminating the entire personality."[99] Cover girl interviews focused on the winner's interests and activities, opinions, and plans. The fact that they were accomplished, studious, or dedicated to family or community service – information the judges did not have when they selected her – seemed only to reinforce the notion that they could see her character in her portrait. Like other beauty contests in this period, the Cover Girl competition was part of what Patrizia Gentile calls the "pageant paradox." By this she means that beauty pageants often claimed to be judging women's poise and charm, reflected in their outward beauty. Mid-twentieth-century pageant organizers presented their events as contests of personality above all, which bestowed a level of respectability that made it socially acceptable for middle-class women to participate. Beauty pageant contestants, Gentile argues, had to "sell sensuality while denying that sensuality and sex were central to beauty and physical attractiveness."[100] In order to present themselves properly, junior councillors had to recognize age-based beauty standards and perform beauty practices like those promoted in the *Journal*. At the same time, they were told it was their personality judges wanted to see; it was admiration, not desire, that contestants should attract from both judges and readers.[101]

While the cover girl received well-documented special treatment following her victory, the *Journal* emphasized that in many ways she was not exceptional. She represented all young Canadian women, as "Canada's Own Cover Girl." If she had poise, charm, and beauty, many other Canadian teenagers shared those model characteristics, according to the *Journal*. In 1944, beauty editor Eva Nagel Wolf insisted the magazine "might have selected a score or more of 'Cover Girls' had there been space to present them here," because so many Canadian teenagers presented what she called a young, fresh, and lovely appearance. She included portraits of thirteen other contestants, each one framed by a miniature magazine cover, to illustrate her point.[102] In each special issue, fashion spreads featured other contestants – also members of Eaton's Junior Council – to imply that many Canadian girls fit the mould even though they had not been selected as the prototype. Introducing 1945 cover girl Joy Hardy, the *Journal* gushed, "It becomes increasingly difficult to pick a cover girl from any 'teen-age group. For Canadian girls seem to become prettier and prettier with each new crop ... They're better groomed ... have more poise ... and they fairly breeze with unselfconscious charm! Joy Hardy is our shining example of all these attractive characteristics."[103]

In setting a standard of teenage appearance, the *Journal* wanted to fashion an identity young readers could admire and achieve using the beauty advice and products advertised in the magazine. Beauty advice in these special issues reflected this desire. In performing a makeover on one Junior Council member, beauty editor Patricia Skinner emphasized that they decided to make her up "as simply as possible so that any girl could copy same without undue expense or effort."[104]

The cover girls' whiteness also shaped expectations about which young Canadians could embody the co-ed. Black, Indigenous, and other racialized teenagers did not see themselves in the depictions of the "typical Canadian girl," whose "fair" and "rosy" skin was celebrated in the *Journal*'s pages. Whiteness was normalized because it went unremarked but was always on display, although ethnicity was sometimes mentioned as an explanation for natural beauty. For example, the September 1946 issue noted that Joy Hardy was born in Toronto to a Scottish mother and a "Winnipegger" father, while the September 1945 issue attributed cover girl Lenore Johannesson's ash-blonde hair and slim good looks to her parents' Icelandic origins.[105] Hardy and Johannesson embodied their families' settler pasts as they performed settler femininity in the present. Presented alongside photographs, comments about the winners' charm and poise underscored the notion that the modern successful co-ed, representative of teenage Canadian femininity, could only ever be white.

The Cover Girl competition also affirmed the co-ed's status as a middle-class consumer. Most obviously, she was always a high school student, as only members of Eaton's Junior Council could participate. This requirement reinforced the connection between youth culture and educational institutions and meant that the cover girl also came from a family that was able to make ends meet without requiring teenage income. The *Journal* described cover girls as coming from smaller families with few siblings. They played tennis, belonged to ski clubs, shopped regularly, and expressed the desire to attend university once they graduated high school. Their families travelled on holidays and consumed regular restaurant meals.[106] All of these characteristics and behaviours marked them as middle or even upper class, as exemplary teenagers rather than typical. They lived lives to which many Canadian teenagers could only aspire.

Aspiring was, of course, the point. Sociologist Mike Featherstone points out that "images invite comparisons: they are constant reminders of what we are and might with effort yet become."[107] Beginning in the mid-1930s, young readers of Canadian women's magazines were invited to imagine themselves as the co-ed depicted on the pages of *Mayfair*, *Chatelaine*, and *Canadian Home Journal*. She embodied what could be called a student lifestyle. Wearing the clothes best suited to the activities associated with school, she engaged in heterosocial activities such as dating, and was admired by male peers and emulated by female ones. She relied on clothing and beauty products to achieve her so-called natural beauty and on magazines to inform her about these commodities. Through her self-management, she cut a confident and purposeful figure, and was held up as both a model for others and a typical young Canadian.

— Calling All Co-eds! —

WHILE ADOLESCENCE WAS ALREADY an established biological and social transition between childhood and adulthood by the 1930s, manufacturers and retailers sought to capitalize on and to commodify this transition by associating school attendance and student status with specific fashions and beauty regimens. Magazines shifted their focus from college-going students in the late 1930s to younger high school girls by 1950, but the focus on using commodities to present a feminine appearance and achieve social success remained. The images and advice they prescribed clearly connected teenage culture with consumption. Female students were ostensibly free to adopt or reject the idealized image of the teenaged consumer as they saw fit, but regardless of whether they ignored them or read them devotedly (as Mary and Cath did), women's magazines helped to spread the idea of the co-ed as a distinct identity, associated school attendance with shopping, and reinforced the practice of turning to popular publications to find advice and products to regulate and shape their appearance in accordance with their age.

2

Act Your Age

Authority and the Meanings of Teenage Consumption

IN NOVEMBER 1957, the *Canadian Home Journal* asked its readers, "How Mature are Teenagers?" For the answer, the magazine turned to six students in Grades 11 and 12, printing snippets of their conversation about signs of maturity among their peers. The students defined maturity in several ways: not being tied to "mother's apron strings," making "the right decision at the right time," thinking about the future more than the present, and doing what was expected and socially acceptable. They equated maturity and adulthood with independence, an ability to make choices, and an awareness of social norms. The magazine summed up their discussion by stating that being mature simply meant "being able to act your age."[1]

Yet being able to act one's age was not merely a matter of individual competencies or judgment. Both socio-economic circumstances and broader social change shaped young people's experiences and choices. Meeting socially constructed age-based expectations was not always possible or easy. Depression, war, and postwar reconstruction fundamentally reshaped childhood and youth in Canada and other Western nations between 1930 and 1960. It was in this context that young people's interactions with the marketplace and their status as consumers began to matter more.

The connection between consumption and maturity shaped discourses of youth both during and after the Second World War. The often subtle and sometimes contradictory representations of teenagers' consumption in newspapers and magazines from the 1940s and 1950s reveal how teenagers' maturity – or ability to act one's age – was linked to consumer choices. The teenaged consumer was just one of many divergent discourses focused on young people during these decades, many of which problematized their upbringing, behaviour, and appearance. To journalists, educators, civic officials, social critics, and medical professionals, teenagers could be, at best, "irresponsible hoodlums who spend most their time making a nuisance of themselves" and at worst, delinquents whose criminality threatened not only their futures but the future of the nation.[2] As Mary Louise Adams notes, young people "could be perceived as trouble simply because they were teenagers. The category of having the potential for trouble slipped easily into the category of being trouble."[3] From the perspective of retail employees, advertising workers, and magazine editors, however, teenagers were no trouble at all. These market actors eagerly presented them as capable authorities when it came to selecting and using consumer goods.

As a group, young people in the 1930s were decidedly unable to act their age. According to Heidi MacDonald, underemployment and unemployment made it much more difficult for people in their late 'teens and twenties to find work, or establish their own households, and "many young men growing up in the Great Depression got stuck in a liminal phase between youth and adulthood."[4] Some young women in urban centres did see their employment opportunities broaden, but low wages and unprecedented levels of male unemployment delayed many marriages, disrupting another marker of the transition from childhood to adulthood. Some families relied on young people's wages to supplement household income; however, most people under the age of twenty-one worked in low-skilled and unskilled labour and poorly paid service jobs.[5] A broad coalition of social and government agencies expressed concern

(53)

about the extended economic dependency of Canadians aged eighteen to twenty-four, a "twilight world of prolonged childhood," and the grave consequences it could have on the nation's future prosperity.[6]

As socio-economic conditions changed for many Canadians during and following the Second World War, the meaning of acting one's age changed, too. Wartime mobilization ended unemployment for many, and income and spending levels rose steadily. While government regulations on production limited the purchase of certain items – particularly automobiles and household appliances – spending on clothing, restaurant meals, cinema tickets, and other smaller items increased between 1939 and 1945.[7] Nevertheless, adults remained concerned about young people's ability to reach maturity successfully. Although young people had made clear contributions to the war effort by raising money through War Savings Certificates, collecting materials during salvage campaigns, preparing first aid supplies, and labouring in fields and factories, juvenile delinquency was perceived to be rising, and older adults worried about how the war's effects on families (specifically enlisted fathers and working mothers) would shape the younger generation.[8]

By the 1950s, the economic circumstances of many young people had much improved. Unemployment remained low until late in the decade, and steady incomes allowed many Canadian families to increase their spending. Economic growth compressed expected transitions to adulthood; rather than struggling to find work and delaying marriage, young people in the 1950s reached these markers of maturity in less time than their parents had. The number of people in their late teens and early twenties who were leaving school, finding work, and marrying increased.[9] With secure incomes and government benefits, many children of the 1940s and '50s grew up in families more closely identified with the goods they purchased than by their fathers' names, deeds, or occupations. The ideal childhood – often termed the normal (and thus expected) childhood – was separate from the adult world. It was defined by school and church attendance, household chores, outdoor play, guided recreation and, increasingly, commercialized leisure. Children could be slowly introduced to adult responsibilities at age-appropriate moments suggested by child development theorists and psychologists.[10] While adults were full persons, "responsible, rational, able members of society," young people were "'human becomings', who are undergoing development and education and who are not yet full members of society."[11] With memories of the Depression and its hardships not far distant, many parents in the 1950s saw their teenaged children as having few responsibilities or worries.

Amid these broad economic and social changes, a subtle but significant shift took place. As retailers, advertisers, and consumer magazines imagined an ideal teenaged consumer in the early 1940s – the white, urban, middle-class, high school student – they emphasized teenagers' maturity and ability to make wise purchasing decisions (with the guidance of consumer magazines). The teenager epitomized the prolonged and carefree childhood many middle-class Canadian adults wanted for their offspring, while their consumption signified that they were sufficiently adult to be addressed directly by retailers. Throughout the war and afterwards, market actors asserted that teenagers were the ultimate authority on their own needs – they did not require parental intervention when making consumer decisions. During the war, these assertions were countered to an extent by concerns that teenagers' purchase and use of faddish clothing dictated by short-lived fashion trends signified their immaturity. Teenagers' competence as consumers had consequences both for their own adult lives and for the nation's future. Following the war, as Canadians embraced what Bettina Liverant calls a "cautious consumerism," teenagers' increasingly direct relationship with retailers and consumer goods was recast as a normal part of growing up, with fads presented as a particularly teenage form of self-expression.[12]

WHO COULD KNOW BETTER?
Teenage Advisory Groups

By the end of the 1930s, it was almost standard practice in American department stores to form advisory groups from among students, according to an industry source quoted in the *Chicago Daily Tribune* in 1941.[13] Organizers of these groups wanted to ensure that the goods and messages being offered in stores or on the pages of magazines were of interest to younger consumers. Beginning in the early 1940s, Canadian retailers including the T. Eaton Company and, in Toronto, the Robert Simpson Company and John Northway & Sons, as well as magazines such as *Chatelaine* and *Canadian Home Journal*, selected high school and college students to offer their opinions on products and to help produce magazine content. These students could help retailers and magazine editors reach other students, a connection that companies publicized in magazines and newspapers to demonstrate that they were well informed about teenage wants and needs.

In the fall of 1940, the T. Eaton Company convened its first Junior Fashion Council, inviting the teenaged daughters, sisters, and friends of Eaton's employees to meet at the Queen Street department store. The Council was the brain-child of Jack Brockie, merchandise display manager at the company's main Toronto store. Brockie had been working at Eaton's for decades. He oversaw the store's annual Santa Claus Parade, arguably the company's most successful marketing event, and was part of a network of retail managers across Canada and the United States who shared marketing practices in industry journals and through private correspondence. Brockie also headed Eaton's public relations department prior to his retirement in 1963. He was well positioned to imagine the value of having a group of young people to consult consistently on teenage habits, preferences, and desires.

Initial meetings of the Junior Fashion Council convinced Brockie that the girls' opinions were useful. Over eight meetings they attended two store fashion shows and completed two surveys about the kinds of clothing and accessories they liked. They were taken on a shopping tour of the store, during which "each girl shopped with an approximate budget in mind and their purchases were recorded." The girls' survey responses were also communicated to the merchandise office for consideration. Brockie reported that "the Councillors give good leads to new fads in school girls' wardrobes."[14] He believed that a well-organized program of weekly meetings would produce a wealth of useful information that the company could use to attract more teenaged customers, both male and female. In 1941, the group met again, this time with representatives selected from Toronto's public high schools. Brockie also expanded the program to include a Junior Executive composed of high school boys. At the same time, Simpson's department store in Toronto began its own advisory group, called the Collegiate Club. Like Eaton's, it drew members from public schools across the city.[15] In 1947, the Junior Fashion Council was renamed simply the Junior Council.

Jack Brockie and the other employees who ran Eaton's Junior Council and Executive described its participants as active authorities on teenaged consumer desires. In publicity documents and meeting minutes, Eaton's employees reiterated that the students deserved the company's attention and could assist the retailer to serve young people more ably. "How were Eaton's to know what to sell them?" an article in the company's Winnipeg store newsletter *Contacts* asked, then concluded that "the most logical approach" was to ask them, "for actually, who could know better what they wanted than the young people who were doing the buying?"[16] The company portrayed the teenager as an authoritative, knowledgable consumer with valuable opinions who was mature enough to engage directly with the marketplace. The company asserted that during the Second World War, "high school kids stopped being children," enlisting in the armed forces, doing vital volunteer work, working in war industries, and supporting their families.[17] Rather than seeing this rapid escalation of duties as a loss of childhood, Eaton's suggested that their experiences made them "important citizens" who were "literate, educated, exuberant, intelligent, and capable." They had "frank and decided" opinions, shopped without their parents, often spent their own money, and were "a group with strong likes and dislikes and a good idea of what they wanted."[18] Although they were under the age of majority (which was twenty-one until 1970), teenagers' presence in Eaton's stores gave them the right to address the company – and to be addressed – as adults.

Brockie and the Junior Council and Executive program's advisors at different stores invited buyers and managers from various departments to bring merchandise to the meetings. A sample of surviving meeting minutes from 1946–51 includes frequent mentions of company employees' soliciting the girls' and boys' opinions about clothing, shoes, accessories, records, and even furnishings. Eaton's employees were reportedly surprised and impressed by the students' comments. In one instance, a buyer who was showing junior councillors a selection of shoes was

(57)

— The Scramble for the Teenage Dollar —

"flabbergasted by the unanimous opinion of the girls that if he concentrated on four patterns he would meet teen-agers' needs." He was also astonished when the same four shoe styles outsold all others in their category that year.[19] His experience was repeated on several occasions to illustrate the Council's effectiveness, including in a story in the *Globe and Mail*.[20]

Boys' opinions on Eaton's merchandise were no less important. In 1947, the Junior Executive advisors shared several examples of boys' assistance with merchandising in their stores. In Montreal, "the boys are very anxious to get blazers specially designed to suit the taste of the high school crowd." The store planned to have samples of the boys' designs made up for their approval. The Winnipeg store noted that their buyers were soliciting junior executives' approval before purchasing stock. The Hamilton advisor reported that he was sending the minutes from every Junior Executive meeting to "all merchandising departments concerned."[21] While shopping was presumed to be a feminine activity, Eaton's assumed that boys would be no less interested than the girls in their appearance, nor in telling the company what they liked and disliked in apparel and other merchandise. "The boys have a big influence in the buying of grads' apparel, the deciding of sweater colours, etc.," the *Globe and Mail* noted in a 1944 profile of the Junior Council and Executive.[22]

In addition to reviewing merchandise brought to meetings, both boys and girls participated in written surveys that asked their opinions on everything from their favourite date outfits to their career plans.[23] Company officials believed surveys were a valuable tool, requesting precise detail from the junior executives and councillors about their preferred stores, brands, how much they spent on clothing each year, and what they found appealing about specific advertisements. Girls were asked to list their favourite colours and fabrics for suits, dresses, and formal gowns.[24] Boys were asked what kind of clothes they typically wore in different situations. "What do you wear at home studying?" the company asked junior executives in Winnipeg, followed by five other questions about what boys might wear "out on a movie and coke date" or "when out with the gang." The boys' answers varied little from "sweater and pants," but the questions demonstrate the company's desire to ensure that its stores stocked the items made up the typical high school wardrobe.[25] Councillors and executives were asked to list their three favourite places to shop for eleven different clothing items, with explanations of their preferences.[26]

Junior Council and Executive members were also placed front and centre when promoting merchandise to younger customers. Several stores began using tags to identify garments that met with councillors' or executives' approval. In 1948, the advisors developed a central policy for use of these tags, to ensure that the same rules were in force at all stores and that the tags truly reflected preferences. The advisors agreed that department managers and buyers should not be able to pressure teenagers to approve specific items, and that "all approvals be obtained on secret ballot to ensure a free and unbiased approval being given on merchandise."[27] Store employees were keen to ensure the authenticity of the tags, which were to be placed only on garments that reflected councillors' and executives' popular opinion.

Eaton's also asked councillors and executives to model clothing in newspaper advertisements, particularly the *Canadian High News*, which was distributed to secondary schools. The students were identified by name and school, and their role as members of Eaton's Junior Council or Executive featured prominently as proof that the company was listening to students and taking them seriously. Rival store Simpson's also used testimony from members of its Collegiate Club in newspaper ads. In one full-page advertisement in the *Globe and Mail* in 1946, a drawing of a girl and boy dressed for a night out appeared next to text in which the girl asked, "Why does Simpson's go over so big with the Hi-Crowd?" Her friend Jerry claimed it was because store employees "take a real interest in us," organizing Friday night gatherings with "super dance bands." The young woman noted that she and Jerry were part of the Collegiate Club, whose members "help advise on what teen-agers like to do, the kind of clothes we want to wear, the kind of things we go for." Because of their advice, she declared, "when Sloppy Joes and sharp ties make way for newer fads, we know Simpson's will be first with the latest and best."[28]

Magazine editors employed similar tactics to lend authenticity to fashion spreads and beauty advice, using surveys and first-person descriptions to present high school and college students as the most informed experts on teenage needs. One strategy was to describe products in a young

(59)

2.1 Junior Executive member Don Beauprie with an unidentified female member of the Junior Council in a photo taken for use in an advertisement for Eaton's Montreal store. A note Don wrote on the reverse reads, "Modelling job – and I got to keep the coat!"

person's voice. A fashion spread in *Mayfair* depicted Jean Wright, a student at University College of the University of Toronto, in the living room of her sorority house. "The minute I'm back from lectures I like to get into slacks," Jean proclaimed, a statement that echoed the popularity of more casual clothing among co-eds in American college dormitories.[29] On several occasions, magazines used endorsements from other female students to advise college- and high school-aged readers. Teenaged readers did not have to believe what adult magazine writers said was popular – they could hear it directly from students themselves. In 1942, *Mayfair* readers were advised to "take a tip from the senior co-eds, before shooting the bundle on your own college wardrobe." Female students from several universities proceeded to propose the best clothing for the ideal college co-ed: "For Campus wear, Beatrice Grant of Queen's thinks the sweater and skirt the ideal outfit. Saddle shoes are worn for campus footwear, although Evelyn McGraw, McMaster senior, claims that the 'loafer' type of shoe is becoming increasingly popular."[30] It was a common strategy in back-to-school issues to circulate a survey to high school students or to "women editors of college publications" at universities across Canada and then report on the most popular styles.[31]

Magazine editors also made use of youth advisory groups, though in a more limited capacity, to promote teenage authority and the magazine's presumed advantage in understanding younger readers and in order to expand their readership. In 1945 and 1946, columnist Lotta Dempsey produced a series of feature articles in collaboration with the *Chatelaine* Teen-Age Council. The Council was formed from groups of high school girls (and a few boys) in several cities across Canada who helped Dempsey to write articles that incorporated their views on various topics, from manners and dating to recreation and declining church attendance. Each article was presented "As Told to Lotta Dempsey," to emphasize the students' influence on the content. As *Chatelaine* explained in introducing the Council in Hamilton, Ontario, "Everything you read in the story is the result of a series of round-table sessions held by the Council ... All the 'dos' and 'don't's' are their own ideas, with no adult prodding."[32] Editor Evelyn Kelly also drew on Council participants for fashion stories in each issue, invoking their authority when presenting the best new styles.

"How do we know?" she anticipated readers asking. "Because we asked them – questionnaired all our Chatelaine Councillors about the kinds of clothes they want for dates and school this season."[33] Photographs of the girls accompanied each piece, and on several occasions *Chatelaine* included a group shot showing them "thrashing out the pros and cons" of a particular issue: What are the causes of juvenile delinquency? Should we go to college?[34] The students were always identified by name, connecting them to their school and community.

The magazine's 'Teen-Age Specials sometimes addressed more serious topics, but the tone was consistently colloquial and conspiratorial. They employed popular slang, favoured local activities, and discussed preferred modes of dress and behaviour. Amid the frequent focus on lighthearted fare, however, the articles gave the impression that high school students had concerns worth taking seriously. As the Winnipeg Council wrote in "Looking Ahead to your First Job," adults liked to think teenagers were silly and carefree, "But we know differently, don't we? We've got a *lot* of things to think about, these last years of high school. And believe us, we're thinking."[35] "How Do You Rate with Your Crowd?" offered etiquette advice from the Hamilton Council, describing various social situations as "our problems." Readers were invited to confide with a confession: "One of our biggest problems is the way our parents treat our friends, without realizing it. You too?"[36] The rhetorical use of "we" and "our" blurred editorial authority and invited readers to see themselves as part of a wider community based on their shared age, activities, and concerns. They were also being encouraged to feel a sense of shared experience at not being taken seriously by the adults in their lives.

Canadian Home Journal editors used many of the same techniques in the Teen Session column, which appeared monthly for several years in the mid-1950s. "Nobody knows more about teen-age problems than teenagers themselves," the *Journal* acknowledged in the first column, which introduced six "typical teen-age boys and girls who will meet each month to talk about teen life." The magazine noted that conversations would be tape-recorded and transcribed "to make sure you get the actual word-for-word report."[37] Rather than compiling these opinions into a narrative piece, as Lotta Dempsey had done, the *Journal* published the Teen Sessions in an abridged interview format with very little editorial comment. The high school students' opinions were attributed to them directly, and the *Journal* frequently reminded readers that the remarks were unaltered and authentic. In 1956, the column included a photograph of the students in conversation around a table with assistant editor Helen Kirk. The caption drew readers' attention to the microphone on the table, which "picks up and records every word."[38] According to the topics covered in Teen Session, teen life consisted of figuring out how to be popular, what to wear to school and on dates, and when it was acceptable to go steady.

The existence of teen advisory councils in the 1940s and '50s suggests a desire on the part of Canadian business interests both to know more about young customers and to present themselves as authorities on teenagers by consulting the source directly. By repeatedly turning to groups of high school students for comments on what "the teenager" was like, what they wore and bought, how they acted, and how they felt about key issues in their society, department stores and magazines reinforced the idea that people in their teens were individuals with valid opinions who could act responsibly. In the eyes of retailers and advertisers, they were mature enough to be addressed directly as consumers, and a group whose needs – extrapolated from the information received from youth advisory councils – deserved to be met.

Did it work? Jack Brockie and his fellow council advisors could not require Eaton's buyers to pay attention to councillors and executives when selecting stock. Writing to J.P. Heffernan, who was in charge of advertising for Eaton's branch stores, Brockie explained that it was up to department managers and buyers to make use of the information gleaned from school representatives:

"If Departments will believe what they read in the analysis of these surveys, they can capture sales and build up good will and satisfaction, but if they feel they are right and youth is wrong, then there is little that we can do about it. We have found in Toronto, that once Departments are convinced that they are helped by the Councils, then things happen and the youngsters are used for all kinds of tests, so that the merchandise we show will appeal to the young shoppers."[39]

Brockie's note to Heffernan suggests the possibility that not all department managers were equally responsive to his urging to heed the advice. Nevertheless, Brockie remained convinced of the students' authority in matters related to teenage consumer desires.

THE SWEATER AND THE SUIT
Fads in Wartime

The idea that teenagers wielded significant consumer authority and economic clout existed alongside representations of them as too immature and irrational to be considered full-fledged consumers. Adult commentators often offered young people's adherence to "fads" as evidence of ill-advised consumer choices. The term *fad* carried negative connotations, implying that a particular product or practice did not conform to the dominant aesthetic and that its popularity reflected poor taste. Furthermore, synonyms such as *craze* and *mania* intimated that those who adhered to fads were passionate, foolish, or suffering from a mental illness. By the 1930s, *fad* also carred a clearly gendered association: purchasing a popular item on a whim was a decidedly feminine or femininizing behaviour. Critics of consumer culture depicted women as the consumers most likely to "flit about, make impulsive decisions, and buy worthless goods."[40] Closer analysis reveals that young men could be subjected to the same scrutiny when they displayed enthusiasm for a fad.

Several teenage clothing trends of the 1940s were labelled fads, provoking anxiety and demonstrating how strongly self-presentation was by this point assumed to be an outward manifestation of an individual's inward character. Both during and after the Second World War, connotations of fads such as the sloppy joe sweater (worn by girls) and the zoot suit (worn by boys) associated these garments with sloppiness and, by association, a carelessness that threatened the future health of the Canadian nation. Reactions to the zoot suit were more severe – the garment sparked well-documented riots between men in uniform and young people in several North American cities – yet denunciation of the sloppy joe was equally persistent. Both garments threatened to undermine a properly gendered display of patriotism and compromised the symbolic power of white, middle-class youth as the embodiment of Canada's future economic security. Critics attempted to curtail the popularity of these garments through rhetoric that linked them to an irrational (and thus feminized) immaturity.

The zoot suit and the sloppy joe sweater have distinct genealogies in the dress history of the twentieth century, but both are tied to the rise of youth culture in the United States in the 1920s and '30s. The zoot suit emulated and exaggerated elements that were already central to the men's garment industry, which was influenced by both the increasing popularity of sportswear and trends among college men for unusual cuts and colours. In 1941, retailer Sears, Roebuck and Company, "the benchmark of everyday, affordable clothes," sold suits for young men with wide legs and large lapels.[41] Zoot suits took these features to the extreme. They featured high-waisted trousers that were wide at the knee and tapered at the ankle, and long jackets with wide, padded shoulders, often in very bright colours or bold patterns.

The rising popularity of sportswear also made sweaters more common in the 1920s and '30s, particularly among female American college students; in 1939, the editors of *Vogue* reported that 80 percent of female college students owned between five and fifteen sweaters. The sloppy joe was an oversized knit pullover or cardigan, sometimes borrowed from a boyfriend or taken from a brother or father. It was commonly worn to mid-thigh, with long sleeves rolled up.[42] Retailers tried to capitalize on the trend, marketing cardigans, pullovers, and even jackets with the "Sloppy Joe" label. By 1944, women's magazines including the *Canadian Home Journal* frequently noted that high schoolers "across the country cling to their beloved Sloppy Joes."[43]

Both trends originated in the United States but were worn by young people in Canada throughout the 1940s and into the 1950s. Canadian wartime regulations shaped reactions. While clothing was not rationed during the war, manufacturers were limited in the kind and amount of fabric they could use to manufacture garments. Clothing styles were also controlled by the Wartime Prices and Trade Board, or WPTB. As the *Globe and Mail* reported to readers in March 1942, the authorized style for a men's suit consisted of "a single-breasted jacket, trousers without cuffs,

— The Scramble for the Teenage Dollar —

and several other restrictions designed to save cloth.'[44] These regulations made the manufacture and sale of zoot suits – with their extreme trouser widths, long coats, and large lapels – illegal. Nevertheless, the suits continued to be worn, and WPTB officials suspected they were being imported from the United States.[45] Sweater manufacture was not prohibited, but wool supply was regulated to ensure that enough was available for both military and civilian needs. In a 1942 administrative order from the WPTB, wool administrator David Dick noted that "it is necessary in the public interest to conserve and limit the supply of wool entering into the production of articles for civilian use."[46] Regulations did not prevent teenaged girls from acquiring sloppy joes, because unlike zoot suits the sweaters did not need to be tailored or purchased new. During the war Canadians were encouraged to repurpose and reuse garments, and the consumer branch of the WPTB set up remake clinics in major cities to help homemakers transform older or unused items of clothing into new outfits for other members of their families.[47] Given their frequent association with second-hand use, one might assume that sloppy joes would be lauded as a patriotic effort to make use of existing materials, but that wasn't the case. Both zoot suits and sloppy joes were decried as fads that demonstrated young people's immaturity.

The zoot suit is probably best known for its role in riots between servicemen and young, predominantly Black and Hispanic male civilians in several North American cities in 1943 and 1944. The clashes, which have been well documented by historians in both the United States and Canada, made the term *zoots* a powerful shorthand for petty criminals and juvenile delinquents. Those wearing zoot suits – *zoot suiters*, they were often called – also wore them to signal class and ethnic solidarity.[48] Critics of the suits were keen to racialize and thus problematize the young men who wore them, pointing to the garment's origins in the Black culture of Harlem as proof of its inferiority. The zoot suit was "the outfit of the urban dandy, unmanly in its various overstated details – a suit for lolling about street corners and smoky billiard halls, for drinking and 'cutting a rug' in dance halls, but not for working or fighting or carrying out the activities that proper adult males were supposed to carry out."[49]

— Act Your Age —

Even before tensions escalated between enlisted and civilian men, the zoot suit was employed to distinguish boys from men in uniform. An article from the *Toronto Daily Star* in December 1942 provides a striking example. It recounted the adventures of sixteen-year-old Torontonian Tom Brown, who trained as a commando and survived the raid on Dieppe only to be discharged because his parents informed the army that he was underaged. Back in class at Central Technical School, Brown was described as restless and eager to return to active duty overseas as soon as possible. The lively story of a teenaged veteran drew clear distinctions between Brown's military and civilian appearance. The front-page headline "Zoot Pants and All, Tom Brown Is Back in School" appeared beneath two photographs of Brown, one as "the Commando" and other as "the Schoolboy." The military uniform is in stark contrast to Brown's school clothes, which included striped trousers with cuffs, baggy socks, pointy shoes, and a boldly printed necktie. The reporter noted that while it was strange to hear a high school student so attired describe throwing grenades, after his service to his country he has the "right to wear zoot-suits if he wants to."[50] Although he was too young to remain in the army, the article implied that Brown's experience overseas authorized him to make choices on his own behalf. This was somewhat ironic, given that Brown told the newspaper he would have chosen to remain in uniform if he had really had a choice. At the same time as he lauded the young man's bravery, the reporter also gently mocked Brown for reverting to his juvenile appearance upon return to his studies.

Similar contrasts appeared in subsequent newspapers in 1943, including a brief piece in April about Oshawa resident Dave Williamson, a parachute trooper who had to "walk the streets in his 'jump suit'" when his regular uniform was at the cleaners. The *Toronto Daily Star* noted that Oshawa residents might have mistaken the long jacket and tapered trousers of his outfit for a zoot suit but reassured readers that Williamson was a member of the 1st Canadian Parachute Batallion, having volunteered on his eighteenth birthday after seven unsuccessful previous attempts.[51] In June, the *Star* ran an article about how strong and athletic high school boys became when they volunteered for the Ontario Farm Service Force over the summer, placing the text adjacent to an article reporting that

(67)

— The Scramble for the Teenage Dollar —

the Japanese were praising American zoot suit rioters.[52] While the placement could have been coincidental, it created a clear contrast between Canadian high school students supporting the war effort and problematic teenaged consumers purchasing garments that gave comfort to the enemy. As the zoot suit gained in popularity and notoriety, it made a useful foil for the patriotic efforts of those wearing the "correct" uniform.

Throughout 1943 and 1944, violent encounters between servicemen and young men in Verdun and Montreal, Quebec, in Vancouver, and in and around Toronto were most often blamed on those whose persistence in sporting zoot suits despite wartime regulations and patriotic duty denoted their immaturity. Young, seemingly able-bodied men dressed in "outlandish" clothes affronted those in military uniform. In restaurants, theatres, parks, and other places of commercial amusement, verbal exchanges repeatedly led to fighting and injuries. In May 1943 in Toronto, after reports of men in uniform "tossing the zoot suiters into Lake Ontario" near the Sunnyside refreshment stand, where young people often gathered to listen to music on Sunday evenings, the police seized the jukebox "to prevent a serious breach of the peace."[53] That same month an estimated two hundred rioters were involved in street fighting in St. Lambert, Quebec, outside Montreal. Those involved alleged that zoot suit–wearing young men had tried to eject those not wearing zoot suits from a restaurant.[54] Later that summer, a skirmish at Burlington Beach, west of Toronto, was explained by one police officer as the fault of young men wearing zoot suits: "As many as 200 zoot-suiters frequented the popular sand strip resort and 'trouble invariably followed,' he claimed."[55]

The following year, clashes in the streets of Verdun, Montreal, and Vancouver were similarly blamed on groups of zoot-suiters, whose habit of "hanging around soda bars and the like" provoked enlisted men.[56] In early June, violence in Montreal spilled over into the smaller town of Verdun when more than a hundred sailors based in the city arrived at the Verdun Dance Pavilion and confronted a group of approximately sixty young people, some of whom were wearing zoot suits. As historian Serge Durflinger notes, the sailors attacked some men whose pre-war suits (with cuffs) they mistook for zoot suits. In response to the brawl, the navy imposed a curfew, cancelled sailors' leave for a week, and prohibited

(68)

— Act Your Age —

them from visiting the pavilion. Despite these consequences, and the fact that zoot suit–wearing civilians were often more injured than servicemen in these clashes, sympathy invariably rested with men in uniform. One Verdun newspaper questioned the sailors' discipline, but the English-language *Guardian* blamed the "clown-like" zoot suits, which were the "symbol of insolence and army evasion, frivolity in a time of war." A magistrate told a young man arrested at the Verdun riot that he should visit his tailor to "avoid further trouble."[57]

These conflicts were contests between two different expressions of masculinity, between the young man who had volunteered for service and the young man who spent money on clothing described variously as impractical, incomprehensible, and impertinent. One "youthful veteran of this war" empathized with servicemen, who had "exchanged their civilian clothes for a uniform for which they are very proud. They feel a lot of these kids wearing the funny clothes should be either in the army, navy, or air force." Another disagreed. If a man worked six days a week, why shouldn't he dress as he liked on his day off?[58] For many Canadians, the zoot suit was synonymous with shirking one's duty. This belief extended beyond the press and into the military leadership; an inquiry into the Verdun riot concluded that men wearing zoot suits were a "sect or clan of a subversive nature who aim at sabotaging the war effort by unwarranted attacks on service personnel."[59] Not only were young men in zoot suits not serving in the military (even if, in some cases, they were too young to do so), they were also spending irrationally. Their consumption was emasculating, commentators implied, with reporters referring to those wearing zoot suits as "longhaired drape-shapes" and one tailor contending that "Canadian boys are too conscious of their strength, they like hard fighting games too much, to go in for such attire."[60] A military uniform suggested the sober assumption of responsibility – a sign of manly maturity – while the zoot suit's perceived excess implied a careless abandon and a focus on personal appearance many considered effeminate.

Just as the zoot suit served as a counterpoint to patriotic masculinity in wartime, the sloppy joe aroused concerns that middle-class women's new roles in the armed forces and as factory and office workers undermined their femininity and threatened their sexual purity. Baggy attire like the

(69)

sloppy joe hid female figures and was often characterized as unfeminine. Loose clothing also meant that young women could avoid wearing girdles, the lack of which implied loose sexual morality to many in older generations. The implication that women were making themselves more masculine was embedded in the term *sloppy joe*, which conjured up the image of a man who cared little about his untidy appearance. The fact that many girls borrowed their sweaters from their fathers, brothers, or boyfriends, or purchased them in men's departments, reinforced the masculine connotations. In 1945, *Journal* writer Eleanor Dare answered a fourteen-year-old's question about why parents made "such a fuss" about sloppy joes: "The older generation thinks they look just what they are called – 'sloppy,' untidy and unfeminine."[61] The sloppy joe directly contravened the association of youthfulness with slenderness, propagated in women's magazines since the 1920s. Indeed, one woman recalled that she purchased her sweaters in the men's department, because "women's sweaters didn't come big enough."[62] The sloppy joe fad privileged comfort over performing femininity, particularly in public.

Fashion editors in several magazines were quick to associate the sweater with immaturity. *Chatelaine* writer Lotta Dempsey advised incoming college students that they should be mature enough to avoid looking sloppy: "You're a big girl now, so you'll tidy up your high-school sloppiness lest you be taken (oh awful thought!) for a child still."[63] Dempsey played on readers' potential insecurities, and differentiated high school and college culture, somewhat artificially, in order to emphasize that "the slop-flop stuff is juvenile."[64] A 1942 advice column in *Mayfair* recommended that college students "forget the saddle shoes and sloppy joes when off the campus." The magazine preferred "neatly shod feet and a tailored dress plus a hat for street wear," suggesting that the more casual "sloppy" look, while acceptable in the school environment, was inappropriate for other outings.[65] By associating sloppy joes with immaturity, fashion editors hoped to convince teenaged girls to adopt a neater appearance.

An increasing number of teenaged girls sought employment during the war, and magazines took particular aim at so-called sloppy young women in articles about job hunting. As the federal bureaucracy expanded to solve a severe labour shortage at the beginning of the war, an unprecedented number of women were recruited, relocated, trained, and employed in war-related work; by 1943, 1.2 million women were working in the formal waged economy, more than one-fifth of them in essential war industries.[66] Magazine writers warned readers that employers would see their appearance as an immediate sign of their capability as an employee, particularly in offices, where appearance signified professional competence.

Critics of the sloppy joe fad sometimes conceded that the oversized sweaters were tolerable attire for wearing around the house or in a dorm room. However, they were always inappropriate in public, and particularly in the workplace. In advice to young job seekers, magazine writers often used the sloppy joe as shorthand for an unacceptable appearance. *Chatelaine* fashion editor Carolyn Damon complained that girls rarely "looked the part" when they attended job interviews. When researching a 1940 article, Damon took a photographer to a National Selective Service office, where government officials interviewed young people prior to placing them in war service jobs. "Sloppy Joes, saddle shoes, un-pressed skirts and frowsy hair were almost the rule rather than the exception," she scolded.[67] Five years later, *Chatelaine* again warned readers that between leaving school and starting work, "you've got to Grow Up." Lotta Dempsey instructed job-hunting teenagers: "Don't wear your sloppy joe, ankle socks and loafers. Please!"[68] In 1946, *Mayfair* writer Ellen Mackie continued to warn college graduates that they needed to "study and understand the requirements of life in a grown-up world" to transition successfully from school to office. Her column was headed with a simple command: "Don't Bring Sloppy Joe!"[69]

Although the sloppy joe was decried for its unfeminine shape, it was praised at least once for its economy. A story entitled "Pop Should Be Pleased," published in *Mayfair* in 1945, suggested that sloppiness might flatten class distinctions. A teenaged boy confronts his father because the boy's mother finds sloppy joes and scuffed saddle shoes "not prettied up enough for parties." The son argues that casual, or "messy," dress is more egalitarian:

> Girls used to spend hours getting ready for hops. They wore high heels and tight thing-mes around their waists. And silk stockings. It cost their families plenty of cabbage. And if you just didn't have the old do-re-me

I guess you stayed home. Well, look at now. Every girl in school can wear her old sweater and skirt, or borrow her brother's. Bobby sox and loafers take care of the pedal division. And she just brushes her hair around her shoulders and never mind the fancy updos.[70]

Casual dress allowed more high school and college students to participate in social activities. Scuffed loafers meant girls could ride bicycles, and borrowed sweaters diminished the need to outspend other girls on expensive clothes. "I think maybe we're democratic," the boy concludes. Appearing feminine required money – particularly for growing teenaged girls who would have to purchase clothing more often if they wanted it to be fitted to their changing figures. Larger clothes could be grown into, but bulky clothes – or clothes that didn't fit within the smooth and tailored aesthetic of the time – could also be a sign of lower socio-economic status. Buying clothing for children in larger sizes was a working-class budget-stretching strategy, particularly during the Depression and war years.[71] Fads like the sloppy joe portended a more inclusive youth culture, at least in theory.

Wartime conditions heightened existing concerns that young people's clothing could reflect poorly on their character. Dress that contravened government regulations and gendered expectations of appearance threatened social stability. By associating fads with immaturity, critics suggested that those who adopted them were childish, despite their new wartime responsibilities. If teenagers chose to be "drape-shapes" or "slop-flops," could they become rational and productive citizens?

The sloppy joe's potential threat to Canada's war effort eventually faded from public consciousness. Following the end of the conflict in 1945, observers believed that women were keen to embrace more fitted (and thus feminine) clothing. Headlines such as "Girls Again Look Like Girls Now That Men Are Available" heralded the end of restrictions on clothing manufacturing and promised longer skirts and more feminine trimmings.[72] Nevertheless, the dictum continued against anything loose or untidy, and therefore unfeminine, as did the assumption that such clothing was juvenile. The zoot suit became even more evidently a mark of criminal behaviour, and newspaper reports of petty crimes and dance-hall fights described those involved as "zoot suit lawbreakers," "zoot suit gangs," and "zoot-suiter types." Clashes in Toronto, Kitchener, and Edmonton between 1949 and 1951 led some to suggest the suits should be illegal.[73] This was more a matter of moral panic than a crime wave. Most of the offences these young people were accused of would not have made the newspapers if journalists were not attuned to juvenile delinquency as a social concern. As Mariana Valverde describes, "The flashy clothing and defiant attitudes of the young people involved seemed to magnify their misconduct and turn it into a major crime." Colourful trousers – or strides, as they were called – made teenagers (and their transgressions) newsworthy. Such was the perceived strength of the connection between deviant dress and deviant behaviour that Toronto city controller Leslie Saunders suggested banning zoot suits to prevent juvenile delinquency.[74]

When news spread in 1954 that young people in Britain were wearing Edwardian suits in a "phantasmagorical parody of clothes fashionable half a century ago," the trend was described as "a recent evolution of the zoot-suited adolescent craze" and blamed for the country's "current teenage problem."[75] Although the zoot suit waned as a fashion, the penchant for associating certain clothing styles with young people's antisocial or undesirable behaviour clearly did not.

TO ANYONE OVER TWENTY, I WAS A MESS
Normalizing Teenage Fads

Alternative positive explanations of teenage fads complicate any easy interpretation of the meanings of young people's consumer desires. George Buri notes in his history of postwar educational reform, "Hope and fear existed side by side in the minds of Canadians" as they contemplated, and then confronted, postwar reconstruction.[76] Similarly, young people's fashion could either focus anxieties about the future or support assertions that the kids were alright. Some experts in child and adolescent development framed teenagers' fondness for fads as characteristic of what they considered normal adolescent development. Middle-class high school trends dismissed as frivolous and immature were in fact a key part of young people's self-expression and provided a sense of belonging among their peers. These aspects of the transition to adulthood grew in importance in the 1940s and '50s as the concept that personality was key to normal social adjustment gained influence among psychologists and educators. As Mona Gleason and Mary Louise Adams explain in separate studies, the term *normal* in this context did not refer simply to common or typical behaviours or attitudes but implied desirable traits or conditions.[77] In normal adolescent development – or positive development toward adulthood – young people learned to get along with others and find outlets for self-expression. Both co-operation and self-realization were considered key to ensuring a peaceful, democratic, and healthy future for Canada.[78]

In consumer magazines, columnists and editors adopted discourses of normality and personality, offering teenagers ways to embrace fads and fit in with their peers while spending responsibly at the same time. The alignment of priorities between advertising professionals and psychologists was not a new one. In the 1930s, some child psychologists were already working alongside (and within) the advertising industry. Even if they didn't employ a child psychologist directly, manufacturers and retailers benefited from using child development theories to frame the supposed benefits of their products for children and youth. The clothing industry used arguments about young children's distinct physiques and need for active play to justify the design and marketing of specific styles for "toddlers," a category the industry invented.[79] Toy companies similarly embraced the ideas of experts interested in reforming children's play, pointing to the ways that particular toys and well-designed playrooms would engage children's imagination and keep them safe inside private homes rather than playing in the streets.[80] Market actors sought to normalize children's consumption by using ideas about their expected physical, mental and social development to promote products.

In similar ways, experts increasingly connected young people's appearance to their social and mental development. Mothers were advised to cultivate "good taste" in a child at an early age, not only because it reflected their competence as mothers but also because children's clothing reflected the child's character and personality. In the late 1920s and '30s, American publications such as *Parents* argued that making one's own purchases at an age-appropriate time helped young

(74)

people develop self-confidence, inner virtue, and judgment. Psychologists had established that peer influence increased in the adolescent years.[81] Increasingly, young people's consumer choices were framed in terms of contributing to their personal development and enhancing the personality they presented to others. Canadian high school and college students were encouraged, in somewhat contradictory fashion, to learn the art of individual self-expression from their peers.

In the 1940s and '50s, the growing importance of a well-adjusted personality made young people's ability to "fit in" or be "normal" key to their successful transition to adulthood. Psychologists and educators noted that the physical and biological changes associated with puberty could make social adjustment difficult, and that these difficulties could persist into adulthood if left unaddressed. Mental health professionals and educational psychologists like the popular and prolific Samuel Laycock linked juvenile delinquency to homes where parents overlooked or ignored their children's psychological needs – needs that included social approval and a sense of belonging alongside affection, independence, self-esteem, and creative achievement.[82] Psychologists associated delinquency with more than criminal behaviour, interpreting teenage misconduct as a symptom of impaired psychological development. Laycock and others charged parents and teachers with helping each child develop a "normal personality" to ensure they grew up to be productive citizens.

Laycock argued in a 1946 article for *Maclean's* that the acquisition and use of consumer goods – while certainly not the only, or most significant, factor in normal development – played a role in assuring young people's proper social adjustment. Laycock was opposed to domineering parenting, arguing that if parents included their children in household decisions, they would be better placed to influence their offspring as they aged. He explained that in early and middle adolescence, physical and social success, evidenced in having friends, playing on sports teams, and so on, was of utmost importance to young people. "Conflicts between adolescents and their parents arise because adolescents are very sensitive to the opinion of their own teen-age crowd," Laycock explained. "They would as soon be dead as out of fashion. If the rest of the gang wears 'sloppy Joes,' your Joannie *must* have an oversize sweater."[83] Failing to recognize the importance of the peer group could harm a child psychologically, his comments implied.

Fashion editors emphasized the potential power of appearance in determining whether teenagers would make friends, and find romance, at school. Such advice made it clear that having a normal school experience depended on conforming to fashion trends and following one's peers. Although it risked undermining the magazine's position as an authority on co-ed style and beauty, most editors allowed that girls were well advised to play "a good game of 'I Spy'" and observe other students before deciding what to purchase. "There may be unwritten laws such as never wearing a hat or carrying a purse which are as strict as savage taboos," *Mayfair*'s Grace Garner warned incoming high school students.[84] Her choice of phrasing certainly suggested that severe social consequences awaited those who didn't "study the laws of your tribe," as another *Mayfair* writer, Adele White, recommended.[85] Similarly, in 1943 Gertrude Stayner advised incoming college students to watch the "popular girls" for cues as to how to dress and behave. "They may terrify you a bit at first," Stayner told readers, "because right now 'they've got something' which you haven't. But after all, they're girls too. They got that something from somewhere – so there's no law against your getting it from them."[86] The implication was that the college co-ed was an identity that could be acquired after girls had noted what their popular classmates were wearing. It was better, magazines stressed, to "travel with the female pack than to be a lone wolf" when it came to appearance.[87]

Several magazine writers framed teenagers' penchant for fads as just a normal part of growing up, something that shouldn't concern adults as they would probably abandon the practice as they aged. In the April 1946 issue of *Canadian Home Journal*, teenaged writer Corinne Langston confessed that she had herself adopted trends that helped her fit in with her peers and "make a hit with the boys":

I draped my slacks and shortened my skirts. I wore plaid shirts and pastel draw-string blouses. I wore my father's sweaters and my brother's jackets and I made certain that my moccasins were well scuffed ... Everyone else did it. Who was I to be different? ... With my hair parted in the middle and

> hanging straight at my sides, with the frames of my personality glasses painted "Pink Lightening" to match my lips and finger nails, I was "hep." To anyone over twenty, I was a mess.[88]

While Corinne acknowledged older people wouldn't understand youthful fads, she asked readers to remember what they had done in their youth that might now seem ridiculous in retrospect: "If you say we are 'boy crazy' and we dress like idiots, remember you yourself squeezed into a bone corset and went on a diet of coca-cola and cigarettes. What for? To get yourself a man! And we're doing it the way it's done now."[89] Fads that older people judged silly or messy appeared to pose less of a threat to young women's femininity if they were being employed to form heterosexual relationships.

Magazines explained that mothers could expect their daughters to embrace fads as they entered their teenage years. Several articles in *Chatelaine* noted that when "there are family storms and tears over scarlet pumps versus sensible black oxfords, and long party dresses as opposed to short ones," daughter was simply "turning into a young woman, of course." Connecting emotions to appearance, magazines argued that the same hormones that were altering a girl's body and moods affected her clothing choices. No longer her mother's "carefree, acquiescent baby," the teenager's mind was purportedly a confusion of styles and colours, "and what she's seen in a movie, and what the richest girl at school wears."[90] While some experts disagreed that there was a demonstrable connection between the effects of puberty and a teenager's social behaviour, such explanations lent an air of scientific authority to columnists arguing that girls' interest in fashion should be acknowledged and channelled as a healthy expression of her personality.[91]

Carolyn Damon acknowledged that dressing a teenaged girl could try her mother's patience but insisted that young women's interest in clothing was a desirable development, and her whims should be indulged while her knowledge of fashion was being refined. Mothers ignored their daughter's wishes at their peril, Damon cautioned, noting that a daughter who was "one of the early blossoming kind" was preferable to the "tomboy" who could become a "dowdy frump" if her interest in clothing and grooming was not properly "stimulated." Magazines reassured women that they could guide daughters gently through their teens with "fashion articles in good magazines, and fashion shows by good shops."[92] Fads were a phase to be tolerated, perhaps even encouraged, to ensure that girls' interest in their appearance, and thus their femininity, was intact.

Throughout the late 1940s and the 1950s, magazine content directed at teenaged girls encouraged them to embrace fads and instructed them on how to adopt their appearance to changing fashion trends but remain conscious of their spending. Although retailers often found fads frustrating because the speed with which they changed made it difficult to adapt store stock quickly enough to capitalize, they also promoted them precisely because of their obsolescence. Fads normalized the idea that one's appearance should change regularly, encouraging greater consumption. As historian Kelly Schrum notes in her examination of American teenaged girls, advertisers, retailers, and fashion editors were not opposed to fads, even those that used products in unintended ways; they "celebrated all indicators of girls' active interest" in clothing and commercialized beauty.[93] Magazines regularly described high school students' style as both "a bewildering blend of sense and nonsense" and an integral and non-threatening part of a teenage lifestyle, a key outlet for girls' creativity and self-expression.[94] Teenagers' awareness of their group's fads was another indication of their clout as consumers rather than of their failure to consume responsibly.

Fads could be acceptable when they fit within a well-designed clothing budget, magazine writers informed young readers. "How are you fixed for money?" Eva Lister asked readers in the *Journal*'s semi-regular column, Teenager's Datebook. She recommended girls track "every cent spent by you (or ON you by your parents)," and look for ways to save money by "sharp shopping." This would leave money available for "just a few luxuries." Lister noted that as a bonus girls who learned to budget would be better equipped to manage a household when they were wives and mothers.[95]

Fashion editors counselled teenagers to embrace less costly and even do-it-yourself fads, which could help them adopt a trend without purchasing more expensive garments such as a dress or a coat of which they might soon tire. "The Collegiate Crowd has scads of fads," the *Canadian Home Journal* noted in 1944, "but wisely confine them to accessories." They tinted their eyeglass rims, painted their shoes, and decorated their handbags.[96] Belts, scarves, and jewellery could help a girl appear stylish at little cost. In the 1950s, *Chatelaine*'s monthly Teen Tempo column regularly offered readers instructions to transform their existing clothes to fit with the latest fashion. From dyeing summer shoes to match a winter formal dress to sewing striped patches from old pyjamas onto blue jeans, the column's editors were eager to show readers how they could change their appearance with a little money and a lot of creativity.[97] For example, editor Cynthia Williams advised teenaged readers who wanted to imitate the Tyrolean Look of Spring 1957, featuring felt circle skirts bedecked with yards of rickrack, embroidery, and appliquéd designs, to "use your own ingenuity (and save tons of money) by designing and sewing different patterns onto your own plain felt skirt." Plain and therefore "dull" shorts could be transformed "with textile paint in a gay, mad print of your own design." Readers who had "grown tired of your tapered pants" could turn them into trendy militia pants by sewing red and white stripes down each side.[98] These homemade fashions sent the message that one's clothing should be kept up to date with fashion trends, regardless of one's financial position. And while they were described as creative projects that allowed teenagers to express themselves and save money, their prescriptive nature required little creative energy. Each do-it-yourself project required some small purchases, and *Chatelaine* expected that the money saved could be used for the clothing, shoes, cosmetics, and other products advertised regularly both in and alongside the column.

Chatelaine insisted that teenagers themselves were the foremost experts on fads in their schools, asking readers to write with "any new fads, fashions, sayings or newsworthy achievements among teenagers in your community" and promising to pay five dollars for usable items. Teen Tempo included forty of these "featured fads" in columns published between 1958 and 1960 alone. The fads were described in the style of a news report without editorial comment and included the names and schools of the students who had submitted them. As in *Chatelaine*'s earlier 'Teen-Age Specials and the *Journal*'s Teen Session columns, the Teen Tempo columnist emphasized teen authority and the desire to allow young readers to communicate directly and authentically with each other.

The featured fads illustrated the supposedly unique ways that young readers were creating their own style using their clothes and accessories. Readers wrote in about how young people in their communities were wearing their shoes, hair ribbons, or jewellery in a particular way to send a message only their peers would understand. In Vancouver, Jean Ferguson and Edie Hedstrom reported, girls at Delbrook High School laced their right shoes upside down to show unrequited love. In Courtenay, British Columbia, girls used sweater colours to broadcast their moods: a pink sweater suggested a secret romance; a white sweater meant someone was "shy but dangerous."[99] Fads also involved modifying one's existing clothing. Students in Greenwood, Nova Scotia, stuck multicoloured adhesive bandages to their shoes, while young female Montrealers reported that they liked to sew felt animals on their jeans.[100] The variety of fads published created the impression of many distinct, localized teenage cultures across the country, each with its own way of doing things that might appear irrational to adults but was central to self-expression. At the same time, the routine appearance of self-reported fads reinforced the idea that quirky fashions were a distinguishing feature of teenage culture rather than threatening omens of social disintegration.

BEGINNING IN THE 1940S, retailers and advertisers – bolstered by child development theories – sought to legitimize their direct appeals to younger consumers and justify teenagers' purchasing choices in various ways. Youth advisory councils helped magazines and retailers to collect and commodify teenagers' opinions on a variety of subjects. Retailers treated the teenager as a distinct and opinionated market throughout the war, regardless of fads or the concerns of experts. To many Canadians, fashions such as the sloppy joe sweater and the zoot suit were emblematic of youth and proof that teenagers did not have the authority or capability retailers and advertisers sought to grant them, but by the mid-1950s, the inclination to adopt quirky fashion trends was becoming a distinguishing feature of the teenager. While some fads were undesirable, many were considered harmless, playful expressions of youth culture. Retailers

— Act Your Age —

like Eaton's jumped at the chance to learn all they could about teenage trends from high school students, hoping to capitalize on the information gleaned to sell more products to young people and to sell itself as the retailer that knew the Canadian teenager best.

3

Students in the Store

Making Space for Teenagers at Eaton's

IT WAS A BRIEF yet illuminating moment for Jack Brockie, the manager of the merchandise display department at Eaton's Toronto stores. While crossing the children's wear floor one day in 1939, he heard the raised voices of a mother and daughter arguing. It was Brockie's job to supervise the appealing presentation of goods to customers, so he paused to listen. The mother held a coat that she wanted to buy for her daughter, but the teenaged girl was insisting that they go and look in the women's wear department for a more grown-up style. Later, Brockie questioned the department manager, who told him this type of family dispute was common. Teenaged girls often disagreed with their mothers about potential purchases, expressed dissatisfaction with the selection, and wanted to shop in departments intended for grown women.[1] Brockie recounted this anecdote nearly thirty years later, during an interview transcribed for the Eaton's archives. It encapsulates the ways that both age and gender helped organize retail space and, as a result, shaped gendered and age-based identities.

Brockie presented this mother–daughter argument – and the reported frequency of such disagreements – as proof that the company needed to reconsider and enhance its relationship with younger customers and reorganize retail spaces to appeal more specifically to girls in their teen years. By the 1930s, Eaton's and most department store retailers across North America and Europe separated merchandise into areas for girls, boys, women, and men. Retailers and manufacturers believed that separate departments that met all a child's clothing needs on one floor were more convenient for mothers. Just as other areas of stores were designed with the middle-class or affluent woman in mind – creating spaces that not only catered to female desire but also constructed shopping as a feminine pursuit – children's wear departments were increasingly organized to appeal to mothers and children. The merchandise and atmosphere marked these areas as distinctly child-related spaces.[2]

From Brockie's perspective, the mother–daughter dispute represented a missed opportunity to satisfy the teenaged girl who wanted to look more sophisticated and was not content to shop in the girls' department even though the clothing fit her. The following year, Brockie initiated the Junior Council (followed by the Junior Executive in 1941) in an effort to better understand young people's consumer desires by consulting high school students about their peers' distinct wants and needs. The retailer had begun to construct and disseminate commercialized age-specific and gendered expectations of the teenager.

The company had in fact been attentive to age in more general ways for decades, marking some spaces as appropriate for children, and specifically middle-class children accompanied by their parents. In the first half of the twentieth century, many American department stores provided child-minding services and children's entertainment, freeing female customers to shop without the presumably inconvenient presence of their offspring. Stores outfitted child-minding areas with toys (also available for purchase in the store), and sometimes offered hair-cutting services.[3] At Eaton's, Christmas and Easter were opportunities for special appeals to children and to childhood. By 1929, the annual Santa Claus Parade brought the retailer's brand to the streets of Toronto, Winnipeg, Montreal, Calgary, and Edmonton with fantastic, whimsical spectacles designed to enchant children and awaken adult nostalgia. After the parade, Santa was installed at Eaton's Toyland, and children and their parents were invited to visit him to share their Christmas wishes and fulfil their consumer desires.[4] Toyland's temporary display connected the store to feelings of excitement and joy for many children.

Appealing to young people was worthwhile because it would please mothers (who presumably made the purchasing decisions) and generate goodwill that retailers hoped would carry into their adult years. Company executives recognized the value of maintaining a good relationship with school-age children. In a 1934 memo, company president R.Y. Eaton, son of store founder Timothy Eaton, argued that "special attention should be given constantly to gain the trade of young people, to win their confidence and to merit their good opinion." Eaton believed that if people became accustomed to shopping at the stores as children, they would be more likely to continue shopping there when they were "in the position of purchasing [for] their own households."[5]

This desire to cultivate loyalty reflected the retailer's paternalist approach to its customers and employees in the first half of the twentieth century. Executives at Eaton's and other large department stores cast themselves and their founders as father figures who modelled Christian morality and capitalist values to those who worked and shopped in their stores. The company was a family and, like a stern but benevolent father, Eaton's provided services such as a staff hospital, sports teams, and social outings, along with discipline by regulating the appearance and behaviour of female staff, in particular. Staff training prescribed particular sales techniques to ensure that customers were also treated in ways befitting their place in the gendered family hierarchy. Men were breadwinners with little time to waste in making purchases, and salespeople should be efficient and not question their requests or choices. Women – described by male sales managers as more irrational and unruly – might require more guidance and subtle suggestion from salespeople. Salespeople should treat children with courtesy and sincerity, endeavouring to spark their desire for consumer goods while acknowledging that mother was holding the purse strings.[6]

In this familial understanding of its customers, Eaton's began to view people in their teen years as new and distinct consumers in the 1940s. They shopped without their parents and made their own purchasing decisions. They sought to fit in with their peers and paid close attention to their appearance. They wanted to look older, more *sophisticated* – a term that implied sexual maturity. They were serious customers and could not be treated in the same manner as children. The company sought to capture their attention and their dollars by inviting them into its stores and creating spaces just for them.

On many Saturday mornings at Eaton's during the school year, junior councillors and executives could be seen holding meetings, reviewing merchandise on the sales floor, and sometimes working in various store departments. The company wanted their employees – and all customers – to know that high school students were welcome at the store and that they had a valuable role to play in the store's operations. The Council and Executive helped Eaton's host regular fashion shows that transformed the stores' auditoriums and restaurants into exclusive spaces in which the ideal female teenaged body was on display. Finally, throughout the 1940s and '50s, Eaton's appealed to high school girls specifically by redesigning retail spaces, creating speciality departments that replicated elements of youth culture and sought to capitalize on teenaged girls' aspirational desire. In all these activities, Eaton's claimed to be serving young people: listening to them and providing them with the goods they needed. At the same time, the company was bringing the teenaged consumer into being.

SATURDAYS AT THE STORE

"You have probably seen these young people with the natty blue blazers and Junior Councillor or Junior Executive crests on their pockets, hustling around the store, and some of you must have wondered who they were."[7] So began a description of the Junior Council and Junior Executive in *Contacts*, the Eaton's Winnipeg employee newsletter, in 1950. The story, titled "Youth Unlimited," informed Eaton's employees about the program, which had been operating in the Winnipeg store since 1946. The piece simultaneously evoked the image of groups of teenagers roaming the store and reassured potentially concerned or just plain curious employees that these young people's "hustle" was legitimate and important. These teenagers weren't loitering or shoplifting. On Saturdays, the

(85)

Junior Council and Executive brought hundreds of high school students into Eaton's stores in six cities across Canada, altering the way the retailer merchandised to teenagers and making them a visible part of the company's retail space (see Figure 3.1).

Apart from the Montreal Junior Executive (see Figure 3.2), which had a dedicated council room, weekly meetings took place in store spaces otherwise occupied by Eaton's customers and employees, transforming them into places where the female councillors and male executives reviewed merchandise, completed surveys, planned fashion shows and dances, listened to guest speakers on a variety of topics, socialized and, undoubtedly, had fun. In Winnipeg, the Junior Council often met in the Grill Room, the store's popular and elegant restaurant, while in Toronto the Georgian Room restaurant at the Queen Street store and the Clipper Room at the College Street store were common meeting places for councillors.[8] The junior executives often met in conference rooms and conducted meetings along the same lines as a corporate board of directors.

These locations reflected and amplified gendered assumptions about retail space. Girls' meetings took place in more decorative, opulent, and consumer-oriented spaces, where high school girls could imagine themselves as adult women at a social lunch. The boys used unadorned meeting rooms whose bareness signified that important business was conducted there without distraction. This gendered use of space was never absolute; the two groups sometimes met together and undoubtedly used the spaces that were available and big enough to fit the thirty to forty people in attendance. Nevertheless, meeting spaces often replicated the gendered roles the company expected of customers and sent distinct messages about how masculinity and femininity were performed in the stores, with girls placed in the feminine and feminizing spaces of shopping and socializing and boys seriously contemplating the business of consumption behind a desk. In both cases, spaces occupied for much of the week by adults were given over to younger people as a sign that the company viewed them as important customers.

In sometimes small and subtle ways, Eaton's indicated teenagers' presence and importance. In its Winnipeg, Montreal, and Hamilton stores, the company installed bulletin boards where junior executives could post

3.1 Members of the Toronto Junior Council watching Rusty Fellows, from the display department of the Eaton's College Street store, adjust a veil as an unnamed fellow councillor models a wedding dress, 1958.

3.2 The Montreal Junior Executive, 1947.

information about high school events. Their "prominent positions in the Men's Wear Shop on the first floor and the Campus Shop on the third floor" ensured that employees and other customers would notice Eaton's taking an interest in high school activities. The bulletin boards signalled that teenagers were welcome in these spaces. In Montreal, advisor W.L. Wornell asked the executives to ensure they "keep us informed of all coming activities in their respective schools."[9] As a source of information about events at different schools, Eaton's hoped the bulletin boards would also draw teenagers into the stores.

Contests and activities designed to introduce students to retailing practices and solicit their ideas also marked pockets of teenage space in the stores. For example, contests held in Montreal and Toronto asked councillors and executives to design newspaper advertisements for store products that they would really like for themselves and to incorporate the Eaton's slogan, "The Store for Young Canada."[10] Contests like this sent the students into store departments to see merchandise, practise selling techniques, and gather inspiration (see Figure 3.3). The results were displayed in various departments and used as copy for local newspaper ads. In 1948, advisors asked councillors in Toronto to design bedrooms using Eaton's merchandise from the Home Furnishings department, selecting ten of the designs for prominent display on the Aisle of Ideas in the College Street store.[11] The same year, windows along Yonge Street showed coats, suits, and sportswear selected by the students with a sign describing them as "Approved by Eaton's Junior Council" alongside portraits of numerous junior executives and councillors. Similarly, Calgary decorated one of its windows with executives' photographs and school crests in 1950.[12] Eaton's employees typically arranged these displays, but at least once in Calgary the executives were given the opportunity to dress the windows themselves and "were quite in favour of this and are looking forward to this opportunity to show what they can do."[13] Putting students' photographs, merchandise selections, and contest entries on display was part of demonstrating to customers that Eaton's saw a place for teenagers in its stores.

Councillors and executives were granted access to the "back-stage parts of the store" in tours designed to familiarize them with the operation of a large department store. In Calgary, meeting minutes described

(88)

— Students in the Store —

3.3 Members of the Junior Executive practising their selling techniques in the Winnipeg store, 1959.

a 1947 tour that started at the top of the elevator shafts and ended with the boilers in the basement. In Montreal, a tour that same year visited the store's kitchens and laundry, its ice cream and candy factories, and the company hospital and employee library.[14] Such tours exposed students to the company's expansive facilities and gave company officials the opportunity to enumerate the potential benefits of employment at Eaton's.

Councillors and executives also provided part-time and volunteer labour in the stores that made them visible and valuable to the company. Some worked regular part-time jobs in various store departments, but for the most part the groups provided Eaton's with a pool of casual labour from which to draw for special events. Particularly at Christmas and Easter, when the stores were busy, meeting minutes included requests for additional assistance, such as at the Edmonton store when a "special sale in the Men's Department which required the services of

8 Junior Executives" drew their weekly meeting to an early close in March 1947. In Toronto, the school representatives were asked to seat guests and serve food at children's parties at Easter. They also marched in the Santa Claus Parade and recruited other young people to do so, being "instructed to look for marchers of a certain age and size."[15] In August 1949, when the Winnipeg store held a sale to celebrate its forty-fourth anniversary, a dozen junior councillors and executives in matching blazers "greeted shoppers with a welcome smile" as the doors opened, handing out commemorative badges.[16] In these instances the students demonstrated that teenagers were part of the Eaton's family, both as employees and as customers.

All these activities brought the student representatives to the attention of Eaton's employees and customers, an awareness that those leading the Council and Executive wanted to encourage. Making students visible in the stores was in keeping with the department store's "highly visual work environment." Employees, particularly female employees, were trained and expected to use phrases and maintain postures, grooming habits, and dress choices that reflected positively on the company and its products as respectable but also "exciting, pleasurable, and accommodating."[17] Similarly, junior councillors and executives were invited to embody youth in the stores in controlled ways that Eaton's believed would benefit its image as the Store for Young Canada.

STORE SPECTACLES
Teenagers on the Runway

No event drew teenagers into the stores as consistently as fashion shows. As early as 1913, the company had used live "mannequin parades" to display clothing, including for children, and by the 1940s and '50s, Eaton's was hosting regular runway spectacles for and by high school students. These shows were of increasing importance to the merchandise display department in Toronto. In 1944, Jack Brockie requested $2,500 for teenage fashion shows, in addition to his budget for the Junior Council and Executive, because a well-designed spectacle could draw hundreds of students – and potential customers – into the store on a Saturday morning.[18] On these occasions, store auditoria and restaurants were transformed into exclusively teenage spaces. The junior councillors and executives were an essential part of producing these events; boys and girls selected garments and distributed tickets, girls modelled, and boys acted as masters of ceremony, disc jockeys, ushers, and chaperones. Fashion shows advertised Eaton's merchandise while presenting the students as authorities on teenage fashion and reinforcing consumers' gendered roles within the store.

Fashion shows at Eaton's were spectacles even though they focused on ready-to-wear, often everyday garments rather than designer creations. Department store fashion shows were typically less artistic and theatrical than more exclusive presentations, and they have attracted less scholarly attention. Yet couture and ready-to-wear fashion shows ultimately serve the same purpose: to project an image that speaks to the audience and sparks their desire to buy the clothing displayed.[19] Furthermore, while fashion shows were not competitions, as the Cover Girl contests hosted by Eaton's and the *Canadian Home Journal* were, the shows did put young bodies on display in similar ways to beauty pageants, exemplifying settler femininity by idealizing the white middle-class teenager as a model for others to emulate.[20]

At its teenage fashion shows, Eaton's endeavoured to create a specific setting such as a schoolhouse or a carnival, using props, music, and decorations. Printed programs invited the audience to "step through the looking glass into a wonderful world of fashion" or "hop on our tandem [bicycle] and merrily roll along with the new Spring silhouette."[21] Many featured live music, comedians, or jugglers, and most organized the parade of garments to reflect a theme (see Figure 3.4). For example, football was a repeated theme at the Toronto store in 1949, 1954, and 1956. At the Fall Fashion Kick-Off, junior executives labelled "fashion quarterbacks" announced the coats, sportswear, and dresses as they were modelled. The program divided the show into quarters, like a football game, and proclaimed that it was a Fall Fashion Chalk Talk for high school students. In another instance, a back-to-school fashion show divided the presentation into schoolday periods and re-created scenes from a day at school. Another used blackboards as backdrops and outfitted the junior executive master of ceremonies in gown and mortar board to play the headmaster. The show opened with dancers breaking through the pages

3.4 Program for a Junior Council Fashion Show in the Eaton Auditorium in March 1950, featuring photographic portraits of four unnamed councillors.

of a giant book and "doing an old fashioned routine to School Days."[22] Eaton's fashion shows were spectacular because they were measured by their visual impact. Not every show was boisterous or colourful but each was designed to inspire the audience and display clothing in motion in ways the retailer hoped the audience would find relevant and inspiring.

The shows' presentation as an exclusively teenage space was an important part of the spectacle. Eaton's emphasized the role of the Council and Executive consistently when planning and reporting on youth fashion shows. From the perspective of the audience, councillors and executives were running the show. Many attendees probably secured tickets from their school representatives. Junior executives directed them to their seats when they arrived and handed them a program that often listed the names of all the student models. Most of the people whom audience members saw during the show were their own age, and they were likely to recognize some as their own Junior Council and Executive representatives.

— Students in the Store —

Reports emphasized the students' role in producing the event. Following a fashion show at the Winnipeg store in December 1950, *Contacts* proclaimed it a success and credited the junior councillors. "Three hundred and fifty high school and college co-eds oh-ed and ah-ed Saturday morning," the report began. It noted that one of the councillors was at the podium, describing garments as they came down the runway. Some of the girls may have had stage fright backstage, but the story reassured readers that "a view from the audience proved that the teen-aged girl of today knows how to look poised and self-assured ... and can smile prettily at a critical audience."[23] A spectacle seemingly created by teenagers for teenagers was meant to demonstrate the retailer's trust in high school students as customers. Although the audience's attention was directed to the models, the ushers and masters of ceremony were also on display for their peers.

Minutes of Junior Council and Executive meetings indicate that the groups spent a significant amount of time planning and preparing for fashion shows. Department store shows were feminine spaces, in which women both consumed the clothing on display and were consumed as models. Men produced the shows – they made the spectacle – while the women who modelled *were* the spectacle. Eaton's maintained these clear gendered roles in its teenage shows, asking councillors and executives to assist in distinct ways that would reinforce heteronormative femininity and masculinity.

Junior councillors were tasked with helping to select clothing they liked, and with modelling the merchandise. Meeting minutes suggest that the girls held regular small fashion displays during their weekly meetings, displaying outfits and practising their modelling skills for each other. A small show took place at an Edmonton Junior Council meeting in 1950, for example, when Miss L. Foster of the Teen Shop brought fifteen dresses along. "Each girl modelled one style for the others," the minutes reported, adding that "the girls had a delightful time, both in modelling and in making frank comments ... about the garment and the model!"[24] The Hamilton Junior Council advisor reported in November 1947 that the councillors were practising modelling every week.[25] In Toronto in 1948, model Dot Fleming spent a meeting preparing the girls for an upcoming fashion show,

(93)

training them in "walking, turning, posing, and position of the arms and hands."[26] Such practice prepared councillors for their role as "poised and self-assured" models in the stores' larger fashion shows, at which their role was to embody the ideal feminine and attractive teenaged girl.

Junior executives were also an active part of the spectacle, but in roles deemed suitably masculine. Beforehand, they were asked to distribute tickets at their schools. In Hamilton, one advisor attempted to stir boys' competitive spirit and offered a prize to the executive who distributed the most tickets to classmates.[27] On the day itself, boys were engaged to seat people in the auditorium, operate the sound system, and escort the female models. For example, boys at the Montreal store were asked "to make themselves available for the Fashion Show on February 22nd to ... operate the Band Box as well as certain ushering duties and escorting the models."[28] Boys dressed in tuxedos to walk with the female models down the runway, often at the culmination of the show when girls were modelling formal dresses.[29] Their participation as "escorts" created the heterosexual fantasy of a romantic evening – a special dance, perhaps – that would encourage girls in the audience to purchase dresses. Boys also dressed to enhance the scene. They wore sports equipment or school team uniforms "to add atmosphere" and were positioned to ensure that female models were the centre of attention.[30] Although the junior executives participating on these occasions were arguably modelling, the term *escorts* was deemed more masculine, and thus more appropriate and appealing to high school boys.

Not all the boys were as opposed to modelling as the company believed. At least once, in 1947, the Hamilton Junior Executive hosted an all-male fashion show. When the event was reported as successful at a meeting of Executive advisors, several advisors from other stores expressed doubt that the boys in their own groups would volunteer to participate in an all-boys show. Instead, Montreal and Toronto groups planned all-male sports-themed "stag parties." Sports equipment and clothing were displayed on mannequins and the audience was treated to talks from local football and basketball coaches. The advisors emphasized that there was to be "no modelling whatsoever, only displays."[31]

Yet there are other indications that not all male high school students viewed modelling as a feminine or feminizing activity. A *Globe and Mail* columnist surveyed high school boys in 1949 and found them in favour of male fashion shows. "The boys in the department store shows are just props," the *Canadian High News* columnist Ian Collins complained. "We need shows of our own." Several male high school students agreed that they would also like a "sneak peek of the fashions before we plan our fall wardrobes" and claimed, "It's not fair to have the shows just for the girls." They suggested that fashion shows were informative and potentially effective ways of encouraging high school boys to shop at the department store. Despite the fact that "not one cry of 'sissy stuff' was raised" among those surveyed, Eaton's employees reportedly told the *Globe* that "male models were awkward, and they wouldn't risk a boys' show for fear of the ribbing."[32] Fashion shows continued to be a key aspect of Eaton's strategy to draw teenagers into its stores, but these exclusively teenage spaces remained overtly feminine.

TOO JUNIOR FOR THE HIGH SCHOOL CROWD
Sartorial Hierarchies and Retail Space

Store fashion shows and Junior Council and Executive activities were designed to draw high school students into Eaton's stores and convince them that the company valued their opinions and custom. In the 1940s and '50s, Eaton's also considered how best to organize its sales floors to appeal more directly to teenaged customers. Specialized departments would cater to and promote the age-specific needs of the "new and distinct" teenaged customer. Eaton's already had several specialized departments. In the 1930s, several stores had areas designed for "business girls," with merchandise advertised as appropriate for young women working in offices. The Toronto store's floor space was temporarily rearranged to accommodate seasonal promotions, such as Toyland at Christmas and a Prep School Shop in August that sold the uniforms of local private schools. By 1940, several American department stores, such as Powers in Minneapolis, had already created sex-segregated departments aimed at high school students.[33] Eaton's followed suit in 1941, creating the Hi-Spot just for teenaged girls.

Specialty shops like these marked what sociologist Daniel Thomas Cook calls a commercial-sartorial hierarchy of age progression. From the

1920s onward, many retailers began selling infants' clothing separately from children's wear and displaying children's clothing in ways that separated smaller sizes from larger ones and associated size with age. Retailers transformed long-standing associations between dress and maturity – such as boys donning long pants or girls wearing longer skirts after reaching puberty – by arranging their merchandise to arouse anticipatory desire in younger customers.[34] If children could see the clothes they would wear when they were older, ideally by walking through racks of merchandise in larger sizes and seeing older children shop, retailers believed they would look forward to the day they too could shop in that part of the store and thus be more grown up. By separating teenage clothing from the children's department, Eaton's reinforced this commercial-sartorial hierarchy. Files from the merchandise display office in Toronto, as well as advertisements for the Toronto stores, reveal how the company worked to create a space and age progression that would appeal to an idealized middle-class high school girl.

When the Hi-Spot opened at Toronto's Queen Street store in September 1941, the company described it as the solution to a familiar problem. In "More about Eaton's," a regular feature of the company's full-page newspaper advertisements, the writer noted that when she toured the new shop the day before it had reminded her of "the good old days when mother dragged us from the Children's Department to the Misses' ... and back again to the Children's ... only to find that no one gave a hoot about the clothing problems of a woman who was tall and fourteen." Remembering her own difficulties finding suitable clothing, the writer assured readers that the Hi-Spot provided the perfect in-between space. The dissatisfied teenaged customer (and, she implied, her tired mother) would get the attention she deserved in the Hi-Spot, where "shopping should become pretty much of a lark for any girl of twelve or up." This was their "very own shop" designed with the input of Eaton's junior councillors.[35]

A full-page advertisement the following week highlighted Hi-Spot features designed to appeal to "high school gals," including a jukebox playing popular music, bar stools at a horseshoe-shaped accessories bar, and an "alumna from our Junior Fashion Council to tell 'all' on what to wear and when." The illustrations featured three young women dancing around a jukebox. Another two are positioned at the accessories bar, one relaxing casually against the counter listening, the other in an animated pose and speaking. All modelled Eaton's merchandise but none were actually shopping. The ad suggested that the Hi-Spot was more of a teen retreat than a shop: "It's where you and all the 'coke crowd' can gather to gossip about clothes and listen to music." The title "Hi-Jinx at the Hi-Spot" also implied that this was a space where teenagers could be carefree, even rambunctious, without censure.[36]

Descriptions of the Hi-Spot as a happening and teen-exclusive space continued in subsequent ads for the speciality shop; it was "our popular 'Junior Deb' centre" and "that lively place on the Third Floor with the uncanny faculty for knowing the right clothes."[37] "This is where they meet when they're on a clothes hunt," the company claimed, assuring "young customers" that they're "always sure of a warm welcome and exactly the right, bright, animated wearables you and your crowd like best."[38] They shopped "alone and coolly independent," Eaton's noted, yet the presence of young but knowledgeable sales staff implied that they would be well advised in their purchases if they left mother at home.[39] The shop was tailored for them, with "fashions with young ideas ... sizes styled to fit 'in-betweens' ... [and] prices keyed to fit 'teenage budgets."[40] Special events for teenagers were planned for the Hi-Spot. In 1943, for example, teenaged film and stage actors Cora Sue Collins and Rosemary Rice signed autographs in the Hi-Spot (see Figure 3.5). Eaton's advertisements mentioned the Hi-Spot as the place for teenaged girls' clothing until 1952.

Despite efforts to make the Hi-Spot a distinct teenage space within its Toronto store, however, Eaton's received criticism from junior councillors and employees alike. In an undated memo to Jack Brockie, employee B. Warner argued that the name did not suit the third-floor department because "the average high school student does not purchase clothes on the 3rd floor but on the 4th." On the third floor, the Hi-Spot was adjacent to the children's and girls' departments, whereas the fourth floor featured the Young Moderns' Shop and College Toggery, sections of the women's department that featured fashions in Junior and Misses' sizes. The minutes of the Toronto Junior Council in September 1948 corroborate that this is where high school girls shopped. Following a fashion

— The Scramble for the Teenage Dollar —

3.5 Eaton's employee Paul Johnson (centre) in the Hi-Spot with American actors Cora Sue Collins (right) and Rosemary Rice (left), as customers await autographs, 1943.

show that featured clothing from the Hi-Spot, Council advisor Miss J. Smith recorded that very few of the councillors knew about the Hi-Spot. "They had difficulty in determining which was the girls' wear section and which was the Hi-Spot," the minutes noted, adding that the girls "felt that the shop should be more definitely separated from the rest of the floor."[41] Although, according to the company's advertising, junior councillors had had a hand in planning the Hi-Spot in 1941, by the time Warner consulted them they were suggesting that the merchandise was "too junior for the … high school crowd."[42]

— Students in the Store —

While the Hi-Spot drew younger students – say, twelve- to fourteen-year-olds with visions of pretty and popular co-eds – those in their later teen years found the association with high school juvenile, perhaps preferring to see themselves as future college students or career women and seeking garments that would allow them to perform that identity. In the commercial-sartorial hierarchy, they disliked shopping on the same floor as other, younger children. The fourth floor featured women's clothing exclusively and was often referred to in advertising as "The Fourth Floor of Fashions." It was a space more associated with mature, stylish, and sophisticated clothing, probably heightening its appeal to teenaged girls.

Eaton's advertising reflected the reality that teenagers could be shopping in various store departments, including the Hi-Spot, the Young Moderns' Shop, and College Toggery. Throughout the 1940s, display ads for the Young Moderns' Shop portrayed a variety of women wearing Eaton's merchandise while at the office, grocery shopping, doing housework, or socializing with friends. It was a shop for the "busy young modern" with a "lithe, youthful figure" of any age.[43] However, several advertisements slipped in references to younger customers, noting that the dresses in the Young Moderns' Shop were "something for 'teen-types to crow about" and fitting for the "lively school-girl, brisk young business woman or the mother of three!"[44] Furthermore, when Eaton's partnered with the *Canadian Home Journal* to host the Canadian Cover Girl promotion, the clothes worn by the winning contestant were selected from College Toggery, not the Hi-Spot. Pictures of junior councillors and the winning cover girl were displayed prominently in the fourth-floor shop during August and September, rather than on the third floor (see Figure 3.6). Teenagers who aspired to the image of a college student or young working woman would be drawn to the fourth floor, away from the Hi-Spot.

The variety of Eaton's shops targeting teenaged customers in the 1940s demonstrates the company's repeated attempts to design a retail space suited to what it believed the high school girl needed. In response to junior councillors' comments about the Hi-Spot, Warner sketched a potential plan for the third floor that created distinct spaces for younger and older teens. She proposed renaming the girls' department "Young World"

3.6 Canadian Cover Girl promotional display in the College Toggery department at Eaton's Queen Street store, 1949.

and dividing the Hi-Spot in two to create a section for a group she called "junior teens" (wearing sizes 12 to 16) and a separate Teen Shop targeting those aged fifteen to twenty, who were likely to wear Junior or Misses' sizes. The space was divided to ensure that customers exiting the elevator would have to pass through the junior teen section to reach Young World, whereas customers visiting the Teen Shop would not need to go through areas dedicated to younger girls. Such an arrangement appeared to try encouraging anticipation in girls not yet able to shop in the junior teen area while also addressing junior councillors' concerns that the Hi-Spot was too juvenile. It's not clear if Warner's suggestions marked the end of the Hi-Spot; her plan for two separate teen shops does not appear to have become a reality. Reorganizing an entire floor to cater to ever more specific age groups could be a risky proposition, particularly if teenaged girls were going to continue to shop in a variety of departments. Warner's plan nonetheless demonstrates junior councillors' value to company executives, who took their criticism about the organization and design of the sales floor seriously.[45]

Another factor in the Hi-Spot's demise might have been the company's decision to create a "completely new section ... devoted to the shopping needs of Young Canada from cradle to college" at Toronto's College Street store. The Young Canada Shops opened on the second floor in March 1951. "Every age group has a separate shop!" Eaton's pronounced, noting as well that the department included "fashions approved by our own Junior Councillors and Executives to please the Hi-Crowd!"[46] As in the main store, all clothing for children and youth would be displayed in one space. This decision meant Eaton's could market the Young Canada Shops to teenagers, children, and parents in the same full-page advertisement.

Specialty shops continued to evolve throughout the 1950s. In 1953, the Young Moderns Shop in the Queen Street store became the Young Toronto Shop, a minor change that suggests Eaton's believed the word *modern* was not resonating with customers. Despite the name change, the target customer remained the slender and fashion-conscious young woman who wore Junior and Misses' sizes. Advertisements directed "Teens and Twenties bound for Collegiate or College" to the Young Toronto Shop.[47] The company seems to have decided that the best way to benefit from the commercial-sartorial hierarchy of age progression was to direct teenaged girls to a space designed for the grown women they wanted to be. In 1957 and 1958, when Eaton's promoted Junior Council and Executive fashion shows, the advertisements featured clothing from the Young Toronto Shop, not the Young Canada Shops. At the same time, the merchandise display department made changes to the girls' department, opening the Pre-Teen Centre on the third floor of the Queen Street store in 1959. Designed for "Miss In-Between" who was "no longer a little girl, not quite a teen," this space was described as a one-stop shop where girls wearing sizes 10 to 14x could find clothes "with the flavor of big sister's fashions!"[48] By displaying girls' clothing in smaller and distinct age segments, the company hoped to speak directly to younger customers and profit from their presumed desire to dress in the same manner as more mature girls and young women.

IN THE 1940S AND '50S, Eaton's made various concerted efforts to draw an ideal teenaged customer into its stores. High school students were recruited for the Junior Council and Executive and asked to advise the company about teenage trends, voice their opinions of Eaton's merchandise, and provide both voluntary and paid labour. Young people were invited to attend and participate in fashion shows, and to shop in departments designed especially for them. The Hi-Spot, Young Canada Shops, and Young Toronto Shop demonstrate how the company persisted in its search to create the space where teenaged girls would most want to shop.

Paternalism and patriarchy shaped retail spaces and the encounters between male department store employees and female customers. At the same time, Eaton's efforts to appeal to high school students demonstrate that age mattered, too; it is likely that some young people exercised more power within the walls of Eaton's than within their own families. Certainly, some of the female students on the Junior Council believed that their time at the store, engaging in weekly meetings and the associated surveys, contests, and other activities, gave them confidence and poise, and made them more style-conscious. "I think that being on the Council makes us feel as if we're on the 'inside track' and part of the store," one councillor told Audrey Brown, the Council advisor, in 1945. Others remarked on their newfound familiarity with the store, with one girl noting that "Eaton's and its employees seem more real after my term as councillor." Girls expressed pride in their positions as school representatives and their gratitude for everything they learned about the company, about fashion, and about other students.[49] The students' appreciation suggests they felt important at Eaton's, and believed the company took them seriously.

4

Tailored for Teens

Selling Age, Gender, and Sophistication

TEENAGERS TODAY select their clothing from a wide array of styles tailored just to them. Many large retailers have separate, teen-specific lines that they advertise on social media platforms and in online shops, as well as in bricks-and-mortar stores. Apparel company Abercrombie & Fitch has Hollister for "guys and girls"; Victoria Secret's popular brand Pink sells underwear, swimwear, casual clothes, and cosmetics to teenaged girls. Without explicitly mentioning teenagers, clothing retailers such as Forever 21 project a youthful vibe and feature young models and small sizes that attract teenaged customers. Yet the practice of tailoring clothing sizes and styles to teenagers is not a new one. The Eaton's catalogue of the 1930s, '40s, and '50s demonstrates the ways in which assumptions about age, gender, and sexuality were used to sell clothing to teenaged girls and boys, as teen-specific clothing sizes and styles emerged.

The mail-order catalogues of the late-nineteenth and twentieth centuries allowed a growing number of Canadians to purchase a wide variety of goods without travelling to the company's urban stores. Through its catalogues in the 1940s and '50s, Eaton's offered young Canadians across the country an image of the ideal teenager similar to the one on display in women's magazines: a well-groomed white student who was wealthy enough to purchase the clothing required to achieve the look being offered. The company used its catalogues as another avenue through which to construct the teenage market, selling clothing in distinct size ranges it claimed would fit young bodies better. Fit referred both to the way garments covered and moulded teen bodies and to their suitability for school and social events, the presumed daily activities of teenaged customers. Clothing styles and colours, as well as catalogue layout and language, were all tailored for teens.

As an historical source, mail-order catalogues are rich records of goods and prices at a specific time. These texts also shaped and reflected shared cultural understanding. In the first half of the twentieth century, the catalogues conveyed and strengthened nationalist messages of a white middle-class Canadian consumer and a paternalistic, civilizing company.[1] The clothing sizes and styles offered set standards by which customers of all ages measured themselves, providing "a touchstone for Canadians" whose "pages depicted an idealized body for both men and women."[2] The catalogue models, most of them drawn but occasionally photographed, varied little in their presentation. They were slender white women, broad-chested white men, and chubby-cheeked smiling white children. Whether people purchased their clothing from Eaton's or not, the glossy pages illustrated how people should dress and look wearing their clothes. The clothing they sold was a "crucial feature in the production of masculinity and femininity," creating and reinforcing ideas about how men and women should dress.[3]

Gender and age intersected on the catalogue pages to provide a powerful prescription of how people should dress to appear appropriately feminine or masculine, youthful or mature. Although women's garments occupied more (and more prominent) space in the Eaton's catalogues, the company clearly wanted boys in their teens to see themselves as consumers who could express their masculinity through their clothing. Distinct size ranges and styles perpetuated and deepened gender stereotypes and idealized body images for both girls and boys, highlighting the idea that teenaged girls dressed to be objects of desire and teenaged boys dressed to get ahead in the working world.

These messages reached beyond those who used mail-order catalogues to purchase goods. Those lacking funds often recalled browsing
its pages wistfully, clipping out images, and copying styles in home sewing projects. In her study of young working women in Depression-era
Toronto, Katrina Srigley likens window shopping and looking though
the catalogue to "forms of 'mental consumption' that allowed women
to imagine themselves dressed in clothes they could not afford but could
sometimes replicate with sewing skills."[4] The catalogues – whose messages connected Eaton's to the strength of the Canadian state – also made
their way into classrooms, where teachers used them for arithmetic and
other lessons.[5]

Several other retailers, including the Toronto-based Robert Simpson
Company and the family-run Quebec firm Dupuis Frères, also produced
mail-order catalogues, but none surpassed the size, scope, and reach of
the Eaton's catalogue in the first half of the twentieth century. The first
catalogue appeared in 1884, and by 1904 it reached more than a million
people nationally.[6] By the Fall and Winter 1930–31 issue, the Eaton's catalogue had expanded into an illustrated and highly detailed tome with
hundreds of pages and twelve thousand items "priced to satisfy a nation."
In addition to a wide selection of men's and women's clothing, outerwear,
undergarments, shoes, and boots, the Eaton's catalogue sold everything
from children's toys to prefabricated houses. The catalogue offered fabric
by the yard, notions for the seamstress, and sewing machines as well.
There was a wide selection of hardware and farm equipment, including
wagons, cream separators, and incubators to hatch chickens. Customers
could furnish their houses. Dishes, household appliances, bedding, and
window furnishings were sold in wide variety. There were bicycles
and scooters for riders of all sizes, ice skates, football helmets, and other
sports equipment. Customers could buy pipes and the tobacco to smoke
in them. Books, typewriters, sheet music, and pianos were all available.
Seeds for the vegetable garden, coffee for the percolator, and tires for
the car – with the Eaton's catalogue, cash, and a shipping address, most
Canadians could purchase a wide assortment of goods. As the company
asserted on the cover of the Spring and Summer 1951 issue, it was "a big
store at your door."

Over the 1930s and '40s, Eaton's published three different catalogues: the Toronto catalogue was also distributed, with minor changes, through the Moncton mail order office to customers in the Maritimes; the Winnipeg catalogue was distributed across Western Canada; and a French translation of the Toronto book was produced in Toronto and distributed in Quebec. The analysis here is based on the Toronto catalogues, because by the 1930s the clothing content of the Toronto and Winnipeg books was increasingly uniform. After 1949, only one catalogue, produced in Toronto, was distributed across the country.[7]

To illustrate the company's varied efforts to construct a teenage market in their catalogues, I sampled dresses and suits in all sizes to develop a set of 883 garments from thirty-seven catalogues published between 1930 and 1960 (alternating between the Spring/Summer and Fall/Winter catalogues). Every tenth dress and suit from each catalogue was included in the sample, which thus represented roughly 10 percent of the total number offered. I recorded verbatim every piece of information Eaton's provided about each garment, including the full description, the size range (smallest and largest size available), the colours offered (and number of colours), and the price. Headings, associated images and their type (drawing or photograph), the position of the model, and any accessories included were all noted.

Dresses and suits were by far the most common items displayed in the catalogues during these decades, and focusing on those garments allowed close attention to the way size ranges and styles changed over time and subtle shifts that suggested the company was trying to reach a different type of customer. As a result, the sample does not shed light on the rising volume of more casual clothing, or sportswear, appearing in Canadians' wardrobes, a development that certainly deserves further scholarly attention.[8] Using dresses and suits as a constant variable makes sense, as it reflects the expectation that continued throughout this period that people would dress more formally in public than they did at home or when engaged in specific activities that required different clothing, such as sports or exercise. Schools enforced dress codes that reflected broader social norms about gendered dress.

— Tailored for Teens —

When read closely, the catalogues demonstrate how Eaton's appeals to teenaged customers grew more focused, and more gendered, over time. Until the 1930s, the company sold clothing for either immature (child) or mature (adult) bodies. There was very little in between. In the mid-1930s, catalogue sizes and styles began to blur the line between these two types of clothing. Eaton's created new size categories and advertised garments that minimized the awkward physical growth of puberty. In the 1940s, the retailer began offering clothing sizes specifically for teenagers and appealed to girls and boys in distinct and gendered ways, emphasizing how the colour, cut, and fit of a garment could enhance one's femininity or masculinity. In the 1950s, Eaton's promised teenagers age-appropriate sophistication, emphasizing the importance of appearance to social success in order to sell garments to boys and girls.

JUNIOR IS A SIZE, NOT AN AGE
Women's, Men's, Boys', and Girls' Sizing

From the 1930s into the 1950s, Eaton's sold clothing in a wide variety of sizes and size categories for men, women, and children of all ages. Every catalogue included detailed instructions, charts, and diagrams to help customers measure themselves accurately. Eaton's contended that size was an objective measure that had little to do with one's age. However, sizes and size categories allowed the company to market clothing to specific groups based on both age and gender. A brief overview of Eaton's size categories demonstrates how they marked a clear boundary between adult and child bodies.

Although the catalogue stressed the ease of ordering clothing that fit, the variety of sizes and size categories made selecting garments challenging, and more so for women than for men. The Eaton's order form asked men to list chest and waist measurements and to indicate their desired trouser length. Women's sizes relied on chest, waist, and hip measurements, with chest being the key variable: size 36 was intended for a woman with a 36-inch chest. Size ranges were also categorized to appeal to different customers: Junior, Misses', Regular Women's, Larger

Women's (sometimes called Short Full-Figure or Full-Figure), and Half sizes (for shorter women).[9] Girls' and Boys' sizes relied on chest and waist measurements but were also associated with age. Girls' size 8, for example, was assumed to fit the average eight-year-old girl. Girls' clothing began at size 6 years (with a 25-inch chest circumference) and increased to size 14 years (with a 32-inch chest circumference). Boys' clothes generally included garments in sizes 6 to 18 years. The smallest suits had a 24-inch chest (size 6), and the largest had a 36-inch chest (size 18). Like many similar stores in Canada and the United States, by the mid-1930s Eaton's had separate but sometimes overlapping categories for infants' garments (up to a year), toddlers' clothing (sizes 1 to 3 years), and children's wear (sizes 3 to 6 years) in its catalogues.[10]

Despite the measurements requested in a catalogue order, it was often difficult to purchase properly fitted garments. Standard sizing allowed clothing manufacturers to ensure consistency and to simplify manufacturing processes by limiting the number of different sizes, but a focus on average or typical measurements constrained the multiplicity of different body shapes and dimensions.[11] One government body reported that fifty different sizes would be needed to accommodate Canadian boys' varied bodies, far more than any manufacturer could economically produce.[12] Some manufacturers based age sizes for boys and girls on data collected by public health agencies, which provided a readily available pool of measurements but tended to result in small sizes because these agencies served children living in poverty, who were more likely to be malnourished.[13] Unfortunately for consumers, clothing sizes were not centrally regulated in Canada until 1969, when the Canadian Government Specifications Board published a set of voluntary standards for children's clothing at the request of the Consumers' Association of Canada.[14] A customer ordering girls' dresses in size 10 from two different manufacturers before that time might well have found that only one, or neither, fit a ten-year-old girl.

Eaton's size categories drew an unambiguous line between clothing for children and clothing for adults. The company assumed that age would be a key factor in body size until the age of 14 for girls and 18 for boys. Girls too large to wear size 14 were expected to buy garments in sizes cut for the physically mature female figure. Boys too large for size

18 had to order their suits in men's sizes. There was no transitional size category until the early 1930s.

Adult bodies had finished growing, and Eaton's insisted that age should not influence consumers' selection. Only size mattered. This was a point the catalogue repeated several times in the 1930s in reference to the Junior and Misses' sizes, the only women's categories for which size numbering did not correlate directly with chest size. Junior included sizes 13 to 19, with a chest ranging from 31 to 37 inches. Misses' sizes began with 14 (a 32-inch chest) and increased to 20 (a 38-inch chest). Junior and Misses' sizes overlapped with Women's Regular sizes in chest measurement but the garments had narrower waists and shorter skirt lengths.[15]

The Junior and Misses' labels certainly implied a link between a woman's age and the size of garment she should buy. The words themselves connote youth: *junior* for something smaller or intended for young people; *miss* for unmarried, and thus typically younger, women. In the 1930s, sometimes the word *years* appeared after the Junior and Misses' sizes, and customers who saw a dress sold in sizes "14 years to 20 years" would probably have assumed that it was intended for someone in their teens. Nevertheless, Eaton's continued to assert that sizes were related to body shape, not age or life stage. In the Spring and Summer 1935 catalogue the company proclaimed, "Junior is a Size, Not an Age," and noted that these categories were "created for slim-fitted adults." It further clarified that Junior Miss sizes suited the smaller woman of any age who felt she could "wear Junior fashions successfully." Several garments in the subsequent pages were carefully described as suited to both "the fashionable Junior Miss and sophisticated older woman with the 'youngish' figure."[16] In both cases, the customer was a woman, rather than a girl.

The Misses' and Junior ranges illustrate how grouping sizes into categories allowed Eaton's to direct particular sales messages to their customers. In tandem with the catalogue illustrations, most often drawn figures in these decades, and the text that accompanied each garment, the size categories provided customers with "a dream of how they would look when they wore Eaton's clothes."[17] This was true of all categories. Women were white, young, slim, and fashionable; their clothing was described most often as new, youthful, charming, chic, graceful, and flattering. Men were white, trim, often chiselled and angular, and strong. They wore suits in conservative styles noted for their value and quality tailoring, reflecting Eaton's belief that male customers were less likely to be persuaded by appeals to fashion. Children were also always white, usually depicted in playful postures, always smiling, often with ruddy cheeks. Their garments were smart and young but also *practical*, a term intended to appeal to the mothers who were buying these clothes. These characteristics remained relatively consistent in each size category over this period. By the early 1930s, however, manufacturers and retailers were already beginning to discuss the potentially different and age-related clothing "needs" of teenaged boys and girls. Articles in the clothing industry's trade publications called for more distinction between the girl of six and the girl of fourteen, and Eaton's followed these broader industry trends.[18]

FULL OF FASHION BUT STILL VERY YOUNG
Senior Girls and Boys

The clear line between children's and adults' clothing began to fade between 1932 and 1935, when the girls' and boys' sections of the Eaton's catalogue distinguished between younger and older children. The range of sizes offered to boys did not change, but the types of garments and the promotional language were increasingly geared toward a teenaged male customer who was no longer a boy but not yet a man. A new Senior Girls' category marked out girls in their early teens as being at an in-between stage that merited its own sizes and a more sophisticated style than Girls' clothing.

The Senior Girls' range began in the Fall and Winter 1932–33 catalogue with the addition of one size to the existing Girls' sizes 6 to 14, as Eaton's announced the introduction of a "specialized style," size 14x.[19] Garments in this size were cut fuller in the armholes, hips, sleeves, shoulders, chest, and waist. Dresses and skirts were also three inches longer than those in size 14, on average.[20] The new size capitalized on anxieties about age-appropriate appearance by implying that girls in their early teens who had outgrown size 14 dresses were not yet old enough to don women's clothing. Eaton's claimed this "new feature" was intended "for the 14-year-old girl who is plump for her age."[21] The implication was that a girl of fourteen, despite being the same size as a grown woman, should not order a dress from the women's section of the catalogue because it would not be age appropriate: 14x was "made expressly for the lassies who have, until now, found it necessary to have garments altered or to wear styles that were too 'old.'"[22] To emphasize the point, Eaton's offered dresses in sizes 10 to 14x with the same frilly necklines and puffed sleeves, and in the same durable, washable materials, as all girls' dresses at the time.[23] The message was that girls who grew at a faster rate were still girls, despite being harder to dress. Eaton's maintained that physical size was key to ensure that clothing fit properly, but it was clear that age was also part of finding the right fit.

In 1935, Eaton's went one step further, creating a Senior Girls' range that was deliberately marketed as being between girls' and women's sizes. In sizes 12 years, 13 years, 14 years, and 14x years, Senior Girls' claimed to offer larger (and implicitly older) age-appropriate styles for girls. For five years, each issue of the catalogue included a separate selection of dresses with this label, intended to appeal to a presumed teenage desire for sophistication while accommodating girls' developing figures and protecting their childlike appearance.

While the word *youthful* was often used to describe women's dresses, it did not apply to Senior Girls' dresses. Advertised as "Not Too Old," these styles played on concern that girls in their early teens who were developing breasts and hips would be able to maintain an appropriately girlish appearance despite their changing figures.[24] The garments combined common features of girls' and women's clothing, creating an in-between style. A printed voile dress labelled "A Chic Fashion" in the Spring and Summer 1935 catalogue, for example, had a longer skirt than other girls' dresses.[25] Long skirts were a traditional marker of sexual maturity for women, and women's dresses and skirts remained longer than girls' dresses and skirts in catalogues throughout the 1930s, '40s, and '50s. The jacket frock also mimicked a women's garment by offering girls a variety of styling choices not typically available in girls' dresses; the separate jacket could be worn with the dress or with other outfits, and had elasticized sleeves that could be worn up or down. It was

4.1 Senior Girls' sizes, with longer skirt lengths than Girls' dresses, Eaton's Fall and Winter 1935–36 Catalogue. Senior Girls' styles were often advertised as more grown-up without being inappropriately sophisticated.

also available in the same "fashion colours" as women's dresses, with exotic-sounding names such as dragon red, Nile green, Formosa blue, fresco rose, and Tahiti green. In contrast, girls' dresses were most often manufactured and sold in a choice of two colours without descriptive names, blue, white, and red being the most common.[26] Senior Girls' dresses were often described in similar terms to women's dresses, using adjectives such as *chic, dashing*, and *modish*. Eaton's wanted to impart a feeling of sophistication to Senior Girls, assuming girls in their early teens were not only larger than their younger sisters but also wanted to look more sophisticated.

At the same time as it mimicked features from women's styles, "A Chic Fashion" shared several characteristics with dresses designed for younger girls, having a round collar, puffed sleeves, and "pert bows." The dress also had a sash, a construction feature common to young girls' dresses because it created a girlish bow at the back and adapted to the growing waist more easily than a fitted waistline. Tie-back waists extended the life of girls' dresses; as a girl grew, the waist could grow with her.[27] Eaton's was also careful to advertise the "sturdy" and "decidedly practical" aspects of Senior Girls' dresses, adjectives that were more typical in descriptions of girls' dresses than women's. By combining girlish features with a more mature style of dress, Eaton's wanted customers to know that Senior Girls' dresses were "full of fashion but still very young."[28] Eaton's frequently highlighted these in-between styles, sometimes featuring them alongside women's dresses.

Eaton's also experimented with boys' size ranges at this time, although the changes were subtler than those seen in girls' clothing and occurred a bit later. Throughout the 1930s, the company had offered boys' suits in wide size ranges that did not clearly categorize boys according to age. For example, the same style of trousers was available in size 6 and size 18.[29] Knee pants and bloomers, garments typically associated with smaller boys, were also available up to size 16.[30] Even though breeching – the practice among middle- and upper-class mothers of outfitting a son in his first suit – had largely fallen out of fashion in Canada by the 1920s, the belief that younger boys should not wear full-length trousers persisted.[31] Long pants gave boys a more masculine appearance as they began to grow up, leaving the maternal protection and more feminized clothing of infancy behind.[32] A suit available in sizes 10 to 16 in the 1933 catalogue was advertised as "an ideal choice for first 'longers,'" suggesting that boys this age might be wearing long pants for the first time. Short pants and bloomers were also advertised as ideal for younger boys because they were "made on roomy sizes that allow free, easy action," making them ideal garments for play.[33] Buying a suit with both bloomers and long pants extended the life of the garment, Eaton's argued; boys could wear the bloomers for play and save the long pants for more formal occasions. Boys were assumed to like this feature too, since they could play in bloomers without worrying about angering their mothers by ruining their trousers. Eaton's advertised its trouser-and-bloomer suits as "practical styles that appeal to the boyhood spirit."[34]

In the late 1930s and early '40s, size ranges for boys began to coalesce into distinct categories: Junior, from size 6 years to size 10 years; Intermediate, from size 10 years to size 15 years; and Senior Boys', from size 14 years to size 19 years.[35] Increasingly, knee pants were sold only in Junior sizes, and bloomers were available in Intermediate but not Senior sizes. Eaton's also distinguished between Junior and Intermediate or Senior Boys by referring to the latter as students. In 1935, a suit for boys in sizes 14 to 18 claimed to have "all the good style points demanded by the student-age youth."[36] The Fall and Winter 1935–36 catalogue included "Students' Two-Pant Suits" in sizes 14 to 19 years, while a page of the 1937 boys' section announced, "Style and Value are 'Classmates' at EATON'S," referring to the presumed student status of the boys who might purchase the suits offered in Senior sizes.[37] The 1940 and 1945 catalogues advertised suits in Intermediate and Senior sizes as "practical for the boy at school" or "a wise choice for service at school."[38] In contrast, descriptions of Junior suits rarely referenced school or students.[39] Junior suits were for play or "for dressing up the 'little man' just like dad!"[40] Even though Junior boys were old enough to attend school, Eaton's preferred to appeal to them (and their mothers) by emphasizing how easy it was to play in the garments. The new sizing categories distinguished between younger and older boys more clearly than in the past, creating stages of boyhood that the company could depict in distinct ways.

By 1940, Eaton's had divided children's clothing into increasingly distinct size ranges based on age. In many ways, these changes reflected decisions made by the catalogue creators to display and promote clothing for young people in more profitable ways. Very little distinguished suits for older boys from those available to their little brothers, aside from the absence of bloomers; they were sold in the same style and colours, regardless of size. By associating sizes 14 to 19 years with suits fit for students, however, Eaton's rhetorically marked Senior sizes as distinct. Senior Girls' clothing was also clearly segregated and presented in a way to appeal to girls in their early teens. Given that the size range was offered only until 1940, we might conclude that this was a failed marketing attempt. Nevertheless, the catalogue continued to sell a more limited selection of girls' garments in sizes 10 to 14x, making a clear distinction between younger and older girls.

THEY'LL NEVER BE AT THE AWKWARD AGE
Modelling Gendered Growth

Although the Senior Girls' section disappeared after 1940, on several occasions in the following years the catalogues promoted garments as specifically designed to transform the awkward adolescent bodies of teenaged girls into graceful and feminine figures. The company never alluded to potentially problematic aspects of boys' figures, despite the fact that the Boys' size range implied continued growth throughout the teen years. Girls, whose clothing was cut to fit more closely to the body, were assumed to grow awkward in puberty and thus more difficult to fit for clothing. Eaton's mentioned girls' awkwardness only when pointing out how a particular dress would shape young female figures, both identifying and solving the "problem" of the teenaged body by reassuring customers that "they'll never be at the 'awkward age' because their clothes are from EATON'S Catalogue."[41]

According to Eaton's, a dress could transform a gawky teenager into the "most popular girl in the crowd." The Spring and Summer 1939 issue dedicated a page of the women's section to "Styles for Teen-Agers," displayed next to the teenaged film actor Deanna Durbin, the "little Canadian-born lady starring in Universal Pictures." The dresses in her clothing line featured shirred waists made of an elastic material, making them "an easy fashion for those sometimes hard-to-fit teens."[42] Although Durbin was seventeen in 1939 and had presumably finished growing, the clothing line, in sizes 10–14, was aimed at girls just entering their teen years. Lisa Jacobson suggests that Durbin's clothing may have appealed more to parents than to teenagers, as Durbin's on-screen characters were the "sweetly innocent" and "wholesome" teens that parents probably wanted their daughters to be.[43]

The Spring and Summer 1941 catalogue further demonstrates the way clothing was intended to transform teen figures. A dress labelled "Fashion Keeps Tabs on Teensters" was included near the front of the catalogue alongside women's dresses and was styled "especially to help eliminate awkward contours" of teenage growth "with tie-backs at the waist to give a fitted look" (see Figure 4.2). The tie-back waist could accommodate a wider or growing waistline or be used to cinch in the waist to conform to ideal slenderness.[44] In another example, Eaton's informed customers that a girls' dress available in sizes 12 to 14x featured fabric (an alpaca-weave rayon that "handles superbly") and design (with "modish tucks at the shoulders and waist," a pleated skirt, and basted hem) chosen specifically to address "the figure problems of growing girls, softening too-bony curves and whittling down too-chubby contours."[45] The dress was thus capable of moulding a "problematic" body into a pleasing shape.

Customers examining the catalogues saw only transformed teenaged bodies rather than awkward ones. The models wearing the dresses advertised were slender, with an hourglass silhouette and long legs. The Deanna Durbin promotion included her glamorous headshot in the top corner, embodying "the very spirit of vivacious, gay, care-free youth!" While teenaged girls were apparently prone to figure problems – an issue always attributed to their bodies, rather than to the clothing sizes or styles – Eaton's wanted customers to believe that their garments could overcome the awkwardness of teen growth. Once the company began selling garments in a new teen-specific size range marketed more directly to girls, rather than to mothers, references to adolescent ungainliness disappeared.

4.2 "Fashion Keeps Tabs on Teensters" dress style demonstrating the idea of an in-between style, Eaton's Spring and Summer 1941 Catalogue. The dress in the bottom left corner of this page, sold in sizes 10–14x, has the silhouette of a woman's dress but the "novelties" of girls' dresses, including "pouchy" pockets at the hips (a feature never advertised on women's dresses), elephant buttons, and a white collar.

— The Scramble for the Teenage Dollar —

A GALAXY OF GAY YOUNG SIZES
Measuring Teenaged Bodies

In the mid-1940s, Eaton's again altered its size ranges to appeal more directly to teenaged customers. Beginning in 1945, girls could order some clothing in Teenster sizes (shortened to "Teen" after 1953), while larger boys could order clothing in the new Grad size range beginning in 1948. An analysis of these size ranges reveals that Eaton's was not trying to better accommodate the teenaged body so much as to attract teenaged customers, a desire apparent elsewhere in the creation of the Junior Council and Executive and in magazine advertising and promotions. Eaton's wasn't alone. Across the retail industry, surveys indicated that girls in their teens had larger wardrobes and spent more money on clothes than their mothers. In 1946, the *Toronto Daily Star* reported that 60 percent of Canadian clothing designers were now producing teen fashions, trying to profit from their consumer clout.[46] While Eaton's continued to insist that sizes were based on body proportions rather than age, their Teenster and Grad clothing used references to school and dating, connecting garments to teenaged customers' social success in gendered ways.

Eaton's Teenster line started small, but within a decade expanded to a dedicated section of the catalogue. The company initially presented eight dresses and four coats in sizes 12, 14, and 16, roughly one-third the number of dress and coat styles offered in Girls' sizes. By 1950, it offered five pages of dresses in Teenster sizes and a wide variety of garments for older girls, including blouses, skirts, and slacks.[47] In 1955, the catalogue grouped all the Teen-sized garments in a new section called Teen Fair, described in the Fall and Winter 1956–57 catalogue as "a galaxy of gay young sizes 12 to 16."[48] Over eight pages, Eaton's displayed Teen dresses, skirt and blouse sets, sweaters, cardigans, slacks, and coats. The section also included a page of "dainty bra's," "sleek girdles," and nylon crinolines.[49] Eaton's had sold lingerie in smaller sizes before, but this was the first time it sold undergarments alongside other clothing instead of placing them in the women's lingerie section. Teen Fair was intended as a one-stop mail-order shop for younger female customers, underlining their growing importance to Eaton's.

(118)

— Tailored for Teens —

Table 4.I ◆ Girls' and Teen size measurements, in inches

	Chest		Waist		Hips		Length	
	Girls'	Teen	Girls'	Teen	Girls'	Teen	Girls'	Teen
10	28	28	24.5	24	29	29	32	36
12	30	30	25.5	25	31.5	32	36	43
14	32	32	26	26	34	34	41	44
14x	33	–	26.5	–	35.5	–	43	–
16	–	34	–	27	–	36	–	45

Source: Eaton's Spring and Summer 1956 Catalogue.

Eaton's hoped the Teenster size range would help girls in their teens find fashions that suited their age and fit well. Introduced in the Spring and Summer 1945 catalogue as "Girlhood Fashions for Growing-Ups," the garments were displayed on their own page just before the girls' section of the catalogue. Eaton's informed customers that Teenster garments were "more fashion conscious and sophisticated than young Sis's clothes" but "not so mature as Juniors' and Misses' fashions." The range had four sizes (10, 12, 14, and 16), expanding the numerical scheme associated with Senior Girls' to include the larger size 16 and potentially increasing the number of girls in their teens who could wear the dresses. Initially, Eaton's claimed that Teenster sizes were "cut fuller in the bust than Children's clothes."[50] This might have been the case in 1945, but by the early 1950s, Girls' and Teenster sizes had the same range of chest measurements and promotions no longer drew attention to specific differences in cut.

Nevertheless, Teenster sizes were intended to create a slightly different silhouette from Girls' sizes (see Table 4.1). While the biggest difference was in skirt length, the Teen size 10 had a smaller waist than the Girls' size 10, and the Teen size 12 had both a narrower waist and wider hips than the corresponding Girls' size. These modifications assumed either that girls' figures were getting curvier or that their garments should strive to accentuate curves as they aged. Indeed, the Misses' size 14 had the same chest and hip measurements as the Teenster size 14, but an even narrower, 25-inch waist. There was a clear progression from a more rectangular torso associated with girls to an hourglass shape associated with the ideal figure of an adult woman. The four new Teenster sizes offered adolescent girls a couple of additional options if their figures conformed to Eaton's expectation of female growth, which many did not. The Teenster size range suggested a recognition (albeit a flawed one) that clothing needed to accommodate teen figures.

In contrast, when Eaton's altered its Boys' size ranges in 1948, it did not change the actual measurements at all, instead referring to larger boys as Grads. While Boys' sizes remained correlated with age, Grad sizes fit chest sizes 32 to 38 inches "for Junior Young Men."[51] Eaton's implied that Grad sizes were new, but the measurements were the same as Boys' sizes 14 to 19 years. A Boys' size 14 had the same chest, waist, and leg measurements as the Grad size 32, and the measurements increased from size to size at the same rate. For the most part, the catalogue continued to offer both Boys' and Grad sizes. Although the two overlapped, Grad sizes had slightly wider waist measurements than Men's sizes, suggesting that Eaton's expected boys in their teen years to have more rectangular torsos than fully grown men.[52]

In 1955, Eaton's expanded the Grad size range to include 40-inch chests, in what the catalogue termed a "Special Service for Man-Sized Youths." The company explained that it had been "keeping an eye on statistics" and had noticed that "teen-agers are taller and huskier for their age than those of previous generations." Eaton's solution was to offer suits that were specially proportioned for these "man-sized youth," so larger boys would not have to buy men's sizes before they had reached the age of maturity, deemed to be roughly nineteen.[53]

Eaton's shifting size ranges hint at a broader belief that girls and boys in their teens could not wear the same clothing as younger children or adults. An age-based style hierarchy was determined less by body measurements than by expectations about teenage appearance. Teens were "still girlish," Eaton's declared on the opening page of the girls' section in 1945, although the Teenster sizes reflected a more mature silhouette than Girls'. Similarly, Grad sizes would save boys – and their parents – money because the suits cost significantly less than similarly sized men's suits.[54]

At the same time, the similarity between Grad sizes and Men's sizes reinforced the idea that even larger boys needed suits made for boys, as opposed to suits made for men. Teenster and Grad sizes may have helped some adolescents find clothing that fit them better, but it was Eaton's marketing of these garments, through their descriptions and visual display in the catalogues, that connected the company's clothing with the image of a popular and attractive teenager.

LOOKING KEEN FOR ALL THE BIG OH-CCASIONS
Dressing for Social Success

Eaton's attempted to set teenaged customers apart from children and adults in their catalogues, using text and images to present teenagers as style conscious and eager to please their peers. The company positioned the bodies of girls and boys between childhood and adulthood in terms of size, but the garment descriptions, colours, and styling also operated to create the image of a sophisticated yet age-appropriate teenager. Teenster sizes emphasized that girls' femininity depended on attracting male attention, while Grad-sized suits promised that being style conscious would enhance boys' masculinity and project future success in the workplace.

These distinctly gendered appeals shared the presumption that teenagers were first and foremost students. Throughout the late 1940s and the '50s, the catalogue associated Teenster and Grad garments with school attendance and activities. "Attention Teeners!" the catalogue announced in 1945, asking girls to "Pick these peppy clothes for your winter activities – at school and after, for comfort indoors and out."[55] Teen-sized dresses were "for a collegiate miss" and "suited to the pep and ginger of a high-schooler perpetually on the go."[56] In 1947, the catalogue proclaimed, "It's always Teen Time at EATON'S" and offered "super duds for school time." Another page was headlined "Styled to a Teen's Taste for the Whirl of School Activities."[57] Similarly, the girls' section of the 1948 catalogue claimed that Eaton's "school togs stand at the head of the class with clothes-conscious teen-agers." The accompanying drawing showed two people walking down the stairs of a school building; the girl adjusts her jacket hood while the boy slings his books over his shoulder.[58] Eaton's referred to older boys as students increasingly in the 1940s, selling suits that were "for the style-wise student," "tops with the Hi-Crowd," and appropriate "whether he is at school, at business or wants a suit for general wear."[59] The term *grad* further associated teenaged boys with school and, crucially, with academic success. Thus, while female teenagers were *schoolgirls*, a term that emphasized their youth, male teenagers were *students* and *junior young men*, suggesting maturity.

Alongside references to the Teenster as student, Eaton's associated girls' garments with their expected role in heterosexual courtship. Teenster dresses were described as ideal for attracting male attention and wearing on dates. Eaton's assumed that girls who could wear Teenster sizes were old enough to date and promoted the belief that dating success depended on one's appearance, such as by labelling a dress "a formula for success for dancing, dating."[60] The Fall and Winter 1946–47 catalogue called a Teenster dress a "compliment catcher – with beau-magnet flattery"; girls could "steal his heart away" just by wearing an Eaton's dress.[61] The Spring and Summer 1947 catalogue included three dresses chosen "to keep a 'teen-ager looking keen for all the big 'oh-ccasions' in her lively life."[62] The description implied that teenaged girls needed to dress for many social events, and at the same time alluded to the excitement, wonder, and pleasure they were assumed to experience as they engaged in such activities.

Eaton's specified exactly what kind of male attention its female customers could expect if they purchased a dress offered in the Spring and Summer 1947 catalogue: "Just listen to 'em whistle when you go by wearing this date timer."[63] The company implied that teenaged girls would be flattered by the catcalls of male strangers, and that attracting unsolicited attention from men was part of what it meant to be a teenaged girl. Dresses that were "plentifully supplied with the lively detail that rates second glances" would ensure girls would be gazed upon with favour while wearing them.[64]

Clearly, Teenster dresses were designed to reveal teenaged girls' bodies, and the catalogue often pointed out how a particular dress highlighted the ideal figure. For example, the "compliment catcher" featured a "pouf of a peplum" and a "belt for a tiny waist."[65] A belt could be used to

— Tailored for Teens —

narrow the figure at the waist, and the peplum (an overskirt or ruffle attached to the waistline) would make the hips appear larger and the waist even smaller, creating a curvier silhouette. Nearly half of the Teenster dresses sampled mentioned that the garment would make waists appear smaller. All three such dresses on a single page of the Spring and Summer 1947 catalogue noted the "nipped in" or "slimming" look that the dresses would give their teenaged wearers.[66] Similarly, in 1955 Eaton's noted that the "waist is minimized by self-covered belt and slide."[67]

Gone were references to awkward adolescent figures, although garments in Girls' sizes 10–14 continued to mention the benefits of elastic shirred waists that could "adjust without fuss to the figure."[68] Teensters were described as having "supple silhouettes" that emphasized the hourglass figure popular in women's fashions in the late 1940s and '50s.[69] While both Girls' and Teen clothing changed shape to reflect the rounded shoulders, small waists, and flaring skirts of what became known as the New Look, Teenster descriptions focused much more exclusively on the wearer's proportions. Eaton's called attention to the tailored nature of Teenster dresses, noting when a dress had a "fitted top" and using words such as *smooth*, *supple*, and *flatter* much more frequently than in Girls' garment descriptions.[70]

For teenaged boys, clothing promised social success in subtler ways. Regardless of size of the garment, descriptions for male clothing were shorter and contained fewer adjectives than those for female clothing. This both reflected and reinforced gendered assumptions about masculine and feminine priorities when shopping; retailers asserted that men wanted to make practical purchases quickly while women were more emotional and impressionable.[71] A suit's style was part of the sales pitch, but Eaton's dedicated very little ink to telling male customers about the best use of a particular suit, preferring to focus on fabric type and construction. This was partially due to the suit's versatility; a man in a three-piece suit could be respectable and perform heteronormative masculinity almost anywhere he went in this period. Nevertheless, the catalogue often referred to "Young Canada" to describe the intended customer of Grad-sized suits, conjuring images of students completing their studies and embarking on successful careers as representatives of the future of the nation.[72] These connotations would have been particularly strong in the first decade following the Second World War.

At the same time, catalogues repeatedly painted the teenaged boy as more concerned about his appearance than younger boys. Durability and value were emphasized for suits in all size categories, but descriptions of style were used to appeal to teenaged boys. Boys' suits were typically referred to with the words *young, best, value, quality, neat, sturdy,* and *serviceable*, while Senior and Grad suits were described in terms such as *smart, tailored, sporty, quality,* and *popular.*[73]

Teenaged boys were still assumed to be more active than their fathers, needing suits that "take everyday punishment well," but they also wanted "snappy styles and fine fabrics."[74] Eaton's promoted Senior Boys' and Grad sizes as "style leaders" for boys who wanted an "up-to-the-minute look" with "Top-Notch Styling."[75] "The good style of this sporty model is sure to catch your eye!" Eaton's declared about a Senior suit that was "cut to make you look your best" with "all the style features that are in demand by the 'teen-age boy."[76] In 1957, Eaton's advertised a suit as an "an up-to-the-minute look that's a sure-fire hit for the style-conscious lad."[77] This description alluded to fashion – the suit was in line with current trends – while avoiding its feminine connotations. The term *style-conscious* suggested that teen boys were deliberately reflecting on and selecting the suits that would fit them best. Consciousness enhanced, rather than threatened, their masculinity; with a suit from Eaton's they could look the part of Young Canada and embody a successful future.

Eaton's also presented teenaged boys with distinct styles not available to younger boys or men. Grads were the only male catalogue customers to be offered draped trousers, one of the few features of the zoot suit that the clothing industry adapted, tamed, and popularized in the late 1940s and early 1950s.[78] These trousers were advertised as being wider at the knee and tapered at the ankle, creating a distinct silhouette. Ankle width was not mentioned in descriptions of most Boys' suits (or in Men's sizes, for that matter), whereas Grad suits sold between 1948 and 1951 made special mention of the "drape effect favoured by Young Canada."[79] In 1949, a suit styled "to-the-minute" advertised pants that were twenty-three inches wide at the knee and seventeen inches at the ankle.[80] In the Fall and Winter 1951–52 catalogue, the drape was more extreme, tapering dramatically from twenty-three-inch knees to a twelve-inch cuff. Eaton's noted that these were the "lines popular with most youths."[81] By offering draped trousers only in suits for older boys, Eaton's was again marking the distinct style preferences of teenaged customers.

While garment descriptions were vital, colour also played an important role in Eaton's teen-specific marketing. The company believed Teenster and Grad customers wanted clothes that would stand out and attract attention. Boys' clothing was typically available in colours such as navy, grey, brown, and black. In the 1940s and '50s, brighter greens and teal began to appear, alongside lighter shades of brown. Although the shift probably reflects broader trends in men's fashions, these colours were offered more often in Grad sizes than in Boys'. Older boys were assumed to be more attracted to a "sporty style in all-wool checked tweed" in green.[82] Between 1945 and 1951, four suits in the sample were available in teal, and three of them were offered only in Senior Boys' and Grad sizes.[83]

Suit descriptions for older boys drew attention to these new colours. In 1949, under the headline "Hi-Styles for Young Canada," Eaton's offered a suit in the "much-wanted brown shade," with "extra slacks in harmonizing Fawn shade."[84] Beyond the implication that brown was popular, the addition of extra slacks in a different shade reflects Eaton's belief that boys wanted to mix and match their clothes. Generally, the catalogue also offered Grads more variety, typically selling Boys' suits in two colours whereas several Senior Boys' and Grad suits were available in three or four.

Like dresses in the earlier Senior Girls' size category, Teenster dresses came in a variety of fashion colours that distinguished them from younger girls' garments. Nearly a third of the Teen dresses sampled from the catalogue were sold in so-called fashion colours, including turquoise, sapphire blue, coral pink, burnt sugar tan, and emerald green.[85] The catalogue stressed that colour was an important way to stand out in a way that was still age appropriate, and Teenster dresses were sometimes much brighter than Women's dresses. In the 1945 Spring and Summer catalogue, the company offered a "swish young party frock" in "catch-eye colors," including lime green. Lime was not a subtle colour, and only one Women's dress in the garments sampled was sold in "Lime Fruit Green (light)," a slightly more subdued version of the bright green shade.[86]

Some Teenster dresses were available in black, another sign that Eaton's wanted to associate these garments with sophistication. For much of the twentieth century, it was unusual for girls to wear black, even for mourning. Generally, the adults who made children's clothes approved of light colours that symbolized innocence and asexuality.[87] Black fell even further out of favour for children's dress when fashion designers such as Coco Chanel began using it to make formal, sophisticated, and often revealing dresses in the 1920s. The association of black with elegance, sexuality, and its ability to slim the figure made it more popular with women and more inappropriate for girls' wear.[88] The Eaton's catalogue reflects this trend; five Girls' dresses in the sample included black trim, but not a single one was sold in black.[89] Junior and Misses' dresses, on the other hand, were often available in black. The solid black "compliments catcher" dress in Teenster sizes reflected a conscious choice to emphasize the garment's sophistication and appeal to teenaged customers eager to appear older. Younger girls were not considered "ready" to wear black, whereas older girls were deemed mature enough to don the darker shade – and attract the ensuing compliments.

The visual display of Teenster and Grad clothing offered Eaton's another opportunity to craft an image of its ideal teenaged customer. Catalogues employed photographs with increasing frequency after the Second World War. Photographs of Girls and Teenster models were rare in the 1930–60 sample before 1946 but appeared in six different catalogues in the 1950s. Boys, on the other hand, were not photographed at all over the three decades. As other companies did, Eaton's continued to use illustrations in its catalogues throughout the 1940s and '50s, particularly for children's clothing. One can imagine that drawing younger people was easier and less expensive than photographing them, but some companies also believed drawings sold more garments because they allowed consumers to imagine themselves in a more glamorous or appealing light.[90] The proportions of drawn figures could be exaggerated to create an appealing illusion.

— Tailored for Teens —

4.3 Teen dresses illustrated in the Eaton's Spring and Summer 1948 Catalogue.

Eaton's used this tactic to great effect in displaying Teenster and Grad clothing. Even after the "streamlined modernist aesthetic" popular in commercial art in the 1920s and '30s had passed, drawn models were much thinner than actual women.[91] Teenster models were drawn tall and thin, yet with hourglass figures that emphasized their chests and hips and slim, high waists that created unrealistically long legs (see Figure 4.3). Statistically, rectangular and pear-shaped figures are much more common than an hourglass shape.[92] Grad models were also drawn tall, with the broad shoulders of full-grown men, and shared the chiselled

4.4 Grad suits from the Eaton's Fall and Winter 1948–49 Catalogue.

features of adult male figures (see Figure 4.4). These models embodied the hard-working and enterprising businessman-in-training, a student who recognized that his clothing projected an image of success. Just as Eaton's dresses were intended to emphasize girls' femininity so they could fulfil their expected roles of wife and mother, Eaton's suits married fashion and consumption to heterosexual masculinity. Catalogue images were evidently intended to sell clothes by displaying garments to best effect, but they also conveyed messages about feminine and masculine appearance. Teenaged girls were very much young women, with fully developed, sexual bodies that should be slender to fit clothing properly. Teenaged boys should aspire to be fit and strong young men. Models showed potential customers an image that many could not imitate.

YOUNG CANADIANS undoubtedly used clothing to communicate their identity, appear more mature, fit in, or have fun; however, their individual choices were also shaped and constrained by the styles and sizes retailers offered. Between 1930 and 1960, Eaton's created an array of new and sometimes overlapping size categories designed to appeal to the teenager. Initially insistent that there was no connection between a customer's age and size, in the early 1930s the company began moving away from a clear division between children's and adults' clothing. By distinguishing Senior Girls and Boys from their younger sisters and brothers, Eaton's suggested for the first time that customers in their teen years warranted their own sizes and styles to match their more grown up but not yet mature bodies and activities. Girls' bodies were conceived as more problematic or awkward than boys', but both were at an in-between stage.

The advent of the Teenster and Grad size categories in the mid-1940s marked a turning point for the retailer, and the catalogues dedicated an increasing amount of space to gendered appeals to teenaged girls and boys. Sizes, garment descriptions, and models worked in tandem to present idealized images of teenage femininity and masculinity. Catalogue text and images presented Teensters as girls with slender figures, ready to date and attract male attention; they were assumed to want slim-fitting and sophisticated garments to win popularity from high school peers and potential beaus. Grads were teenaged boys preparing to assume manly responsibilities; they were sold suits using appeals to subtle style and their status as almost-men. Although Teenster and Grad clothing differed slightly from adult sizes, the company made little effort to reflect the actual dimensions and variety of shapes of teenaged boys and girls. Rather than tailoring their clothing to teens, Eaton's was fashioning an ideal teenaged customer and expecting young Canadians to fit the mould.

5

Eaton's Goes to School

Commodifying Students and Educating Consumers

IN 2020, the computer and office supplies retailer Staples Canada announced its tenth annual Superpower Your School contest to reward schools for their "environmental leadership and creativity" with prizes of $20,000 in new technology. Hundreds of schools entered the contest, hoping for a chance to secure equipment that strained school board budgets could not afford.[1] Staples is only one of numerous large Canadian and multinational corporations to maintain close relations with schools. These companies claim to be assisting and empowering students by providing equipment, sponsorship, cafeteria food, field trips, or curriculum materials. At the same time, by placing their names and products in school hallways and classrooms, they familiarize students with their brands at a young age, encouraging consumption and, ultimately, increasing their own profits.

Such examples of classroom commercialization in North America are numerous and well documented (as are the less numerous attempts to resist corporate influence in schools).[2] As Catherine Gidney argues in

Captive Audience, "the incorporation of advertising and marketing into schools reinforces corporate aims, fuelling consumer desire and a culture based on material accumulation that often counters schools' emphases on intellectual creativity, personal development, and individual well-being."[3] Although corporate–school partnerships have increased dramatically in the last thirty years, school commercialization has a longer history in Canada. When Eaton's began recruiting female junior councillors and male junior executives from schools in Toronto (and later Winnipeg, Hamilton, Calgary, Edmonton, and Montreal), it initiated a long and seemingly co-operative relationship between Canada's largest department store retailer and urban school boards and secondary schools. How did the retailer commodify student representatives while positioning its promotional activities as educational – and thus beneficial to students – in the 1940s and '50s?

Eaton's efforts in schools went beyond those of other corporations in the first half of the twentieth century, many of which regularly offered free teaching aids to cash-strapped teachers and schools.[4] Dozens of schools in four provinces participated in the Junior Council and Executive program, ostensibly sold on the benefits of helping Eaton's select representatives from among the student body and allowing the company to promote itself in school corridors and at extracurricular events. Councillors and executives were selected from among their peers because of their popularity and ambition, surveyed extensively on their purchasing preferences, and asked to promote the Eaton's brand in their schools. As representatives of their schools, they engaged in eight months of weekly meetings and activities. Eaton's intended to capitalize on students' peer networks and engage councillors and executives in promotional and merchandising efforts.

High school students were clearly valuable to Eaton's, imbuing the image, activities, and even bodies of student representatives with exchange value. Dressed in matching blazers with Eaton's lapel pins, they were emblems of the company in the stores and in their schools. This was not new terrain. The company consistently commodified its female employees in the first half of the twentieth century, advertising to them, enticing them to buy and use its merchandise, and using their images and appearance in its publicity.[5] The Junior Council and Executive program was another facet of this corporate commodification. Eaton's sought out sixteen- to eighteen-year-olds, asked for their assistance in serving the high school market, used their voluntary and paid labour in stores and at promotional events, and then took credit for being the store preferred by teenaged consumers.

Eaton's efforts to commodify the teenaged student occurred in the context of rising concern in the 1940s about whether high schools were preparing students for futures as workers and consumers. Did the curriculum teach subjects that made young people useful employees? How could young people be encouraged to remain in school until graduation? Representatives of Canadian industry and business joined government and social agencies, religious groups, and unions in considering these questions. Eaton's contributed to debates about making secondary education more practical and asserted that it was capable of offering students enriching experiences in the business world. The company framed its activities with the Junior Councils and Executives – visits to store departments, meetings with managers and buyers, field trips, and fashion shows – as opportunities to prepare boys and girls for their adult roles (in distinctly gendered ways). Canada's largest department store went to school, so to speak, to profit from students' peer influence and promote itself as an educational partner.

COOLHUNTING IN THE HALLS

Today, market researchers use the term *influencers* to describe individuals with the potential to shape their peers' consumer choices. Influencers don't simply endorse a company's products. They enjoy socializing or communicating with others, can do so effectively, and have earned the widespread trust of their peers. They are often trendsetters, those who are willing to take risks and purchase new merchandise or adopt a different style earlier than others, signalling a product's popularity to retailers. Author Malcolm Gladwell examines how successful advertising campaigns from the 1980s and '90s relied on finding out what people with influence thought was cool. This coolhunting "is not about the articulation of a coherent philosophy of cool. It's just a collection of spontaneous observations and predictions that differ from one moment to the next and from one coolhunter to the next."[6] Today's influencers are likely to be online "micro-celebrities" who leverage their followers on social media platforms and are, in many ways, brands themselves. Alhough they they did not yet have the sobriquet, influencers were also an important part of marketing in the pre-internet age.[7]

In the 1940s, Eaton's wanted to find those who could translate youth culture for the company, people who could inspire others and project an image that others would want to emulate. High school was the ideal place to find influencers because that is where young people were spending more time and engaged in a range of activities. As Mary Louise Adams notes, if people in their teen years "were contained within the state-run education system, they provided research material for inquisitive professionals – including psychologists, psychiatrists, physicians, sociologists and journalists."[8] Workers in the advertising and retail industries could be added to this list of experts keen to capitalize on a somewhat captive audience.

Although Eaton's would never have described its efforts as coolhunting, the employees who ran the Council program sought students who were not merely interested or enthusiastic but also influential in their peer groups. The company wanted outgoing, popular students as councillors and executives. To ensure that incoming councillors and executives were known and liked by their peers, outgoing school representatives were asked to identify several classmates who could replace them. These names were forwarded to school principals for approval and then to the company for final selection. "Popularity with the student body" was important, Eaton's reminded the students, to "ensure the candidate would have the support of the students themselves, as well as the principals and teachers."[9]

Several stores also used application forms to gather detailed information from potential representatives prior to selecting a boy and girl from each school. In Winnipeg, Eaton's employee and Junior Executive advisor T.M. Miller kept some of the forms completed by boys in 1950 and 1951, in separate files for successful and unsuccessful applicants. The application form (which was identical for boys and girls) included date of birth, age, grade level, home address, and clothing size, followed by questions about the student's hobbies and ambitions. Applicants were asked to include their favourite subjects, their part-time jobs, and their father's occupation. They were asked what activities and sports they participated in at school and in the larger community. Reference letters and academic averages were also requested. While the surviving forms from Winnipeg constitute only a small sample of the hundreds of students who applied and served in the groups across the country, the centralized nature of the program (with a national secretary in Toronto and regular meetings between program co-ordinators) suggests that other stores most likely used similar criteria to select junior councillors and executives. The questions and answers reveal the company's desire to select popular and influential students who could grant them access to what they believed was a lucrative base of customers.

Eaton's evidently sought young people whose influence was firmly rooted in their high school culture. To that end, six of the application's thirty questions related to extracurricular activities, hobbies, and sports. Academic achievement was less important than a good knowledge of, and experience with, the social activities of their schools and peer groups. In meetings with store executives, council advisors were warned not to "over emphasize either scholastic or athletic ability, but [to] find a boy or girl who is typically an all around student and who has the cooperation and support of the student body."[10] Executive advisor W. Lloyd Wornell wrote to Montreal's high school principals asking for their cooperation in nominating potential candidates. He noted that leadership and "executive qualities," followed by popularity among students and staff, were the highest priorities to consider when encouraging boys to apply.[11]

Analysis of the applicants' answers to these questions suggests that Eaton's employees preferred students who held multiple official school positions. Successful applicants were captains of school sports teams, class or school presidents, or yearbook editors – and sometimes all three.[12] Of the twenty-five boys chosen as executives in Winnipeg in 1951, twenty-two held more than one leadership position at school, and eleven listed three or more such roles. Forty percent of successful applicants were or had been class or school president. By contrast, nearly half of the forty-three unsuccessful applicants listed only one school position, and six did not list any.[13] Students who participated in or led school clubs and councils would not only be positively disposed to joining the Junior Executive program but would ensure that Eaton's had the ear of students who organized school activities and were visible leaders at school.

Equally important to program co-ordinators, if not more so, were answers to two questions designed to parse applicants' knowledge of their school's social networks. Students were asked to list the "school activities you are interested in" and the "social functions you have in your school." Both questions gauged their awareness of extracurricular events at school, rather than their participation. The second question, in particular, measured candidates' social savvy. Were they aware of the main events of the school's calendar, and thus able to help the company advertise at these events? Answers included dances, parties, debates, and other events common at urban high schools in the 1940s and '50s. Fifteen-year-old David Williamson's answer on his 1951 application was typical: "February Frolics, Sadie Hawkins dance, 2 class parties a year, the Holly Hop, Graduation exercises and dance, Grade X Wind-up, [and] many similar functions."[14] Some boys even listed social functions to which they would not have been invited, such as a mother–daughter tea. Eaton's was looking for young people with social connections and peer influence. In the process of finding them, the company extracted information about each school's social events that would potentially be useful for planning marketing activities to coincide with them.

During weekly meetings at the store, Eaton's made no secret of the fact that it wanted councillors' and executives' opinions. The students' personal preferences were a valuable commodity to the company, which used the feedback it received about merchandise and advertising to target teenaged consumers. The company also sought to benefit from students' peer influence at school. Student representatives could disseminate product information to their classmates. Events such as fashion shows were one way of accomplishing this goal, as audience members were positioned to admire and emulate their peers on the runway. Occasionally the company asked students to exert their influence more subtly, by giving them merchandise samples to wear to school. For example, at a

5.1 Members of the Montreal Junior Executive selling tickets to the Red Feather Frolic, 1947.

May 1948 meeting of the Toronto Junior Council, Mr. Sharpless from the shoe department asked that six councillors be fitted with a new style of saddle shoe. The minutes reported that "the girls are going to wear these shoes to school all the time," to show them off to their friends and tell them where to get their own pairs.[15]

Councillors and executives also granted the company access to their schools through the sponsorship of school events, including athletic competitions and dances (see Figure 5.1). In several cities, Eaton's created a Band Box, which was described as a portable sound system equipped with current popular recordings and branded with the the company logo. Junior executives were able to reserve the Band Box for school dances, where they acted as DJs (see Figures 5.2 and 5.3). The Montreal executives reported "tremendous student enthusiasm for the service,"

5.2 A dance at Montreal West High School in full swing, with members of Eaton's Junior Executive operating the Band Box. The date is unclear – either 1947 or 1948.

5.3 Don Beauprie (standing, left) and other members of the Montreal Junior Executive operating the Band Box.

which was reserved by a different school at nearly every meeting.[16] In Hamilton, it was used twenty-six times in three months; however, advisor C. Knapman complained that the company was not getting enough credit for providing the Band Box and reminded the executives "to give a little more time and care to the announcement [about the company's sponsorship,] which should be made just before intermission."[17] Executives also sold and distributed tickets at school for company-sponsored teen dances and fashion shows.

Eaton's invited councillors and executives to tell the company how it could support high school activities, and the students offered numerous suggestions. For example, in December 1943 the Toronto Junior Executive decided to hold a photo contest called "Eyes of Youth." Jack Brockie's memo notes that high school camera clubs were becoming more numerous, and that the executives believed the competition "was a splendid way in which they could contact the students of their school individually and become better known."[18] The junior executives might not have been avid amateur photographers, but they recognized that an Eaton's-sponsored contest would give them an opportunity to make camera club members part of their peer network. In other cases, the support was more transactional, as when a Toronto councillor asked if the store could supply her swim team with seventy bathing suits. In response, the manager of the sportswear department brought a "smart, trim, jersey-lined suit" to a meeting, prompting another councillor to place an order for her school team as well.[19]

The value of students' school activities to Eaton's was demonstrated in 1952 when the Winnipeg program advisor, T.M. Miller, suggested cancelling any advertising in the *Canadian High News*, a newspaper distributed at secondary schools in several cities. The ads reached only three thousand Winnipeg students, and Miller believed they were not worth the cost. Instead, the funds could be used "to much greater advantage in doing direct Public Relations with the schools."[20] Students brought the company's name and products into school hallways, and Eaton's executives believed they provided a type of advertising that money simply couldn't buy.

TRULY REPRESENTATIVE OF THE
CANADIAN HIGH SCHOOL YOUTH?

Despite Eaton's claim that its councillors and executives were "truly representative of the Canadian High School Youth," they embodied only a small minority of Canadians in their teen years.[21] The program was designed to be exclusive by limiting membership to upper-year high school students. This meant that Eaton's was already choosing from the small but growing number of people still attending school in Grades 11 and 12. They were also among those whose families were more economically secure.

Students' socio-economic status, as measured by their fathers' occupations listed on the application forms from Winnipeg, nevertheless appears to have played a less prominent role in their selection than their ambitions and extracurricular record. Approximately one-third of both successful and unsuccessful applicants in 1951 were the sons of labourers. Seven boys who became junior executives that year were the sons of retail employees or clerks, while another six had fathers in the civil service or the professions.[22] One was the son of a business owner. The fathers of the other two applicants were deceased. Although Eaton's did not appear to favour boys from more affluent families, it is telling that none of the applicants' fathers was unemployed. While we know little more about the representatives' families, their fathers' occupations suggest that they approximated the postwar ideal of a breadwinning father whose income supported his wife and offspring in relative material comfort.

Councillors and executives were among the more accomplished and ambitious high school students. Since participation required a letter of recommendation from the school principal or guidance counsellor, applicants were students with average or above-average grades. They participated in multiple extracurricular activities and held leadership positions at school and in community organizations. Many also had part-time jobs. When asked about their plans on the application forms, three-quarters set their sights on attending university after graduation. Among successful applicants for the 1950 and 1951 Junior Executive in Winnipeg, only four did not intend to continue to university, and two of those responded that they would instead enter "business."[23] While university aspirations did not necessarily translate into university attendance, the desire to pursue postsecondary education suggests that these were not typical high school students at a time when fewer than 10 percent of young people aged eighteen to twenty-one were enrolled in university programs in Canada.[24]

By referring to its junior councillors and executives as representative of Canadian high school youth, Eaton's privileged the white, middle-class Protestant teenager. Membership rolls and group photographs show that these young people were predominantly, if not exclusively, of European heritage. At Eaton's Montreal store, the program was run in English despite the large number of French-speaking high school students in the city. As a result, initially councillors and executives were students of the English Protestant school board and few, if any, were French-speaking Catholics before the mid-1950s, when the program began to expand into French Catholic schools. This was not the case in Toronto and Winnipeg, where the groups did have representatives from Catholic schools. In Winnipeg in 1951, T.M. Miller also noted that two of his executives were Jewish. Racialized teenagers and those of various ethnic and religious backgrounds could and did attend Canadian public high schools in the 1950s, but Eaton's did not idealize them as typical teenaged consumers. Just as many young people did not see themselves in the pages of consumer magazines, they were unlikely to be represented in the Junior Council and Executive program.

EATON'S AND THE SCHOOLS
Maintaining Good Relations

Eaton's relied to a considerable degree on co-operation from school authorities to operate the Council and Executive program. Company employees worked hard to maintain these relationships in the face of concerns that the retailer might be seen to be taking advantage of, or corrupting, students. Every part of the program was designed to garner goodwill from schools, beginning with the application process. Rather than issuing an open call for applicants, group advisors worked within the existing institutional power structure, contacting local high school principals and guidance counsellors each spring to solicit their assistance in selecting the next year's councillors and executives from within the student body. In Montreal, W. Lloyd Wornell wrote to school officials, "If you consider it feasible, the students may be allowed to forward names of suggested candidates. This slate of candidates to be considered by you when drawing up the final slate."[25] While students could propose applicants, the final choice rested with the principal, who would receive application forms for their preferred candidates to complete. Advisors were reminded at a joint meeting in May 1950 that "all selections must have the authorization of Principal and staff."[26] Eaton's knew that its activities in the schools would be better received if the students chosen were well liked by their teachers.

Once representatives were selected, the Eaton's employees who acted as Council and Executive advisors maintained regular contact with local schools. Many of the activities the company used to reach student consumers also generated goodwill with school administrators. It regularly donated or lent items to schools, for example, including five-dollar gift certificates as prizes at school dances, blue Eaton's curtains to decorate school auditoriums for events, and items requested by teachers from United Nations flags to wool. Although Eaton's did not honour every request – Mr. Schoales, teacher at Runnymede Collegiate, became "quite indignant" when he learned it would not donate classical music recordings to the school library following his request in 1948 – company records reveal repeated donations to more than a dozen Toronto schools in the 1940s and '50s, and several more to schools in the Greater Toronto area.[27] Eaton's offered to print tickets, posters, and programs for school events free of charge and included the store's name on each one. It provided decorations for school events eagerly and often. In Toronto, the company created and circulated 38,000 class timetables to students through their Council and Executive representatives during the first week of school. Council advisors were encouraged to pursue these opportunities to put the company name in front of students because, while "board of education rules do not permit any commercialism in the schools proper," the schools "turn a blind eye on this type of advertising that we are doing."[28]

Despite its success at convincing schools to co-operate, Eaton's was aware that it might be criticized. Council advisors were warned to design activities carefully because "school principals will always ... want to guard against the exploitation of students for commercial purposes."[29] It was relatively common for national and international firms to donate teaching aids from posters and pamphlets to filmstrips and lesson plans, all prominently branded. Teachers used these aids to fill gaps in their classroom resources, particularly before higher levels of provincial and federal government funding to public schools were put in place in the 1960s. However, teaching aids and other programs that brought brands into the classroom were sometimes regarded with suspicion by parent–teacher associations and denounced by social critics like Vance Packard in his popular 1950s book, *The Hidden Persuaders*.[30] Eaton's was keen to avoid this kind of scrutiny.

Not surprisingly, specific complaints about the Eaton's program either went unrecorded or have not survived, but advisors did make passing references to conflicts with schools, and at least one school ended its relationship with the company. St. Andrew's College, a private boys' school in Toronto, had a student representative on the Junior Executive in the 1940s but in 1953 discontinued a practice of displaying Eaton's sports equipment in the school, deeming it "too commercial," according to a staffer in the company's public relations office.[31] The minutes from the Junior Council and Executive meeting in May 1948 recorded a similar problem, noting that "some groups ... are prevented from tying in with various sporting events because of the opposition from local school authorities."[32] (Those present at the meeting also indicated that Eaton's received greater publicity from sporting events than from social events such as dances.) It is unclear from the records whether school authorities were opposed to commercial sponsorship generally or to Eaton's in particular.

In response to these criticisms, Eaton's staff worked hard to maintain good relations with school administrators. From Eaton's head office in Toronto, Jack Brockie cultivated personal contacts with principals and school board officials in order to ensure the program's success. At Brockie's request, the assistant principal at Malvern Collegiate Institute in Toronto, Milton Jewell, spoke to advisors in 1946, coaching them on the best way to approach school administrators; he encouraged advisors to describe the program as a service to the schools.[33] To that end, some

— Eaton's Goes to School —

5.4 Commercial High School principal Mr. F.N. Stephen speaking with Mr. J. Clifford, Eaton's advertising supervisor, at an event organized for school principals at the Toronto store, October 18, 1947.

advisors asked councillors and executives to invite their principals to dinners and presentations held in their honour at the store. Here, school administrators would meet store managers and executives, learn more about what the students were doing in the program, and receive the company's gratitude for their co-operation (see Figure 5.4). These principals' meetings were planned "in an attempt to tie-in and cooperate closely" with school officials.[34] In a letter written in September 1947, Toronto Board of Education superintendent C.W. Robb amicably advised Brockie to send any Eaton's promotions directly to school principals, as board practice prohibited teachers from circulating "material of an advertising nature" in their classrooms. Robb went on to say that "the Board of Education has been indebted to the T. Eaton Company on so many occasions in the past that I am of the opinion that this rule could be stretched a bit."[35] Robb did not state how Eaton's had helped the school board specifically, but his words imply that the company had succeeded in generating enough goodwill to promote its goods and activities to students when he might normally restrict such activities.

Brockie's close relationship with Superintendent Robb also proved beneficial when a school board east of Toronto opposed the company's attempts to draw members for a new Junior Council and Executive from its school. The Toronto Board of Education wrote to school authorities in Belleville, Ontario, endorsing the program in hopes of convincing them to allow Eaton's to proceed.[36] The minutes of the Junior Executive advisors' conference in 1946 indicate that other stores also encountered unnamed "problems" with local school authorities. The delegates decided to "make up a confidential report of these individual situations with information on how they were handled" so that advisors could help each other avoid the perception they were exploiting high school students. The report, if generated, does not survive.[37] In 1947, the advisors also recommended the creation of distinct stationery to be used in the conduct of Junior Council and Executive business and thus "keep any commercial taint out of Eaton's dealings with the schools," presumably because school officials would not see the Eaton's name and logo on letters, memos, and application forms associated with the program.[38]

The ambitious Junior Council and Executive program required the consent of school authorities in several provinces. The challenge of maintaining good relationships are alluded to only elliptically in the surviving records, but it is clear that Eaton's employees were conscious of the need to preserve these ties in order to sustain the company's privileged access to high school students. Eaton's not only attempted to avoid overt advertising but also responded to growing concerns about the purpose of secondary education by emphasizing and enhancing what it saw as the educational merits of the program.

A MORAL RESPONSIBILITY TO EDUCATE

Describing the launch of the Junior Council in a public relations pamphlet written in 1960, Eaton's admitted its initial motivation had not been "altogether altruistic," but asserted that the company quickly realized its "moral responsibility" to these students, "whose education could be greatly broadened through intimate contact with executive level representatives of the largest and most successful retailing enterprise in

Canada."[39] While increased sales and profit margins were the ultimate goal of the Junior Council and Executive, the program's potential educational value held increasing interest for Eaton's in the context of emerging debates about what and how high school students should learn to prepare them for adult roles as citizens, workers, and consumers.

In the 1940s, when many jobs did not require a postsecondary degree, Canadians often viewed a high school diploma as an academic achievement leading to university. Yet secondary schooling was coming to be seen as part of a basic education and therefore beneficial for all young people, regardless of their aspirations, academic ability, or class status. Educators, psychologists, child development experts, and social commentators argued that compulsory high school attendance would prevent juvenile delinquency and produce citizens who were well adjusted and able to participate in the workforce.[40] Eaton's was one of numerous corporations in Canada to participate in discussions about how the high school curriculum could be broadened to be more "practical" and appealing to students, many of whom still left school at age sixteen without graduating. Experiential learning and vocational guidance were among the methods proposed by youth organizations, government-sponsored commissions, and non-governmental agencies.[41] Briefly examining the efforts of one such group, the Canadian Education Association, helps to explain Eaton's belief in its moral responsibility as more than just a convenient strategy to appease school authorities. While the company's public image undoubtedly benefited from the perception that it was providing educational opportunities to Canadian students, these efforts were part of a larger conversation about how best to prepare young people for adulthood in the postwar world.

From 1946 to 1951, the Canadian Education Association, an umbrella organization dedicated to producing and sharing educational research across provincial boundaries, conducted an intensive study of the nation's secondary schools. It formed the Canadian Research Committee on Practical Education, which conducted numerous surveys and wrote several reports on why young people left high school before graduation. Its members asked employers across industries to identify the skills or qualities they desired in young workers, and quizzed graduates about their success finding employment. Reporting on its findings in the journal *Canadian Education* in 1951, the Research Committee argued that better schooling meant more practical schooling. This was seen to involve fewer core academic requirements and more electives "to suit the varied interests and aptitudes of the pupils," a recognition of the value of part-time work, and the objective of moving beyond an exclusive focus on fundamental literacy and numeracy to encompass an understanding of the political and economic workings of a democratic country.[42]

The Research Committee's work involved the close participation and financial support of some of the country's largest extractive, manufacturing, and retail companies, as well as trade associations, labour unions, and agricultural interests. In fact, the *Financial Times* reported in 1948 that the group was created at the behest of, and financed by, industry groups such as the Canadian Retail Federation and the Canadian Manufacturers' Association.[43] Industry representatives – all male – helped to set the research agenda and arrive at recommendations about how best to define and meet secondary students' needs. Over the committee's duration, fifty-seven firms and associations gave a total of $65,000 to conduct surveys, compile opinions, and discuss results. Included on the list of contributors were Canada's leading trade organizations, various large manufacturers of textiles, household appliances, pulp and paper, and steel, and numerous mining companies. Several department stores supported the committee's work, including the Robert Simpson Company, the Hudson's Bay Company, and Quebec retailer Dupuis Frères. Eaton's $1,200 contribution was the largest of any retailer, an indication of its interest in supporting the project's aims.[44]

Among the Research Committee's numerous surveys, one was directed at Canadian retailers and designed to solicit their opinions about the "appropriate education for retail business." The five-page questionnaire asked retailers a slew of questions, from whether a high school diploma was necessary to work efficiently in merchandising and sales to whether a high school course focused on the retail industry would better prepare young people for work in their companies. Should such a course be taught by teachers or by people with "practical retail experience"? Retailers were also asked their opinion on a co-operative training plan "whereby senior students in this special Retail course would be given practical training by part-time work experience while attending school part-time."[45] The responses to this survey have not survived, but the questions reveal a desire to provide students with experience that would help them secure post-graduation employment.

In addition to bringing high school education more closely in line with industry expectations of workers, the Research Committee believed that high schools should be doing more to value students' part-time work. This marked a shift from attitudes during the Depression and the Second World War, when various commentators believed teenagers were drawn into "blind-alley occupations" and got into trouble when they had "money to burn."[46] Teenagers didn't need a job to learn how to handle money, syndicated parenting columnist Angelo Patri insisted in 1946. They had enough to do to keep up to the standards of the classroom, and chores and a small allowance could serve their financial needs. Full-time jobs for young people were plentiful during the war, and many left school before graduation. Critics blamed rising rates of juvenile delinquency on these teens' higher incomes and lack of schooling.[47]

In contrast, the Research Committee recommended including part-time work in the general high school program, particularly for students who did not intend to attend university. W.A. Osbourne, vice-president of an Ontario boiler-making firm, told the 1947 convention of the Canadian Education Association that opportunities for summer employment "should be an important and intelligently planned part of the student's education and his adaptive process."[48] Responding to a Research Committee's report entitled *Your Child Leaves School*, a group of educators and industry advisors in Alberta also suggested that schools should recognize part-time jobs as "a desirable thing: it should probably be encouraged, even permitting students to miss periods to hold a job."[49] Work experience could have broad educational value.

Surveys of graduates affirmed that it was common for them to have held part-time jobs during their high school years, and that those who did were actually more likely to complete their high school education. This seems to have been borne out among the boys who applied to become junior executives in Winnipeg in 1951: two-thirds of those selected worked weekend or summer jobs.[50] Graduates reported that they believed their part-time jobs had helped them secure employment after graduation by increasing their self-confidence and giving them a sense of what it meant to work.[51] In its final report, the Research Committee recommended that secondary schools could better retain students by "recognizing the value of part-time work not only as a means of income, but as providing training and experience, and also as assisting the student to make his choice of occupations."[52] Rather than a blind alley, a part-time job after school, on weekends, or during summer holidays could offer a clear path to future secure employment.

When organizations such as the Canadian Youth Commission reported that "the young people of Canada want the schools to get closer to the *working world*," companies such as Eaton's claimed to be listening.[53] Given the company's financial support of the Research Committee's work, it was probably not a coincidence that the Junior Council and Executive program was increasingly framed as an opportunity for practical retail experience. Department stores had ready access to people who could teach students about the retail industry, Eaton's pointed out, along with the means to employ students part time and give them a "big chance to get a real behind-the-scenes, first-hand look at some aspect of a trade, career or profession they may want to follow up later."[54] With the encouragement of school officials, the company modelled the Junior Executive on corporate directors' meetings in order to foster the "business attitude" staff believed would serve male students well in the future.[55] In Montreal, both the Council and the Executive created subcommittees to handle communication with schools and track teenage trends in music and clothing. The national secretary reported that these committees would "provide each member with ample opportunity to obtain experience in committee work and its responsibilities, to develop leadership and poise, and to enable the councillor to obtain a more comprehensive knowledge of some particular phase of retail merchandise."[56] (They would also, of course, serve the company by collecting and disseminating useful marketing data more efficiently.) Even fashion shows were described as "educational in preparing students for the Business World."[57]

Councillors' and executives' activities in the stores could be seen as both marketing and educational opportunities, from contests for the best

— Eaton's Goes to School —

advertising copy or floor display to tours of store departments and visits to local manufacturers. Councillors and executives frequently worked part time in the stores, and educators' increasing favour of this practice allowed Eaton's to present it as a valuable educational experience. Eaton's also suggested that its constant surveying of teenagers for their product preferences – "the informal equilateral exchange of information between bright, opinionated school 'kids' and knowledgeable, experienced business executives" – benefited the students themselves.[58] The Council and Executive meetings were intended to be a window into the retail world.

A GENDERED CONSUMER EDUCATION

Through its Junior Council and Executive program, Eaton's assumed that female and male representatives required different kinds of lessons about consumption for their presumably gendered futures. The window into the retail world offered a panorama of opportunity for boys and a rather more blinkered view for girls: male students would be corporate managers or executives themselves someday; female students might also work in retail, most likely on the sales floor, but were ideally destined to be wives and mothers who purchased goods for their families. For Eaton's male and female employees who organized these activities for the students, these gendered roles were of equal import. If retailing was an evolving industry that boys could better understand through experience, then outfitting and running an efficient, comfortable home required training and skill that girls could acquire, in part, through Council activities. The minutes from Council and Executive meetings at six stores between 1946 and 1951 reflect the company's belief that it could prepare teenagers for their distinctly gendered future relationship to the consumer marketplace.[59]

In publicity materials related to the Council program, Eaton's emphasized that all high school representatives gained valuable knowledge about the retail industry through their participation. However, meeting minutes reveal that boys spent more time than girls learning about store operations and listening to retail industry experts. These encounters placed more emphasis on business operations than on selecting and purchasing products. At the Edmonton store, junior executives made a list

(149)

of speakers they wanted to invite to their meetings, including experts on the stock market, law, and Trans-Canada Airlines operations. They also wanted a tour of the airport. Advisor John Mooney noted that such talks would be "instructional from the view point of assisting the representatives in planning a career."[60] Company employees visited the junior executives often as well, with the 1947 minutes recording presentations about the operations of various Eaton's departments, from receiving and customer service to merchandising, advertising, and staff welfare. From January to April 1947, the Winnipeg Executive hosted six guest speakers, the Toronto Executive had seven, and between them Montreal, Hamilton, Edmonton, and Calgary hosted an additional fifteen. These presentations reportedly provided boys with insight into sales strategy, merchandising, and advertising. For example, in the same year the supervisor of the shoe department in the Toronto store spoke to junior executives about the way shoes were priced, the benefits and drawbacks of high-heeled ladies' shoes, and the names of Canadian shoe designers. In Montreal, a visit from the manager of the chinaware and glassware department focused on the basic principles of merchandising.[61] This information assumed that the boys would one day be selling shoes and housewares, not buying them.

Field trips offered young executives another opportunity to become familiar with business operations. Between 1946 and 1951, twenty-five different field trips were mentioned in meeting minutes. The boys made excursions to local manufacturers and other corporate concerns, in addition to visits to different Eaton's departments. The Montreal group visited the Eaton's Clothing Factory and a scarf manufacturer. The Hamilton group visited the Firestone plant, and the Edmonton executives toured the offices of the *Edmonton Journal* newspaper. Tours of local businesses exposed the boys to company products and operations. The Winnipeg Junior Executive visited the Gerhard Kennedy Sportswear plant, the *Winnipeg Free Press* offices, and the Eaton Mail Order Building. At the Gerhard Kennedy plant, they were shown bolts of cloth and different sewing machines, watched demonstrations, and learned how styles and colours were chosen for manufacture. At the same time, Kennedy "urged the Junior Executive to make known their wants and needs in clothes so that manufacturers and retailers might supply those needs."[62] Field trips were both education and advertisement; they gave retailers a captive audience and an opportunity to establish rapport with young consumers while teaching students about business operations and the skills they might need to join the industry.

In contrast, the guest speakers and field trips mentioned in the minutes of the Junior Council meetings at various stores reveal the assumption that high school girls were not destined for the corporate world. Their future role as shoppers and homemakers nevertheless required no less special training. Donica Belisle shows that, from the turn of the twentieth century, home economists were arguing that proper, expert consumer education for future wives and mothers was the only way to ensure Canadian families would be healthy and stable in an increasingly "complicated new world of mass consumption."[63] By the 1930s, home economics curricula – first at the postsecondary and then at the high school level – had shifted their focus from making do with less to making discerning choices when selecting goods for the home. The Eaton's Council program mirrored these goals, deepening connections between industry and classroom that began in home economics programs at Canadian universities across the country.[64] It is entirely possible that some of the Eaton's employees who organized the girls' activities and field trips during their weekly meetings were themselves graduates of these programs, trained to believe that proper consumption – spending that upheld standards set by white, middle-class women – was an act of citizenship and the duty of Canadian women. Animated by the ethos of home economics, Junior Council meetings at Eaton's sought to shape high school students' consumption habits and, specifically, to channel their spending into the department store.

Councillors were taught how products should be used and cared for. For example, after a thorough talk about the diversity and proper care of girdles (with samples for the girls to examine), the Toronto junior councillors were invited to be fitted in the foundations garment department, linking their new product knowledge to the point of sale. In the Calgary store, Mrs. Hannah from the hosiery and neckwear department showed a film on nylon hose and explained different types and styles of stockings to the girls, and Miss Breauchle from cosmetics "gave a talk and demonstration on the cleansing of skin, the application of make-up, and the use of various other beauty aids."[65] When Mr. Savage, from Eaton's jewellery department, spoke with Toronto councillors, the minutes reported that the highlight of his visit was when "one of the girls was fortunate enough to wear a one hundred thousand dollar necklace for about thirty seconds."[66] The talk sparked councillors' desire to own jewellery. Similarly, when Mr. Fellows brought a variety of items from Eaton's College Street store to show the Toronto councillors, he showcased household furnishings and appliances that were versatile and easy to clean. In thanking him for his visit, councillor Pat Cook "said that when she was ready to furnish a house she would be sure to come and see him."[67] These guest speakers emphasized the use of fashion, beauty, and household wares, focusing on information useful to those purchasing – rather than making or selling – products.

The sample of Council meeting minutes preserved in the Eaton's archive does not record any trips to factories or other companies outside Eaton's. Instead, new councillors were often given a tour of the store, which staff advisors described as "another step in familiarizing the Council and Execs with the behind the scene work in a department store."[68] In Winnipeg, girls visiting the store's research bureau were reportedly very interested in the way the employees, most of them male, scientifically tested materials before giving the "stamp of approval from Eaton's."[69] Brand awareness and assurances of quality were front and centre, while the skills required to work in the research bureau were not discussed.

Although councillors often heard female guest speakers in business and other occupations, the presentations rarely offered career advice, focusing instead on girls' as potential consumers. For example, Miss Marjorie Hunt of Lever Brothers visited the Toronto Council with samples of Lux soap flakes and a talk called "Pageant of Fashion" that used dolls as props to illustrate period costumes. Similarly, Miss Vivien Combe from Eaton's merchandise display department brought samples of china, linen, crystal, and silverware and encouraged the councillors to buy items that were beautiful and useful for their hope chests: "'Beautility' ... is a good word to keep in mind when shopping," she told the female students.[70]

(152)

Both women worked for large companies but neither discussed her job. A significant number of women, including married women, worked outside the home in the 1950s, but Junior Council activities shared the focus of high school home economics courses, emphasizing preparation for a future role as a homemaker and, as such, an expert consumer.

EATON'S RELATIONSHIP to dozens of schools across Canada in the 1940s and '50s illuminates the history of corporate involvement in Canadian classrooms. It demonstrates efforts to commodify students' peer influence, secure teenaged customers' loyalty, and associate the company with progressive education and good corporate citizenship. Eaton's contribution to debates about the purpose of secondary education points to the efforts some Canadian corporations made to shape the school curriculum. By presenting itself as an educator, Eaton's transformed the teenaged consumer into embodied evidence of the company's goodwill and dedication to young people while simultaneously putting students to work for the corporate image.

Its interactions with the schools demonstrate Eaton's efforts to appeal to both female and male students as potential customers. However, the different activities assigned to each group underlined the belief that consumption was more central to teenaged girls' identities than it was to teenaged boys' sense of themselves. The Junior Council and Executive program continued at several Eaton's stores for decades. In the mid-1960s, stores in Halifax, Saskatoon, and Calgary requested information about organizing their own, and Eaton's executives in Toronto agreed that the groups were "a nucleus for youth activities and a channel to youth tastes and preferences in merchandise."[71] Maintaining close relationships with schools remained beneficial for the company and, it continued to insist, for students as well.

Conclusion

IN 1999, *Business Week* magazine proclaimed that the children of baby boomers – those between the ages of five and twenty when the article was published – were poised to challenge the success of their parents' preferred brands. Through the size and influence of Generation Y, these millennials were "forcing" marketers to listen and to develop "a new kind of advertising as well as a new kind of product." These young people were less homogenous as a group, marketers declared. They were more cynical about traditional marketing techniques and less loyal to established brand names than their parents. Those wishing to sell to them couldn't address them as "kids" and had to bring their messages to the places where these young people congregated, "whether it's the Internet, a snowboarding tournament, or cable TV."[1]

Sound familiar? The article reads very much like "The Scramble for the Teen-Age Dollar," John Clare's 1957 article in *Maclean's*. Both attempted to make generational distinctions and appealed to the novelty of young people as a powerful consuming force with tastes and preferences only market research could decode. Market actors have "discovered" a distinct youth market repeatedly since the 1950s, heralding the generational agency and novel economic clout of people in the present generation of teens. Twenty-first century retailers and advertisers continue to spend millions courting the favour of young people whose cultural capital, reflected in their social media profiles, makes them ideal brand ambassadors as well as prolific consumers. Market research companies continue to generate knowledge about the teenager to shape advertising campaigns. Young people's assertiveness continues to legitimize these campaigns, with arguments that today's teens are "discovering trends and deciding for themselves" sounding very much like mid-century department stores' arguments about serving their authoritative teenaged customers.[2]

— Conclusion —

The preceding chapters have demonstrated that advertising to teenagers has a long history in Canada. By 1957, retailers and advertisers had all the pieces in place to foster teenagers' increased spending: distinct size ranges and styles for male and female catalogue customers; monthly magazine columns dedicated to the clothing, fads, and social etiquette of the high school girl; and an elaborate national network of Junior Councils and Executives, sponsored and organized by the largest retailer in the country, generating industry knowledge about the teenaged consumer and professing the desire to serve them. The teenagers of 1957 were in the process of growing up, but the teenager as a commercial persona had already matured – been fleshed out, so to speak, by market actors in previous decades. This teenager was a white, middle-class, heteronormative, and usually urban high school student, ideally situated to consume clothing, beauty products, and music recordings, among other commodities.

Now, as then, teenagers' savvy – a term that invokes their ability to differentiate products and brands, to decide what they like and reject what they don't – is presented as a justification for ongoing intensive market research on this age group. Beginning in the 1940s, Eaton's claimed to be merely meeting the needs of its younger customers, rather than cultivating them:

> Youth must be served, and Eaton's endeavour to do this by meeting them on their own ground, meeting and understanding them. It would have been impossible to contact these important citizens of Canada as individuals but it is possible to talk to them through the council and executive groups who are truly representative of the Canadian High School Youth.[3]

Such statements publicly expressed the company's faith in high school students as avid, style-conscious, and competent consumers who demanded to be recognized. The intention was to legitimize the retailer's numerous campaigns and solidify the idea that teenagers constituted a market: a group with distinct needs that could only be met through acts of consumption. By labelling high school students as "important citizens" even though they were not yet old enough to vote, Eaton's declared itself to be acting in teenagers' best interests. At the same time, of course, this

(155)

approach supported efforts to profit from increased sales and customer loyalty. The Junior Council and Executive program gave teenaged members considerable clout within the stores while transforming them into commodities Eaton's could use to promote its corporate image and sales inside the country's urban high schools.

Now, as then, young people are also surrounded by images of what the teenager looks like: images that are meant to prompt comparison and self-evaluation. Beginning in the late 1930s, the desirable image was that of the co-ed, a fashionable and popular student who was an independent, responsible shopper and part of an opinionated cohort that retailers ignored at their peril. Magazine columnists, editors, and store employees consistently privileged white settler femininity and excluded racialized, queer, and working-class people in their teen years from the commercialized look and lifestyle of the Canadian teenager. The characteristics of the teenaged consumer – shopping alone, purchasing their own clothing, and identifying with particular styles and brands – emerged from early market research efforts such as the Junior Council and Executive, which gave Eaton's and its associated advertisers insider knowledge of high school culture.

After decades of market actors presenting consumption as central to "good" childhoods and successful transitions to adulthood, and claiming to empower young people to express themselves using consumer goods, the consequences of their actions deserve closer scrutiny. There is ample evidence to suggest that growing up in consumer society can be detrimental. Young people's ability to keep up materially with their peers has been shown to have negative psychological effects.[4] In times of economic uncertainty and austerity – the recession of the 1980s, the global financial crisis of 2008, or the rising cost of living following the COVID-19 pandemic – young people also face higher rates of unemployment than their elders and are therefore especially vulnerable to rising rents and food prices.[5]

At the same time, as the volume of advertising has risen in recent decades, so have levels of consumption, not to mention the environmental impact of clothing production and waste. Clothing sales have doubled since 2000, fuelled by online advertising and shopping.[6] The persona of

— Conclusion —

the teenager as an agentive consuming subject has persisted through several generations. The problem, historian Jon Savage notes, is that this persona "is, and has been tied to, a way of life that is becoming unsustainable."[7] Alternative imaginings of the teenager are needed but potentially difficult, given that people have been taught to connect their self-expression and citizenship – their right to choose – to consumption from a young age. With their history of crafting the persona of the teenager, we cannot expect marketing professionals to do this work; their repeated discovery of the teenager is in essence an effort to maximize corporate profits rather than take responsibility for the potentially negative consequences of consumerism.

Further inquiry into the histories of young people's experiences as consumers could provide teenagers today with different models of youth culture. Much work remains to be done, particularly regarding the purchasing decisions and meaning-making efforts of Canadian teenagers themselves. Student-generated sources, such as high school newspapers and yearbooks, might offer important glimpses into the ways that young people have used and related to consumer goods. Certainly, existing scholarship using sources from university campuses suggests that this evidence can point to young people's preferences, priorities, and actions in an institutional environment.[8] Similarly, Linda Mahood's study of youth mobility demonstrates the value of oral histories in enriching our understanding of young people's decisions.[9] Teenagers and young adults choose to travel and hitchhike for a variety of reasons not captured in periodicals or government records. What could the memories of those who were teenagers in the 1950s, '60s, and beyond tell us about the meaning of consumer goods, and the practices of consumption, in the shifting process of growing up?

Young Canadians' participation as workers in the consumer economy also deserves historians' attention. The mall is not only where teenagers shop but also often their workplace. In the 1970s, Paul Willis argued that high schools were instrumental in inculcating working-class values into teenaged boys, preparing them for a lifetime of manual and wage labour. More recently, geographer Linda McDowell revisited Willis's arguments and posited that high school students today are "learning to serve" more than "learning to labour." The service-oriented nature of a large segment of the North American economy has increased the importance of consumption to how we work and earn money.[10] We need to investigate further the ways in which institutions such as schools have taught children to consume and prepared them for roles in a consumer economy, replicating patterns of class, gendered, and racialized inequity in the process.

Children cannot be separated from the expectations, imaginations, and actions of adults and the institutions within which their lives are structured. The meaning of the term *teenager* continues to be remade; most recently, the COVID-19 pandemic rendered many expected teen experiences – from daily school attendance to playing sports, socializing with friends, and forming romantic attachments – difficult or impossible. Social interactions occurred online during periods of lockdown, and the consequences will not become clear until more time has passed. What is clear is that the commercial persona of the teenager also occupied these online spaces, reaching out to young consumers even (or especially) in a time of crisis, promising to serve them.

Youth must be served, indeed, but by whom? And to what end? Historians can serve young people by continuing to explore the ways in which age has been socially constructed by corporate interests that are ultimately motivated by profit margins. In marketing, age has intersected with gender, class, and race to shape Canadians' identities and experiences. By telling these stories, we encourage young people to question how they have been and are represented. In so doing, I hope we can open a space in which they can value themselves for who they are.

Notes

Introduction

1 John Clare, "The Scramble for the Teen-Age Dollar," *Maclean's*, September 14, 1957, 18, 19, 112.

2 James Onusko, *Boom Kids: Growing Up in the Calgary Suburbs, 1950–1970* (Waterloo, ON: Wilfrid Laurier University Press, 2021), 1.

3 Onusko, *Boom Kids*, 1; Doug Owram, *Born at the Right Time: A History of the Baby Boom Generation* (Toronto: University of Toronto Press, 1996), 136–58.

4 Owram, *Born at the Right Time*, 141. On the influence of baby boomers in the 1960s, see also Thomas Frank, *The Conquest of Cool: Business Culture, Counterculture, and the Rise of Hip Consumerism* (Chicago: University of Chicago Press, 1997).

5 Sidney Katz, "Going Steady: Is It Ruining Our Teen-Agers?" *Maclean's*, January 3, 1959, 9; Eric Hutton, "Is 'Car Craziness' a Menace to Our Teenagers?" *Maclean's*, June 6, 1959, 13.

6 Bettina Liverant, *Buying Happiness: The Emergence of Consumer Consciousness in English Canada* (Vancouver: UBC Press, 2018), 3.

7 Cynthia Comacchio, *The Dominion of Youth: Adolescence and the Making of Modern Canada, 1920–1950* (Waterloo, ON: Wilfrid Laurier University Press, 2006), 8–13. On Canada's department stores, see Donica Belisle, *Retail Nation: Department Stores and the Making of Modern Canada* (Vancouver: UBC Press, 2011). On the growth of consumer culture and women's consumer identities in the interwar decades, see Cheryl Krasnick Warsh and Dan Malleck, eds., *Consuming Modernity: Gendered Behaviour and Consumerism before the Baby Boom* (Vancouver: UBC Press, 2013); Jane Nicholas, *The Modern Girl: Feminine Modernities, the Body, and Commodities in the 1920s* (Toronto: University of Toronto Press, 2015); Katrina Srigley, *Breadwinning Daughters: Young Working Women in a Depression-Era City, 1929–1939* (Toronto: University of Toronto Press, 2010). Recent works discussing the intersection of gender, race, and class in consumer identities include Cheryl Thompson, *Beauty in a Box: Detangling the Roots of Canada's Black Beauty Culture* (Waterloo, ON: Wilfrid Laurier University Press, 2019); Donica Belisle, *Purchasing Power: Women and the Rise of Canadian Consumer Culture* (Toronto: University of Toronto Press, 2020); and Donica Belisle, "Eating Clean: Anti-Chinese

— Notes to pages 6–9 —

Sugar Advertising and the Making of White Racial Purity in the Canadian Pacific," *Global Food History* 6, 1 (2020): 41–59.

8 Liverant, *Buying Happiness*, 212.

9 Several studies demonstrate that Canadians' concerns about prices, access to goods, and household finance motivated their political activism and demands for policy changes. See Magda Fahrni, *Household Politics: Montreal Families and Postwar Reconstruction* (Toronto: University of Toronto Press, 2005), 108–23; Michael Dawson, *Selling Out or Buying In? Debating Consumerism in Vancouver and Victoria, 1945–1985* (Toronto: University of Toronto Press, 2018), 70–88; and Joy Parr, *Domestic Goods: The Material, the Moral, and the Economic in the Postwar Years* (Toronto: University of Toronto Press, 1999), 84–100.

10 See, generally, Kelly Schrum, *Some Wore Bobby Sox: The Emergence of Teenage Girls' Culture, 1920–1945* (New York: Palgrave Macmillan, 2004); and Grace Palladino, *Teenagers: An American History* (New York: Basic Books, 1996). In the British context, see Melanie Tebbutt, *Making Youth: A History of Youth in Modern Britain* (London: Palgrave, 2016), 132. See also David Fowler, *The First Teenagers: The Lifestyle of Young Wage-Earners in Interwar Britain* (London: Woburn Press, 1995).

11 Alys Eve Weinbaum et al., eds., *The Modern Girl around the World: Consumption, Modernity, and Globalization* (Durham, NC: Duke University Press, 2008), 1–21.

12 Liverant, *Buying Happiness*, 212; Parr, *Domestic Goods*, 29–38.

13 Comacchio, *The Dominion of Youth*, 12.

14 See, for example, Katrina Srigley, "Clothing Stories: Consumption, Identity, and Desire in Depression-Era Toronto," *Journal of Women's History* 19, 1 (2007): 82–104; Craig Heron, "The High School and the Household Economy in Working-Class Hamilton, 1890–1940," *Historical Studies in Education/Revue d'histoire de l'éducation* 7, 2 (1995): 217–59; and Comacchio, *The Dominion of Youth*.

15 G. Stanley Hall, *Adolescence: Its Psychology and Its Relations to Physiology, Anthropology, Sociology, Sex, Crime, Religion and Education* (New York: Appleton, 1904), vol. 1: 128, quoted in Kent Baxter, *The Modern Age: Turn-of-the-Century American Culture and the Invention of Adolescence* (Tuscaloosa: University of Alabama Press, 2008), 49–50. Several historians have explored Hall's ideas and their consequences. See, for example, John Demos, *Past, Present, and Personal: The Family and the Life Course in American History* (New York: Oxford University Press, 1986), 92–113; Baxter, *The Modern Age*, 44–72; and Comacchio, *The Dominion of Youth*, 20–22.

16 The origins of *teenager* have been variously attributed to the early nineteenth century (rare), to the 1920s (in the 2011 Oxford English Dictionary), and to a 1941 issue of the American magazine *Popular Science Monthly*. Despite uncertain origins, most sources agree that common usage began in North America in the 1940s. See Katherine Bell, "Teenagers," in Katherine Bell, ed., *The Sage Encyclopedia of Children and Childhood Studies* (Thousand Oaks, CA: Sage, 2020), 1551–54.

(160)

— Notes to pages 9–14 —

17 Mary Louise Adams, *The Trouble with Normal: Postwar Youth and the Making of Heterosexuality* (Toronto: University of Toronto Press, 1997), 40.

18 Daniel Thomas Cook, *The Commodification of Childhood: The Children's Clothing Industry and the Rise of the Child Consumer* (Durham, NC: Duke University Press, 2004), 18–20.

19 Belisle, *Retail Nation* 14, 82–107. Rod McQueen also discusses the cultural importance of the store in more detail in *The Eatons: The Rise and Fall of Canada's Royal Family* (Toronto: Stoddart, 1999), 2–5. The company's extensive records have also been used to write numerous histories, including Russ Gourluck, *A Store Like No Other: Eaton's of Winnipeg* (Winnipeg: Great Plains Publications, 2004); Patricia Phenix, *Eatonians: The Story of the Family behind the Family* (Toronto: McClelland and Stewart, 2002); Joy Santink, *Timothy Eaton and the Rise of His Department Store* (Toronto: University of Toronto Press, 1990); George Parkin de Twenebroker Glazebrook, Katharine B. Brett, and Judith McErvel, *A Shopper's View of Canada's Past: Pages from Eaton's Catalogues, 1886–1930* (Toronto: University of Toronto Press, 1969); and Mary-Etta MacPherson, *Shopkeepers to a Nation: The Eatons* (Toronto: McClelland and Stewart, 1963).

20 Steve Penfold, *A Mile of Make-Believe: Eaton's and the Santa Claus Parade* (Toronto: University of Toronto Press, 2016), 20.

21 See Belisle, *Retail Nation*, ch. 1 for an examination of the expansion of various department stores to the 1930s.

22 Belisle, *Retail Nation*, 80–81.

23 Penfold, *A Mile of Make-Believe*, 13, 161–62.

24 Penfold, *A Mile of Make-Believe*, 52.

25 Cook, *The Commodification of Childhood*, 18.

26 Wendy Mitchinson, *Fighting Fat: Canada, 1920–1980* (Toronto: University of Toronto Press, 2018), 275–76.

27 J.M. McCutcheon, "Clothing Children in English Canada, 1870–1930" (PhD diss., University of Ottawa, 2002), 203–72.

28 For histories of rural and colonial Canada, see Beatrice Craig, *Backwoods Consumers and Homespun Capitalists: The Rise of a Market Culture in Eastern Canada* (Toronto: University of Toronto Press, 2009); Douglas McCalla, *Consumers in the Bush: Shopping in Rural Upper Canada* (Montreal and Kingston: McGill-Queen's University Press, 2015); and Belisle, *Purchasing Power*.

29 Adams, *The Trouble with Normal*, 5.

30 "Un manteau de grand chic pour l'adolescente," Dupuis Frères Autumn and Winter 1945–46 Catalogue, 2; "Exaltation," Dupuis Frères Spring 1948 Catalogue, 2.

31 Penfold, *A Mile of Make-Believe*, 13.

32 Dawson, *Selling Out or Buying In?*

33 Penfold, *A Mile of Make Believe*, 12–13.

34 Stuart Hall, "Introduction," in *Representation: Cultural Representation and Signifying Practices*, ed. Stuart Hall (London: Sage/Open University, 1977), 3.

— Notes to pages 14–17 —

35 See, for example, Valerie Korinek, *Roughing It in the Suburbs: Reading* Chatelaine *Magazine in the Fifties and Sixties* (Toronto: University of Toronto Press, 2006); Heather Ann Molyneaux, "The Representation of Women in 'Chatelaine' Magazine Advertisements: 1928–1970" (MA thesis, University of New Brunswick, 2002); and Erin Spencer, *Lipstick and High Heels: War, Gender, and Popular Culture* (Kingston, ON: Canadian Defence Academy Press, 2007).

36 Neil Sutherland, *Children in English-Canadian Society: Framing the Twentieth-Century Consensus* (Toronto: University of Toronto Press, 1976), 13–36.

37 On employment, see Lorna F. Hurl, "Restricting Child Labour in Late-Nineteenth-Century Ontario Factories," *Labour/Le Travail* 21 (Spring 1988): 87–121; on school-leaving regulations, see Comacchio, *The Dominion of Youth*, 100; on restricting the age of marriage, see James G. Snell and Cynthia Comacchio Abeele, "Regulating Nuptiality: Restricting Access to Marriage in Early Twentieth-Century English-Speaking Canada," *Canadian Historical Review* 69, 4 (1988): 466–89.

38 For example, Sutherland, in *Children in English-Canadian Society*, 227–41, discusses how reformers wanted to change labour laws related to women to help ensure "healthy mothers" for Canadian children. Some also promoted town planning regulations to improve the amount of sunlight and fresh air children received in their homes.

39 On age grading in Canadian schools, see R.D. Gidney and W.P.J. Millar, *How Schools Worked: Public Education in English Canada, 1900–1940* (Montreal and Kingston: McGill-Queen's University Press, 2013), 30–31. Gidney and Millar note that the correlation between age and school grade became stronger after 1940. On the increased number of peer-based summer camps, see Sharon Wall, *The Nurture of Nature: Childhood, Antimodernism, and Ontario Summer Camps, 1920–1955* (Vancouver: UBC Press, 2009).

40 See Marta Gutman and Ning de Coninck-Smith, "Introduction: Good to Think With – History, Space, and Modern Childhood," in *Designing Modern Childhoods: History, Space, and the Material Culture of Children*, ed. Gutman and de Coninck-Smith (New Brunswick, NJ: Rutgers University Press, 2008), 4–5.

41 Cook, *The Commodification of Childhood*, ch. 3.

42 For a succinct examination of children and debates about childhood in a global context, see Peter N. Stearns, *Childhood in World History* (New York: Routledge, 2006).

43 Adams, *The Trouble with Normal*, 40.

44 Laura Ishiguro, "'Growing Up and Grown Up ... in Our Future City': Discourses of Childhood and Settler Futurity in Colonial British Columbia," *BC Studies* 190 (Summer 2016): 15–19.

45 Ishiguro, "Growing Up and Grown Up," 15.

46 Michael Gauvreau, "The Protracted Birth of the Canadian 'Teenager': Work, Citizenship, and the Canadian Youth Commission, 1943–1955," in *Cultures*

(162)

of Citizenship in Post-war Canada, 1940–1955, ed. Nancy Christie and Michael Gauvreau (Montreal and Kingston: McGill-Queen's University Press, 2003), 213.

47 Kristine Alexander, "Childhood and Colonialism in Canadian History," *History Compass* 14, 9 (2016): 399. For a discussion of images of Indigenous peoples in advertising, see Daniel Francis, *The Imaginary Indian: The Image of the Indian in Canadian Culture* (Vancouver: Arsenal Pulp Press, 1992), especially ch. 8.

48 Lisa Jacobson, *Children and Consumer Culture in American Society: A Historical Handbook and Guide* (New York: Bloomsbury, 2007), 64–69; Gary Cross, *The Cute and the Cool: Wondrous Innocence and Modern American Children's Culture* (Oxford: Oxford University Press, 2004), 10–16.

49 Viviana Zelizer, "A Grown-Up Priceless Child," in *Situating Child Consumption: Rethinking Values and Notions of Children, Childhood and Consumption*, ed. Anna Sparrman, Bengt Sandin, and Johanna Sjöberg (Lund, Sweden: Nordic Academic Press, 2012), 74.

50 See, for example, Juliet Schor, *Born to Buy: The Commericialized Child and the New Consumer Culture* (New York: Scribner, 2004); Susan Linn, *Consuming Kids: Protecting Our Children from the Onslaught of Marketing and Advertising* (New York: Anchor Books, 2005); Tim Kasser and Susan Linn, "Growing Up under Corporate Capitalism: The Problem of Marketing to Children, with Suggestions for Policy Solutions," *Social Issues and Policy Review* 10, 1 (2016): 112–50, https://doi.org/10.1111/sipr.12020.

51 See Cynthia Comacchio, "Dancing to Perdition: Adolescence and Leisure in Interwar English Canada," *Journal of Canadian Studies* 32, 3 (1997): 5–35; Neil Sutherland, "Popular Media in the Culture of English-Canadian Children in the Twentieth Century," *Historical Studies in Education* 14, 1 (2002): 1–33; Adams, *The Trouble with Normal*; Mona Gleason, "'They Have a Bad Effect': Crime Comics, Parliament, and the Hegemony of the Middle Class in Postwar Canada, 1948–1960," in *Pulp Demons: International Dimensions of the Postwar Anti-Comics Campaign*, ed. John A. Lent (Vancouver: Fairleigh Dickinson University Press, 1999), 129–54. On television, in particular, see Katharine Rollwagen, "The Young Medium: Regulating Television in the Name of Canadian Childhood," *Canadian Historical Review* 101, 1 (2020): 27–48.

52 Vance Packard, *The Hidden Persuaders* (New York: Pocket Books, 1980), 147–55; Keith Wailoo, *Pushing Cool: Big Tobacco, Racial Marketing, and the Untold Story of the Menthol Cigarette* (Chicago: University of Chicago Press, 2021), 75–78.

53 Belisle, *Purchasing Power*, particularly ch. 4; Nicholas, *The Modern Girl*, particularly ch. 1; Laurie K. Bertram, *The Viking Immigrants: Icelandic North Americans* (Toronto: University of Toronto Press, 2020), particularly ch. 1.

54 Sparrman, Sandin, and Sjöberg, eds., *Situating Child Consumption*, 10. In "How 'New' Is the New Social Study of Childhood? The Myth of a Paradigm Shift," *Journal of Interdisciplinary History* 38, 4 (2008): 553–76, Patrick Ryan points out that this was not really a paradigm shift.

— Notes to pages 19–26 —

55 On cigarettes, see Jared Rudy, *The Freedom to Smoke: Tobacco Consumption and Identity* (Montreal and Kingston: McGill-Queen's University Press, 2005); Daniel Robinson, *Cigarette Nation: Business, Health, and Canadian Smokers 1930–1975* (Montreal and Kingston: McGill-Queen's University Press, 2021); and Sharon Cook, *Sex, Lies, and Cigarettes: Canadian Women, Smoking, and Visual Culture, 1880–2000* (Montreal and Kingston: McGill-Queen's University Press, 2012).

56 Among the most recent contributions to this debate are Stephanie Olsen et al., "A Critical Conversation on Agency," *Journal of the History of Childhood and Youth* 17, 2 (2024): 169–87; and Mona Gleason, "'Children Obviously Don't Make History': Historical Significance and Children's Modalities of Power," *Journal of the History of Childhood and Youth* 16, 3 (2023): 343–60. Both are responses to Sarah Maza's "The Kids Aren't All Right: Historians and the Problem of Childhood," *American Historical Review* 125, 4 (2020): 1261–85.

57 Cook, *The Commodification of Childhood*, 15.

Chapter 1: Calling All Co-eds!

1 Mary Peate, *Girl in a Sloppy Joe Sweater: Life on the Canadian Home Front during World War II* (Montreal: Optimum Publishing International, 1988), 87.

2 Peate, *Girl in a Sloppy Joe Sweater*, 88.

3 See, for example, Simone Weil Davis, *Living Up to the Ads: Gender Fictions of the 1920s* (Durham, NC: Duke University Press, 2000); Nancy A. Walker, *Shaping Our Mothers' World: American Women's Magazines* (Jackson: University Press of Mississippi, 2000); Nan Enstad, *Ladies of Labor, Girls of Adventure: Working Women, Popular Culture, and Labor Politics at the Turn of the Twentieth Century* (New York: Columbia University Press, 1999); Kathy Peiss, *Hope in a Jar: The Making of America's Beauty Culture* (Philadelphia: University of Pennsylvania Press, 1998); Jennifer Scanlon, *Inarticulate Longings: The* Ladies' Home Journal, *Gender, and the Promises of Consumer Culture* (Routledge: New York, 1995); Jane Nicholas, *The Modern Girl: Feminine Modernities, the Body, and Commodities in the 1920s* (Toronto: University of Toronto Press, 2015), especially ch. 2.

4 Christopher Wilson, "The Rhetoric of Consumption: Mass-Market Magazines and the Demise of the Gentle Reader, 1880–1920," in *The Culture of Consumption: Critical Essays in American History, 1880–1980*, ed. Richard Wightman Fox and T.J. Jackson Lears (New York: Pantheon, 1983), 42.

5 Ellen Gruber Garvey, *The Adman in the Parlour: Magazines and the Gendering of Consumer Culture, 1880s–1910s* (Oxford: Oxford University Press, 1996), 136.

6 Fraser Sutherland, *The Monthly Epic: A History of Canadian Magazines, 1789–1989* (Markham, ON: Fitzhenry and Whiteside, 1989), 131, 156.

7 Sharon Zukin, *Point of Purchase: How Shopping Changed American Culture* (New York: Routledge, 2004), 169–96.

(164)

— Notes to pages 26–30 —

8 Rachel Alexander, *Imagining Gender, Nation and Consumerism in Magazines of the 1920s* (New York: Anthem Press, 2022), 58.

9 In 1930, *Chatelaine*'s circulation was 122,000 and *Canadian Home Journal*'s circulation was 132,000. Sutherland, *The Monthly Epic*, 249. After the *Journal* ceased publication in 1958, Maclean Hunter Limited purchased the subscription list, which likely contributed to *Chatelaine*'s increased readership by 1960. Sutherland, *The Monthly Epic*, 254.

10 Sutherland, *The Monthly Epic*, 156–60, 248.

11 Valerie Korinek, *Roughing It in the Suburbs: Reading* Chatelaine *Magazine in the Fifties and Sixties* (Toronto: University of Toronto Press, 2000), 4.

12 Penny Tinkler, *Constructing Girlhood: Popular Magazines for Girls Growing Up in England, 1920–1950* (London: Taylor and Francis, 1995), 65–66.

13 Penny Tinkler, "*Miss Modern*: Youthful Feminine Modernity and the Nascent Teenager, 1930–1940," in *Women's Periodicals and Print Culture in Britain, 1918–1939: The Interwar Period*, ed. Catherine Clay, Maria DiCenzo, Barbara Green, and Fiona Hackney (Edinburgh: Edinburgh University Press, 2018), 153.

14 On American teenage magazines, see Kelly Massoni, *Fashioning Teenagers: A Cultural History of* Seventeen *Magazine* (Walnut Creek, CA: Left Coast Press, 2010), and Samantha Yates Francois, "Girls with Influence: Selling Consumerism to Teenage Girls, 1940–1960" (PhD diss., University of California Davis, 2003). On depictions of younger consumers, see Lisa Jacobson, *Raising Consumers: Children and the American Mass Market in the Early Twentieth Century* (New York: Columbia University Press, 2005).

15 Stuart Hall, "Culture, the Media, and the 'Ideological Effect,'" in *Mass Communication and Society*, ed. James Curran, Michael Gurevitch, and Janet Wollacott (London: Edward Arnold, 1977), 340–41.

16 Alys Eve Weinbaum et al., eds., *The Modern Girl around the World: Consumption, Modernity, and Globalization* (Durham, NC: Duke University Press, 2008), 1.

17 Nicholas, *The Modern Girl*, 23.

18 Liz Conor, *The Spectacular Modern Woman: Feminine Visibility in the 1920s* (Bloomington and Indianapolis: Indiana University Press, 2004), 12–13.

19 Cheryl Thompson, *Beauty in a Box: Detangling The Roots of Canada's Black Beauty Culture* (Waterloo, ON: Wilfrid Laurier University Press, 2019), 12–13, 84–86.

20 Cheryl Thompson, "'I'se in Town, Honey': Reading Aunt Jemima Advertising in Canadian Print Media, 1919 to 1962," *Journal of Canadian Studies* 49, 1 (2015): 205–37.

21 Patrizia Gentile, *Queen of the Maple Leaf: Beauty Contests and Settler Femininity* (Vancouver: UBC Press, 2020), 9.

22 Lynn Peril, *College Girls: Bluestockings, Sex Kittens, and Coeds, Then and Now* (New York: W.W. Norton, 2006), 109–12, 116.

23 "College Classics for September," *Mayfair*, September 1936, 42.

— Notes to pages 30–33 —

24 Grace Garner, 'Teens and Twenties column, *Canadian Home Journal*, July 1937, 29; September 1937, 22; and October 1937, 4.

25 Grace Garner, "You're A Big Girl Now! Hi-ho for High School, Teens and Twenties," *Canadian Home Journal*, September 1938, 16.

26 "'Teens' Routines," *Chatelaine*, September 1943, 33; "Teen-Agers Love These," *Chatelaine*, September 1946, 34, 38; "The Teens Get Ideas," *Chatelaine*, September 1945, 64.

27 "Teen-Agers Club," *Mayfair*, August 1945, 93–97; Eva Nagel Wolf, "Teen-Agers Take Note!" *Canadian Home Journal*, September 1946, 76.

28 Advertisement for Phillips' Milk of Magnesia, *Chatelaine*, October 1940, 31; Advertisement for Shredded Wheat, *Chatelaine*, July 1940, 51; Advertisement for Singer Sewing Centres, *Chatelaine*, June 1940, 20.

29 *Mayfair*, August 1945, 33.

30 Kelly Massoni, "'Teena Goes to Market': *Seventeen* Magazine and the Early Construction of the Teen Girl (As) Consumer," *Journal of American Culture* 29, 1 (2006): 33.

31 Tinkler, *Constructing Girlhood*, 7.

32 Nearly half of the *Chatelaine* items found were published in either August or September issues. Similarly, more than three-quarters of the college and teenage items found in *Canadian Home Journal* appeared in those months, and *Mayfair* published such articles in its August and September issues exclusively. In *Chatelaine*, other than the Teen Tempo column, 35 of 77 college- and teen-focused items (45.5 percent) were published in August or September; in *Canadian Home Journal*, other than the regular Teenager's Datebook and Teen Session, 129 of 147 items (87.7 percent) appeared in August or September issues; and in *Mayfair* all 57 items were published in those months.

33 A RetailMeNot.ca survey of parents in 2017 found that Canadian parents spent more on average on back to school shopping than they did on Christmas gifts. Jeff Doucette, "Back to School Shopping in Canada, 2019," *Field Agent*, August 1, 2019, https://www.fieldagentcanada.com/blog/back-to-school-2019. Another RetailMeNot survey of Canadian parents, this one conducted on July 13 and 14, 2016, found that the 1,506 respondents spent roughly $450–$500 on back-to-school shopping that year. Male respondents reported spending more ($523) than female respondents ($413).

34 "Teen Page: New Term, New Time," *Chatelaine*, October 1949.

35 "This Month, Meet the Girl behind Our New Teen-Age Page," *Chatelaine*, September 1956.

36 Korinek, *Roughing It in the Suburbs*, 35–36.

37 Cynthia Comacchio, *The Dominion of Youth: Adolescence and the Making of Modern Canada, 1920–1950* (Waterloo, ON: Wilfrid Laurier University Press, 2006), 101–2; R.D. Gidney and W.P.J. Millar, *How Schools Worked: Public Education in English*

— Notes to pages 33–37 —

Canada, 1900–1940 (Montreal and Kingston: McGill-Queen's University Press, 2012), 30–34.

38 George Buri, *Between Education and Catastrophe: The Battle over Public Schooling in Postwar Manitoba* (Montreal and Kingston: McGill-Queen's University Press, 2016), 154; Gidney and Millar, *How Schools Worked*, 21–22.

39 Paul Axelrod, *Making a Middle Class: Student Life in English Canada during the Thirties* (Montreal and Kingston: McGill-Queen's University Press, 1990), 21.

40 M. Wisenthal, "W340-438, Full-Time University Enrolment, by Sex, Canada and Provinces, Selected Years, 1920 to 1975," *Historical Statistics of Canada*, ed. F.H. Leacy (Ottawa: Statistics Canada, 1983), https://www150.statcan.gc.ca/n1/en/catalogue/11-516-X.

41 Thomas D. Snyder, ed., *120 Years of American Education: A Statistical Portrait* (Washington: National Office of Education Statistics, 1993), 7.

42 Peate, *Girl in a Sloppy Joe Sweater*, 65–66.

43 Ellen Mackie, "Don't Bring Sloppy Joe!" *Mayfair*, August 1946, 72.

44 Grace Garner, "Course in Social Studies (Teens and Twenties)," *Canadian Home Journal*, October 1938, 18.

45 Gertrude Stayner, "Gertrude Stayner Says Do Your College Shopping Early," *Mayfair*, August 1941, 26.

46 For more on the ways in which the Junior League reproduced and reinforced social class in the first half of the twentieth century, see Elise Chenier, "Class, Gender, and the Social Standard: The Montreal Junior League, 1912–1939," *Canadian Historical Review* 90, 4 (2009): 671–710.

47 George Colpitts, "The Domesticated Body and the Industrialized Imitation Fur Coat in Canada, 1919–1939," in *Contesting Bodies and Nation in Canadian History*, ed. Patrizia Gentile and Jane Nicholas (Toronto: University of Toronto Press, 2013), 136.

48 Colpitts, "The Domesticated Body," 136, 139.

49 "College Careers," *Mayfair*, September 1937, 39.

50 "Campus Cutey," *Mayfair*, September 1940, 23.

51 Advertisement for Northways, *Mayfair*, September 1940, 8.

52 "Campus News!" advertisement for Simpson's, *Mayfair*, August 1942.

53 Advertisement for Eaton's "College Toggery," *Mayfair*, September 1940. The wool coat advertised was $49.75 and the fur coat was $195.00.

54 "Extra Credits in a College Wardrobe," *Mayfair*, August 1943, 36.

55 Axelrod, *Making a Middle Class*, 27. The average annual tuition for an arts course in 1938 was $125.

56 Gertrude Stayner, "The Most out of College," *Mayfair*, August 1942, 47.

57 Evelyn Kelly, "Their Styles Are Young and Gay," *Chatelaine*, September 1948, 96–97.

58 Lotta Dempsey, "Go Back a Smarter Girl," *Chatelaine*, September 1944, 12–13, 64.

— Notes to pages 37–43 —

59 Margaret Thornton, "Prep Course in College Fashions," *Canadian Home Journal*, September 1951, 17.
60 "Majoring in Classics," *Mayfair*, September 1940, 29; "Extra Credits in a College Wardrobe," 36.
61 Thornton, "Prep Course in College Fashions," 17.
62 "Campus Clothes," *Mayfair*, September 1938, 51.
63 "Campus Clothes," 39.
64 Deirdre Clemente, *Dress Casual: How College Students Redefined American Style* (Chapel Hill: University of North Carolina Press, 2014), 43.
65 Lotta Dempsey, "The Teens Talk Out," *Chatelaine*, February 1945, 27.
66 "Candidly Collegiate," *Mayfair*, September 1938, 41.
67 See, for example, "Go Back a Smarter You," *Chatelaine*, September 1944, 12–13, 33.
68 Clemente, *Dress Casual*, 90.
69 "Housecoats and Slacks Drafted for Room Service," *Mayfair*, August 1943, 34.
70 "Extra Credits in a College Wardrobe," 36.
71 "Housecoats and Slacks," 34.
72 Advertisement for Bard's, *Mayfair*, August 1943, 37; and *Mayfair*, August 1947.
73 Grace Garner, "Course in Social Studies," *Canadian Home Journal*, October 1938, 18.
74 Nicholas, *The Modern Girl*, 63. See also Peiss, *Hope in a Jar*, especially ch. 6; and Joan Jacobs Brumberg, *The Body Project: An Intimate History of American Girls* (New York: Random House, 1997).
75 See, for example, Enstad, *Ladies of Labor*; Katrina Srigley, *Breadwinning Daughters: Single Working Women in a Depression-Era City, 1929–1939* (Toronto: University of Toronto Press, 2010).
76 Nicholas, *The Modern Girl*, 77–78.
77 Advertisement for Elizabeth Arden, quoted in Michelle J. Smith and Jane Nicholas, "Soft Rejuvenation: Cosmetics, Idealized White Femininity, and Young Women's Bodies, 1880–1930," *Journal of Social History* 53, 4 (2020): 913.
78 Jane Nicholas, "On Display: Bodies and Consumption in the 'New' Canadian Cultural History," *History Compass* 17, 2 (2019): 3, https://doi.org/10.1111/hic3.12519.
79 Wolf, "Teen-Agers Take Note!" 76.
80 Jean Alexander, "Honors Course in Beauty," *Chatelaine*, August 1942, 29.
81 "Majoring in Beauty," *Mayfair*, August 1941.
82 "Birthdays Don't Count!" advertisement for Ivory Soap, *Ladies Home Journal*, March 1942, 12.
83 Alexander, "Honors Course in Beauty," 30, emphasis in original. See also "Majoring in Beauty."
84 "Majoring in Beauty."
85 Adele White, "Ask Your Doctor," *Chatelaine*, September 1944, 30.
86 Eva Nagel Wolf, "Hitch Your Wagon to a Star!" *Canadian Home Journal*, September 1945, 59–60.
87 Vivian Wilcox, "Discover Your Secret Beauty," *Chatelaine*, April 1958, 31.

(168)

— Notes to pages 43–53 —

88 Advertisement for Elizabeth Arden, *Chatelaine*, September 1944, 30.

89 Advertisement for Helena Rubenstein, *Mayfair*, September 1947, 103.

90 "Both Young Moderns Cheer the Same Thorough Skin Care," advertisement for Ponds, *Chatelaine*, February 1940, 21.

91 "Some Days I'm Happy!" advertisement for Kotex, *Chatelaine*, March 1942, 39; "Are You in the Know?" advertisement for Kotex, *Chatelaine*, September 1946, 35.

92 "Some Days I'm Happy!" 39.

93 "Chin Up!" advertisement for Kotex, *Chatelaine*, September 1942, 32.

94 Gentile, *Queen of the Maple Leaf*, 9.

95 Gentile, *Queen of the Maple Leaf*, 15.

96 Gail Anderson, "One Year Later: Cover Girl, Co-ed," *Canadian Home Journal*, September 1946, 3.

97 Conor, *The Spectacular Modern Woman*, 132, 136.

98 "*Canadian Home Journal* Spotlights the Cover Girl," *Canadian Home Journal*, September 1946, 5.

99 "Close Up of Our Cover Girl," *Canadian Home Journal*, September 1949, 5; "*Canadian Home Journal* Spotlights the Cover Girl," 5.

100 Gentile, *Queen of the Maple Leaf*, 46–47.

101 Conor, *The Spectacular Modern Woman*, 164.

102 Eva Nagel Wolf, "The Collegiate Crowd Chooses That Cover Girl Look," *Canadian Home Journal*, September 1944, 56.

103 "*Canadian Home Journal* Spotlights the Cover Girl," 5.

104 Patricia Skinner, "Take Another Look When You Leave High School," *Canadian Home Journal*, September 1949, 60.

105 Kathryn Adams, "Cover Girl at Home," *Canadian Home Journal*, September 1946, 65; Rita McLean Farquharson, "Cover Girl's Mother," *Canadian Home Journal*, September 1945, 2.

106 "Close-Up of Our Cover Girl, Beverly Joselin," *Canadian Home Journal*, September 1949, 4; Adams, "Cover Girl at Home," 65.

107 Mike Featherstone, "The Body in Consumer Culture," in *The Body: Social Process and Cultural Theory*, ed. Mike Featherstone, Mike Hepworth, and Bryan S. Turner (London: Sage, 1991), 179.

Chapter 2: Act Your Age

1 "How Mature Are Teenagers?" *Canadian Home Journal*, November 1957, 50.

2 Sidney Katz, "It's a Tough Time to Be a Kid," *Maclean's*, December 15, 1950, 7.

3 Mary Louise Adams, *The Trouble with Normal: Postwar Youth and the Making of Heterosexuality* (Toronto: University of Toronto Press, 1997), 48.

4 Heidi MacDonald, "'Being in Your Twenties, in the Thirties': Liminality and Masculinity during the Great Depression," in *Bringing Children and Youth into*

— Notes to pages 53–57 —

Canadian History: The Difference Kids Make, ed. Mona Gleason and Tamara Myers (Toronto: Oxford University Press, 2017), 156.

5 Cynthia Comacchio, *The Dominion of Youth: Adolescence and the Making of Modern Canada, 1920–1950* (Waterloo, ON: Wilfrid Laurier University Press, 2006), 140–45.

6 Katrina Srigley, *Breadwinning Daughters: Single Working Women in a Depression-Era City, 1929–1939* (Toronto: University of Toronto Press, 2010), 38; Michael Gauvreau, "The Protracted Birth of the Canadian 'Teenager': Work, Citizenship, and the Canadian Youth Commission, 1943–1955," in *Cultures of Citizenship in Post-war Canada, 1940–1955*, ed. Nancy Christie and Michael Gauvreau (Montreal and Kingston: McGill-Queen's University Press, 2003), 204. Many of those concerned drew on data from J.E. Robbins' report, *Dependency of Youth: A Study Based on the Census of 1931 and Supplementary Data*, Census Monograph no. 9 (Ottawa: Dominion Bureau of Statistics, 1937).

7 Graham Broad, *A Small Price to Pay: Consumer Culture on the Canadian Homefront, 1939–1945* (Vancouver: UBC Press, 2013), 7.

8 Jeffrey Keshen, *Saints, Sinners, and Soldiers: Canada's Second World War* (Vancouver: UBC Press, 2004), 202–7.

9 Jordan Stanger-Ross, Christina Collins, and Mark J. Stern, "Falling Far from the Tree: Transitions to Adulthood and the Social History of Twentieth-Century America," *Social Science History* 29, 4 (2005): 640–42.

10 See Neil Sutherland, *Growing Up: Childhood in English Canada from the Great War to the Age of Television* (Toronto: University of Toronto Press, 1997); and James Onusko, *Boom Kids: Growing Up in the Calgary Suburbs, 1950–1970* (Waterloo, ON: Wilfrid Laurier University Press, 2021).

11 Barbro Johansson, "Subjectivities of the Child Consumer: Beings and Becomings," in *Childhood and Consumer Culture*, ed. David Buckingham and Vebjorg Tingstad (London: Palgrave Macmillan, 2010), 80.

12 Bettina Liverant, *Buying Happiness: The Emergence of Consumer Consciousness in English Canada* (Vancouver: UBC Press, 2018), 12.

13 "College Shops Open with New Smart Styles," *Chicago Daily Tribune,* August 4, 1941, 16, quoted in Deirdre Clemente, *Dress Casual: How College Students Redefined American Style* (Chapel Hill: University of North Carolina Press, 2014), 30.

14 J.A. Brockie, "Report: Junior Fashion Council," 1940, Archives of Ontario, T. Eaton Company fonds, J.A. Brockie files (hereafter AO F 229-151), file 87 – Junior Fashion Council 1944–1945.

15 "Teen-Agers Club," *Mayfair,* August 1945, 93.

16 "Youth Unlimited: The Story of Eaton's Junior Council and Executive," *Contacts,* July 1950, 6.

17 "Students and a Store," draft copy, December 29, 1960, Archives of Ontario, Eaton's Archives Office subject files (hereafter AO F 229-162), box 40, file 1323 – Promotions – Youth – Junior Councils & Executives, 1.

18 "Youth Unlimited," 6.

— Notes to pages 58–66 —

19 "Students and a Store," 3.

20 Ken McTaggert, "An Outsider Looks at the Inside of Eaton's," *Globe and Mail*, September 20, 1944, 24.

21 "Minutes of Junior Executive Advisers' Meeting, February 1947," Toronto, February 1947, AO F 229-151, box 3, file 92 – Jr. Exec. Conference.

22 McTaggert, "An Outsider Looks at the Inside of Eaton's," 24.

23 Jack Brockie, Merchandise Display Department, letter to J.P. Heffernan, Branch Stores Advertising, March 27, 1947, AO F 229-151, box 3.

24 "Report of Belleville Clothing Questionnaire," undated, AO F 229-151, box 3.

25 "Junior Executive Questionnaire," 1947, Archives of Ontario, T. Eaton Company fonds, T.H. Miller's files relating to the Winnipeg Junior Council and Executive (hereafter AO F 229-198).

26 "Survey No. 4: Teen-Age Shopping Habits and Advertising," undated, AO F 229-151, box 3.

27 Junior Executive and Council advisors' meeting minutes, Toronto, November 1947, AO F 229-151, box 3, file 93 – Jr. Exec. & Jr. Council Meeting.

28 "Why We Enjoy Shopping at Simpsons," advertisement for Simpsons, *Globe and Mail*, August 24, 1946, 12.

29 "Housecoats and Slacks Drafted for Room Service," *Mayfair*, August 1943, 34; Clemente, *Dress Casual*, 90–91.

30 "Changing College Life," *Mayfair*, August 1942, 22.

31 Gertrude Stayner, "Calling All Coeds ... from Coast to Coast," *Mayfair*, August 1943, 26–27, 38.

32 "Chatelaine's Teen-Age Council," *Chatelaine*, April 1945, 64.

33 Evelyn Kelly, "Young Country, Young Fashions," *Chatelaine*, September 1946, 8.

34 "Should We Go to College?" *Chatelaine*, September 1946, 3.

35 Lotta Dempsey, "Looking Ahead to Your Job," *Chatelaine*, May 1945, 12, emphasis in original.

36 Lotta Dempsey, "How Do You Rate with Your Crowd?" *Chatelaine*, April 1945, 64.

37 Teen Session, *Canadian Home Journal*, May 1956, 68.

38 Teen Session, *Canadian Home Journal*, June 1956, 68.

39 "Report of Belleville Clothing Questionnaire," undated, AO F 229-151, box 3.

40 Donica Belisle, "Crazy for Bargains: Inventing the Irrational Female Shopper in Modernizing English Canada," *Canadian Historical Review* 92, 4 (2011): 597.

41 Kathy Peiss, *Zoot Suit: The Enigmatic Career of an Extreme Style* (Philadelphia: University of Pennsylvania Press, 2011), 23–24.

42 Clemente, *Dress Casual*, 124–26.

43 June Lawford, "The Collegiate Crowd Chooses Fads and Fashions," *Canadian Home Journal*, September 1944, 9.

44 "Old-Time Suits Yield to New," *Globe and Mail*, March 25, 1942, 8.

45 "Zoot Suit's Day Wanes, in Opinion of Tailors," *Globe and Mail*, June 12, 1943, 5.

— Notes to pages 66–71 —

46 Canada, Wartime Prices and Trade Board, *Canadian War Orders and Regulations, 1942* (Ottawa: King's Printer, 1942), 80.

47 "Remake Revue Proves Conservation Triumphs," *Globe and Mail*, March 19, 1943, 12.

48 Peiss, *Zoot Suit*, 2. For more on zoot suits, see Luis Alvarez, *The Power of the Zoot: Youth Culture and Resistance during World War II* (Berkeley: University of California Press, 2008); Serge Durflinger, *Fighting from Home: The Second World War in Verdun, Quebec* (Vancouver: UBC Press, 2006); and Keshen, *Saints, Sinners, and Soldiers.*

49 Comacchio, *The Dominion of Youth*, 183.

50 Allan May, "Zoot Pants and All, Tom Brown Is Back in School," *Toronto Daily Star*, December 5, 1942, 1.

51 "It's Jump Suit, Not Zoot Suit, That Draws Eyes," *Toronto Daily Star*, April 29, 1943, 8.

52 "Service as Commando Held Ideal Conditioner for High School Boys," and "U.S. Zoot-Suiters Strong, Courageous Says Jap on Radio," *Toronto Daily Star*, June 18, 1943, 12.

53 "All Calm on 'Hep Cat Alley' When Police Seize Juke Box," *Toronto Daily Star*, May 31, 1943, 1.

54 Comacchio, *The Dominion of Youth*, 185.

55 "Zoot-Suiters and Servicemen," *Globe and Mail*, August 10, 1943, 2.

56 "Zoot-Suit Riots Rage in Montreal, Many Hurt," *Globe and Mail*, June 5, 1944, 1.

57 *Guardian* and *Messenger/Le Messager* articles, both from June 8, 1944, quoted in Durflinger, *Fighting from Home*, 160–62.

58 "Zoot Suit's Day Wanes," 5; J.V. McAree, "Why Can't a Guy Wear a Zoot Suit?" *Globe and Mail*, June 28, 1943, 6.

59 Comacchio, *The Dominion of Youth*, 185.

60 "Thirty-Two Arrested in Zoot-Suit Fracas," *Globe and Mail*, August 7, 1944, 2; "Zoot Suit's Day Wanes," 5.

61 Eleanor Dare, "I'd Like to Know!" *Canadian Home Journal*, September 1945, 55.

62 Helen McLean, "Who Roared in the 20's? Time We Trotted Out an Era of Our Own," *Globe and Mail*, 27 February 1958, 18.

63 Lotta Dempsey, "Go Back a Smarter Girl," *Chatelaine*, September 1944, 33.

64 Lotta Dempsey, "The Teens Talk Out," *Chatelaine*, February 1945, 25.

65 "It Might Be a Good Idea," *Mayfair*, August 1942, 18.

66 For comparison, in 1939, 600,000 women worked in the formal waged economy. Jennifer Stephens, *Pick One Intelligent Girl: Employability, Domesticity, and the Gendering of Canada's Welfare State, 1939–1947* (Toronto: University of Toronto Press, 2007), 39.

67 Carolyn Damon, "First Job," *Chatelaine*, February 1940, 24.

— Notes to pages 71–77 —

68 Lotta Dempsey, "First Job!" *Chatelaine*, December 1945, 13, 40. See also Margaret Vollmer, "The "Last Year's" Wardrobe," *Canadian Home Journal*, September 1943, 69.

69 Ellen Mackie, "Don't Bring Sloppy Joe!" *Mayfair*, August 1946, 72.

70 Lotta Dempsey, "Pop Should Be Pleased," *Mayfair*, August 1945, 91.

71 Sutherland, *Growing Up*, 29.

72 "Girls Again Look Like Girls Now That Men Are Available," *Globe and Mail*, August 13, 1946, 10.

73 "Bread, Water Soon Softens Teen-Age Toughies at Don," *Toronto Daily Star*, January 16, 1946, 23; "Jail One, Fine 7 $100 As Zoot-Suiters Tried after Brawl at Dance," *Toronto Daily Star*, August 25, 1949, 1; "Zoot Suit Gangs to Be Kept Away," *Toronto Daily Star*, September 7, 1949, 13; "Mayor Urges Whipping For Gang Offenders," *Globe and Mail*, June 19, 1950, 8; "A Ban on Zoot Suits?" *Globe and Mail*, July 3, 1951, 6; "Professor Recommends Short Sentence, Labour for Zoot-Suiter Types," *Globe and Mail*, September 16, 1953, 5.

74 Mariana Valverde, "Building Anti-Delinquent Communities: Morality, Gender, and Generation in the City," in *A Diversity of Women: Women in Ontario since 1945*, ed. Joy Parr (Toronto: University of Toronto Press, 1995), 28.

75 Peter Whitney, "Edwardian Supplants Zoot-Suit," *Globe and Mail*, May 7, 1954, 19.

76 George Buri, *Between Education and Catastrophe: The Battle over Public Schooling in Postwar Manitoba* (Montreal and Kingston: McGill-Queen's University Press, 2016), 19.

77 Mona Gleason, *Normalizing the Ideal: Psychology, Schooling, and the Family in Postwar Canada* (Toronto: University of Toronto Press, 1999), 12–13, 72–73; Adams, *The Trouble with Normal*, 12–15.

78 Catherine Gidney, "From a 'Disciplined Intelligence' to a 'Culture of Care': Shifting Understandings of Emotions and Citizenship in Twentieth-Century Educational Discourses," *Canadian Historical Review* 103, 4 (2022): 543–48.

79 Daniel Thomas Cook, *The Commodification of Childhood: The Children's Clothing Industry and the Rise of the Child Consumer* (Durham, NC: Duke University Press, 2004), 85–88.

80 Lisa Jacobson, *Raising Consumers: Children and the American Mass Market in the Early Twentieth Century* (New York: Columbia University Press, 2004), 162.

81 Cook, *The Commodification of Childhood*, 136.

82 Gleason, *Normalizing the Ideal*, 86–87.

83 S.R. Laycock, "Parents Are Such Problems," *Maclean's*, October 15, 1946, 13.

84 Garner, "You're a Big Girl Now!," 16.

85 Adele White, "College Girl's Private Primer," *Mayfair*, September 1940, 31.

86 Gertrude Stayner, "The 'College Girl' Is You," *Mayfair*, August 1943, 44.

87 White, "College Girl's Private Primer," 50.

88 Corinne Langston, "We 'Teen-Agers,'" *Canadian Home Journal*, April 1946, 62.

89 Langston, "We 'Teen-Agers,'" 62.

— Notes to pages 77-84 —

90 Carolyn Damon, "Growing Up!" *Chatelaine*, March 1939, 23; Carolyn Damon, "From Six to Sixteen," *Chatelaine*, March 1940, 25.

91 Adams, in *The Trouble with Normal*, 46–47, discusses several sociologists and anthropologists who criticized psychologists for their lack of "causal connection between the physical phenomenon of puberty and the social behaviour of young people during the adolescent period."

92 Damon, "Growing Up!" 23; Damon, "From Six to Sixteen," 28.

93 Kelly Schrum, *Some Wore Bobby Sox: The Emergence of Teenage Girls' Culture, 1920–1945* (New York: Palgrave Macmillan, 2004), 147–49.

94 June Lawford, "The Collegiate Crowd Chooses Fads and Fashions," *Canadian Home Journal*, September 1944, 8.

95 Eve Lister, "How Are You Fixed for Money?" *Canadian Home Journal*, November 1954, 4.

96 Lawford, "The Collegiate Crowd Chooses Fads and Fashions," 8.

97 Cynthia Williams, Teen Tempo, *Chatelaine*, November 1956, 84; Susan Cooper, Teen Tempo, *Chatelaine*, July 1957, 20.

98 Cynthia Williams, Teen Tempo, *Chatelaine*, December 1956, 76; Susan Cooper, Teen Tempo, *Chatelaine*, June 1958, 28; Susan Cooper, Teen Tempo, *Chatelaine*, August 1958, 26.

99 Susan Cooper, Teen Tempo, *Chatelaine*, January 1958, 23; Susan Cooper, Teen Tempo, *Chatelaine*, March 1959, 12.

100 Susan Cooper, Teen Tempo, *Chatelaine*, March 1959, 12; Susan Cooper, Teen Tempo, *Chatelaine*, April 1958, 46.

Chapter 3: Students in the Store

1 Interview with Mr. J.A. Brockie, October 3, 1968, Archives of Ontario, T. Eaton Company fonds, Eaton's Archives Office subject files (hereafter AO F 229-162), box 40, file 1323 – Promotions – Youth – Junior Councils & Executives.

2 On department stores as feminine spaces, see Cynthia Wright, "Feminine Trifles of Vast Importance: Writing Gender into the History of Consumption," in *Gender Conflicts: New Essays in Women's History*, ed. Franca Iacovetta and Mariana Valverde (Toronto: University of Toronto Press, 1992), 229–60; Donica Belisle, *Retail Nation: Department Stores and the Making of Modern Canada* (Vancouver: UBC Press, 2011), ch. 5; Susan Porter Benson, *Counter Cultures: Saleswomen, Managers, and Customers in American Department Stores, 1890–1940* (Urbana and Chicago: University of Illinois Press, 1988).

3 Benson, *Counter Cultures*, 85, 89; Daniel T. Cook, "Spatial Biographies of Children's Consumption," *Journal of Consumer Culture* 3, 2 (2003): 152–53.

4 Steve Penfold, *A Mile of Make-Believe: A History of the Eaton's Santa Claus Parade* (Toronto: University of Toronto Press, 2016), 23–26, 46.

(174)

— Notes to pages 84–91 —

5 Mr. R.Y. Eaton to Mr. D.E. Startup, December 28, 1934, Archives of Ontario, J.A. Brockie files (hereafter AO F 229-151), box 3, file 109 – Miscellaneous.

6 Belisle, *Retail Nation*, 163–81.

7 "Youth Unlimited: The Story of Eaton's Junior Council and Executive," *Contacts*, July 1950, 6–7.

8 Russ Gourluck, *A Store Like No Other: Eaton's of Winnipeg* (Winnipeg: Great Plains Publications, 2004), 113–14.

9 Report from Junior Executive meeting, Montreal, March 8, 1947, *Junior Executive Bulletin*, Archives of Ontario, T. Eaton Company fonds, T.H. Miller's files relating to the Winnipeg Junior Council and Executive (hereafter AO F 229-198), box 1, file 21 – Junior Executive Bulletin, Spring 1947.

10 Report from Junior Executive meeting, Toronto, February 15, 1947, *Junior Executive Bulletin*.

11 Report from Junior Council meeting, Toronto, January 24, 1948, AO F 229-151, box 2, file 88 – Junior Council.

12 Report from Junior Executive meeting, Calgary, January 18, 1950, AO F 229-151, box 3, file 95 – Junior Council and Executive.

13 Report from Junior Executive meeting, Calgary, March 1, 1947, *Junior Executive Bulletin*.

14 Report from Junior Executive meeting, Calgary, March 1, 1947, and Junior Executive meeting, Montreal, January 25, 1947, *Junior Executive Bulletin*.

15 Penfold, *A Mile of Make-Believe*, 49.

16 Report from Junior Executive meeting, Montreal, March 8, 1947, Junior Executive meeting, Toronto, March 29, 1947, and Junior Executive meeting, Edmonton, March 1, 1947, *Junior Executive Bulletin*; "A Badge, Sir?" *Contacts*, August 1949, 2.

17 Donica Belisle, "Sexual Spectacles: Saleswomen in Canadian Department Store Magazines between 1920 and 1950," in *Feminist History in Canada: New Essays on Women, Gender, Work, and Nation*, ed. Catherine Carstairs and Nancy Janovicek (Vancouver: UBC Press, 2013), 139–40.

18 "Budget Notes," 4 July 1944, AO F 229-151, file 84 – Merchandise Office 1944. C$2,500 in 1944 was equal to approximately C$48,000 in 2023 when adjusted for inflation.

19 Caroline Evans, "The Enchanted Spectacle," *Journal of Dress, Body and Culture* 5, 3 (2001): 271–310.

20 Patrizia Gentile, *Queen of the Maple Leaf: Beauty Contests and Settler Femininity* (Vancouver: UBC Press, 2020), 85–86.

21 Programs from "Ride into Spring on Eaton's Junior-Teen Tandem of Fashion," undated, and "Eaton's Fashion Fantasy of Caravan Colours," undated, Archives of Ontario, T. Eaton Company fonds, Eaton's Auditorium Programmes and Handbills (hereafter AO F 229-135), file 3 – Eaton Auditorium Programmes – Miscellaneous, 1945–1973.

(175)

— Notes to pages 92–97 —

22 "Junior Council Show Calls the Signals for Fall's Touchdown-Winning Fashions," AO F 229-135, file 3; "Fall Fashion Kick-Off," 1954 and 1956, AO F229-135, part 2; "Eaton's Rings the School Belles," undated, AO F 229-135, file 3. A description of the "School Days" show was included in the minutes of joint meeting of the Junior Council and Executive, Toronto, September 16, 1950, AO F 229-198, box 1, file 51 – Toronto Executive Meeting Minutes.

23 "Eaton's Tenth Junior Council Stages Fashion Show," *Contacts*, December 1950, 25.

24 Report from Junior Council meeting, Edmonton, February 27, 1950, AO F 229-151, box 3, file 95 – Junior Council and Executive.

25 Junior Council and Executive advisers' meeting minutes, November 1947, AO F 229-151.

26 Report from Junior Council meeting, Toronto, February 21, 1948, AO F 229-151, box 2, file 88 – Junior Council.

27 Report from Junior Executive meeting, Hamilton, March 12, 1947, *Junior Executive Bulletin*.

28 Report from Junior Executive meeting, Montreal, February 15, 1947, *Junior Executive Bulletin*.

29 Report from Junior Executive meeting, Toronto, March 15, 1947, *Junior Executive Bulletin*.

30 Minutes of joint meeting of the Junior Council and Executive, Toronto, September 16, 1950.

31 "Minutes of Junior Executive Advisers' Meeting, February 1947," Toronto, AO F 229-151, box 3, file 92 – Jr. Exec. Conference; Report from Junior Executive meeting, Toronto, January 4, 1947, *Junior Executive Bulletin*.

32 Naomi Bristol, "Male Mannequins: Schoolboys Want Fashion Shows with Latest in Black Jackets," *Globe and Mail*, September 16, 1949, 4.

33 Daniel Thomas Cook, *The Commodification of Childhood: The Children's Clothing Industry and the Rise of the Child Consumer* (Durham, NC: Duke University Press, 2004), 131.

34 Cook, *The Commodification of Childhood*, 116, 137.

35 "More about Eaton's," advertisement for Eaton's, *Globe and Mail*, September 18, 1941, 24.

36 "Hi-Jinks at the Hi-Spot," advertisement for Eaton's, *Globe and Mail*, September 25, 1941, 24.

37 Advertisement for Eaton's, *Globe and Mail*, October 3, 1942, 32; Advertisement for Eaton's, *Globe and Mail*, December 12, 1942, 28.

38 "Paging Junior Debs ... At the Hi-Spot," advertisement for Eaton's, *Globe and Mail*, March 4, 1944, 26; "At the Hi-Spot," advertisement for Eaton's, *Globe and Mail*, March 18, 1944, 24.

39 "On the September Slate," advertisement for Eaton's, *Globe and Mail*, September 6, 1944, 5.

— Notes to pages 97–106 —

40 "First to Eaton's, Then to School!" advertisement for Eaton's, *Globe and Mail*, August 23, 1948, 28.

41 Report from Junior Council meeting, Toronto, September 28, 1948, AO F 229-151, box 2, file 88 – Junior Council.

42 B. Warner, "Hi-Spot" memo to Jack Brockie, undated, AO F 229-151, box 3, file 109 – Miscellaneous.

43 "Minx-Modes Keep in Mind Your Dates and Duties," advertisement for Eaton's, *Globe and Mail*, October 18, 1943, 26.

44 "Light-Hearted Minx-Modes," advertisement for Eaton's, *Globe and Mail*, May 15, 1943, 28; "Minx-Modes Plan a Two-Part Summer," advertisement for Eaton's, *Globe and Mail*, May 21, 1943, 28.

45 B. Warner, "Hi-Spot" memo to Jack Brockie.

46 Advertisement for Eaton's, *Globe and Mail*, March 15, 1951, 32.

47 Advertisement for Eaton's, *Globe and Mail*, September 5, 1953, 32.

48 Advertisement for Eaton's, *Globe and Mail*, March 20, 1959, 34.

49 Audrey I. Brown, memo to Jack Brockie regarding councillors' comments on the Junior Fashion Council, June 1945, AO F 229-151, box 2, file 87 – Junior Fashion Council 1944–1945.

Chapter 4: Tailored for Teens

1 Donica Belisle, *Retail Nation: Department Stores and the Making of Modern Canada* (Vancouver: UBC Press, 2011), 45–81.

2 Wendy Mitchinson, *Fighting Fat: Canada, 1920–1980* (Toronto: University of Toronto, 2018), 216.

3 Joanne Entwistle, *The Fashioned Body: Fashion, Dress and Modern Social Theory*, 2nd ed. (Cambridge: Polity Press, 2015), 143.

4 Katrina Srigley, *Breadwinning Daughters: Young Working Women in a Depression-Era City, 1929–1939* (Toronto: University of Toronto Press, 2010), 29.

5 Eleanor Thompson, "Eaton's Mail Order Catalogue – Oral History Project," Canadian Museum of History, Library and Archives (hereafter CMH LA), History Records, box 1-164, file 6.

6 Belisle, *Retail Nation*, 48.

7 Lorraine O'Donnell, "Visualizing the History of Women at Eaton's, 1869 to 1976" (PhD diss., McGill University, 2002), 270–74; Catherine M. Cole, "Comparative Analysis of the Toronto and Winnipeg Editions of the Eaton's Mail Order Catalogues, 1905–1945," CMH LA, History Records, box 1-164, files 41–45.

8 For an analysis of the role of sportswear in the Eaton's catalogue, see Betsey Baldwin, "Athletic Wear and Fashion in Canada, 1900–1950, through the Eaton's Catalogue," 1999, CMH LA, History Records, box 1-164, file 11.

(177)

— Notes to pages 108–13 —

9 Wendy Mitchinson, in *Fighting Fat*, 224, suggests that although there was no consistency in women's sizing between 1920 and 1976, the measurements used for women's sizes did not vary drastically between 1930 and 1960.

10 Daniel Thomas Cook, *The Commodification of Childhood: The Children's Clothing Industry and the Rise of the Child Consumer* (Durham, NC: Duke University Press, 2004), 85–86, 104.

11 On the role of standards in reducing diversity based on any number of set values and assumptions, see Susan Leigh Star and Martha Lampland, "Reckoning with Standards," in *Standards and Their Stories: How Quantifying, Classifying, and Formalizing Practices Shape Everyday Life*, ed. Martha Lampland and Susan Leigh Star (Ithaca, NY: Cornell University Press, 2009), 3–24; Wendy Mitchinson also makes this point in her analysis of catalogue sizes in *Fighting Fat*, 216.

12 This was according to a report of the Canadian Government Specifications Board in the 1950s, recounted in Robert F. Legget, *Standards in Canada* (Ottawa: Information Canada, 1971), 96.

13 Martha Jane Ulrich, "A Comparison of the Body Measurements of Girls from 6 to 14 with the Measurements of Dresses of Corresponding Size" (MSc thesis, Department of Textiles and Clothing, Kansas State College of Agriculture and Applied Science, 1938), 3.

14 Legget, *Standards in Canada*, 94–96.

15 Eaton's Spring and Summer 1951 Catalogue (Toronto: T. Eaton Company, 1951), 29.

16 Eaton's Spring and Summer 1935 Catalogue (Toronto: T. Eaton Company, 1935), 5.

17 Mitchinson, *Fighting Fat*, 216.

18 Cook, *The Commodification of Childhood*, 107–8.

19 Eaton's Fall and Winter 1932–33 Catalogue (Toronto: T. Eaton Company, 1932), 57.

20 Although Eaton's mentioned that 14x dresses were cut wider, the catalogue did not include the precise measurements.

21 Eaton's Fall and Winter 1932–33 Catalogue, 57.

22 Eaton's Fall and Winter 1932–33 Catalogue, 57.

23 See, for example, "Chic Jumper Effect," Eaton's Fall and Winter 1933–34 Catalogue (Toronto: T. Eaton Company, 1933), 29; "Puffed Sleeves," Eaton's Spring and Summer 1933 Catalogue (Toronto: T. Eaton Company, 1933), 27; "And When There's a Party–," Eaton's Fall and Winter 1932–33 Catalogue, 57.

24 Eaton's Fall and Winter 1938–39 Catalogue (Toronto: T. Eaton Company, 1938), 32.

25 Eaton's Spring and Summer 1935 Catalogue, 17. See also Jo B. Poaletti and Carol L. Kregloh, "The Children's Department," in *Men and Women: Dressing the Part*, ed. Claudia Brush Kidwell and Valerie Steele (Washington: Smithsonian Institute Press, 1989), 38.

26 "You'll Save Here," Eaton's Spring and Summer 1935 Catalogue, 17; "Pique Suit," Eaton's Spring and Summer 1935 Catalogue, 17; "New High Collar," Eaton's Fall and Winter 1935–36 Catalogue (Toronto: T. Eaton Company, 1935), 15; "Low

— Notes to pages 113–14 —

Priced Rayon Rough Crepe," Eaton's Spring and Summer 1937 Catalogue (Toronto: T. Eaton Company, 1937), 48; "Summer Charm!" Eaton's Spring and Summer 1939 Catalogue (Toronto: T. Eaton Company, 1939), 74.

27 Eaton's Spring and Summer 1935 Catalogue, 17.

28 Eaton's Spring and Summer 1939 Catalogue, 74.

29 See, for example, "All-Wool Blue Serge Trousers," Eaton's Fall and Winter 1929–30 Catalogue (Toronto: T. Eaton Company, 1929), 209; "Khaki Drill Outing Trousers," Eaton's Spring and Summer 1931 Catalogue (Toronto: T. Eaton Company, 1931), 180.

30 See, for example, "Double-Breasted Suit of Brown Tweed – A Saving for Junior," Eaton's Spring and Summer 1932 Catalogue (Toronto: T. Eaton Company, 1932), 95; "Blue Botany Suits with Golf Bloomers and Longs," Eaton's Spring and Summer 1932 Catalogue, 97; "Blue Cheviot Suits One or Two Longs," Eaton's Fall and Winter 1933–34 Catalogue, 159; "Smart Double-Breasted Style All-Wool Blue Cheviot," Eaton's Fall and Winter 1934–35 Catalogue (Toronto: T. Eaton Company, 1934), 190; "Dressy!" and "Norfolk Style," Eaton's Spring and Summer 1935 Catalogue, 2; "All Wool and Decidedly Smart," Eaton's Spring and Summer 1939 Catalogue, 91.

31 J.M. McCutcheon, "Clothing Children in English Canada, 1880–1930" (PhD diss., University of Ottawa, 2002), 244.

32 Paoletti and Kregloh, "The Children's Department," 31–33. Size and age were both factors when deciding to put a boy in long pants; a large boy might be breeched at a younger age than a smaller boy because he was beginning to look more like a man.

33 Eaton's Spring and Summer 1930 Catalogue (Toronto: T. Eaton Company, 1930), 14.

34 Eaton's Fall and Winter 1929–30 Catalogue, 202.

35 These age sizes occasionally deviated slightly, such as when a suit was sold in size 5 to 10 years instead of 6 to 10, or from 10 to 16 years instead of 10 to 15.

36 "All-Wool Worsted Carefully Tailored," Eaton's Fall and Winter 1935–36 Catalogue, 183.

37 Eaton's Spring and Summer 1935 Catalogue, 182; Eaton's Spring and Summer 1937 Catalogue, 135.

38 "Pleated Pants with Zipper Fly," "Striped Tweed! Pleats! Zipper!" "Double-Breasted," and "Blue Cheviot," Eaton's Spring and Summer 1940 Catalogue (Toronto: T. Eaton Company, 1940), 122–23; "Students' Suit," Eaton's Spring and Summer 1945 Catalogue (Toronto: T. Eaton Company, 1945), 106.

39 A suit sized 6 to 10 years appeared on a page headlined "Dress Him Right for School or Play!" in the Spring and Summer 1944 Catalogue (Toronto: T. Eaton Company, 1944), 106.

40 A page of Junior suits was headlined as "Juniors' Play, Dress Togs" in Eaton's Spring and Summer 1949 Catalogue (Toronto: T. Eaton Company, 1949), 160. See also "Rayon Gabardine Suit," Eaton's Spring and Summer 1951 Catalogue, 163.

— Notes to pages 115–22 —

41 Eaton's Fall and Winter 1941–42 Catalogue (Toronto: T. Eaton Company, 1941), 129.

42 Eaton's Spring and Summer 1939 Catalogue, 14.

43 Lisa Jacobson, "Advertising, Mass Merchandising, and Children's Consumer Culture," in *Children and Consumer Culture in American Society: A Historical Handbook and Guide*, ed. Lisa Jacobson (New York: Bloomsbury Publishing, 2007), 12.

44 Eaton's Spring and Summer 1941 Catalogue (Toronto: T. Eaton Company, 1941), 6.

45 Eaton's Fall and Winter 1940–41 Catalogue (Toronto: T. Eaton Company, 1940), 6.

46 "Teen-Agers 'Big Business,'" *Toronto Daily Star*, June 15 1946, 12, quoted in Cynthia Comacchio, *The Dominion of Youth: Adolescence and the Making of Modern Canada, 1920–1950* (Waterloo, ON: Wilfrid Laurier University Press, 2006), 186.

47 Those wearing Girls' sizes, in comparison, had fifteen coats and twenty-seven dresses to choose from in Eaton's Fall and Winter 1946–47 Catalogue (Toronto: T. Eaton Company, 1946), 124–25. See also Eaton's Fall and Winter 1950–51 Catalogue (Toronto: T. Eaton Company, 1950), 172–86.

48 Eaton's Fall and Winter 1956–57 Catalogue (Toronto: T. Eaton Company, 1956), 135. The Teen Fair section appeared in each catalogue sampled except the Fall and Winter 1958–59 Catalogue (Toronto: T. Eaton Company, 1958), when the section was titled Campus Corner. Nevertheless, Campus Corner was exclusively for Teen-sized garments.

49 Eaton's Fall and Winter 1956–57 Catalogue, 142.

50 Eaton's Spring and Summer 1945 Catalogue, 74.

51 Eaton's Fall and Winter 1948–49 Catalogue (Toronto: T. Eaton Company, 1948), 185.

52 In the Fall and Winter 1948–49 Catalogue, Grad size 36 had a 31.5-inch waist, compared to 30 inches for the Men's size.

53 Eaton's Spring and Summer 1955 Catalogue (Toronto: T. Eaton Company, 1955), 237; Eaton's Fall and Winter 1956–57 Catalogue, 306.

54 Eaton's Spring and Summer 1955, 237; Eaton's Fall and Winter 1956–57 Catalogue, 306. Men's suits (with two pairs of trousers and no vest) in a sample from the 1955 and 1956 catalogues cost between $37.50 and $62.50. Grad suits in the same catalogues cost $21.95 and $33.95.

55 Eaton's Fall and Winter 1945–46 Catalogue (Toronto: T. Eaton Company, 1945), 76.

56 Eaton's Spring and Summer 1945 Catalogue, 74.

57 Eaton's Spring and Summer 1947 Catalogue (Toronto: T. Eaton Company, 1947), 88, 94–95.

58 Eaton's Spring and Summer 1948 Catalogue (Toronto: T. Eaton Company, 1948), 118, 119.

59 Eaton's Spring and Summer 1948 Catalogue, 118; Eaton's Spring and Summer 1947 Catalogue, 119; "Pleated Pants with Zipper Fly," Eaton's Spring and Summer 1940 Catalogue, 122.

60 Eaton's Fall and Winter 1946–47 Catalogue, 124.

— Notes to pages 122–24 —

61 Eaton's Fall and Winter 1946–47 Catalogue, 124; Eaton's Spring and Summer 1949 Catalogue, 140.

62 Eaton's Spring and Summer 1947 Catalogue, 89.

63 Eaton's Spring and Summer 1947 Catalogue, 89.

64 Eaton's Fall and Winter 1953–54 Catalogue (Toronto: T. Eaton Company, 1953), 2.

65 "Compliment Catcher," Eaton's Fall and Winter 1946–47 Catalogue, 124.

66 "Sweetheart of a Frock," Eaton's Spring and Summer 1947 Catalogue, 89.

67 "The New, Long-Waisted Look," Eaton's Spring and Summer 1955 Catalogue, 145. For other examples, see "In Gabardine, No Less!" Eaton's Fall and Winter 1948–49 Catalogue, 166; "Gay Cotton Calico Dress," Eaton's Spring and Summer 1953 Catalogue (Toronto: T. Eaton Company, 1953), 137; and "Dreamy Romantic," Eaton's Fall and Winter 1960–61 Catalogue (Toronto: T. Eaton Company, 1960), 71.

68 "Long-Sleeve Cotton Plaid," Eaton's Fall and Winter 1951–52 Catalogue (Toronto: T. Eaton Company, 1951), 163. For other examples, see "Bewitchingly Be-bibbed," Eaton's Spring and Summer 1949 Catalogue, 145; "Hi There, Sailor," Eaton's Fall and Winter 1946–47 Catalogue, 129; and "Winsome Twosome," Eaton's Spring and Summer 1959 Catalogue, 139.

69 "For the Teens," Eaton's Fall and Winter 1953–54 Catalogue, 2.

70 On the New Look, see Claudia Brush Kidwell, "Gender Symbols or Fashionable Details?" in *Men and Women*, ed. Kidwell and Steele, 138; "Prettied-Up for Dressing-Up," Eaton's Spring and Summer 1945 Catalogue, 74.

71 Donica Belisle, "Crazy for Bargains: Inventing the Irrational Female Shopper in Modernizing English Canada," *Canadian Historical Review* 92, 4 (2011): 595–600.

72 "All-Wool English Worsted," Eaton's Fall and Winter 1948–49 Catalogue, 185; Eaton's Spring and Summer 1953 Catalogue, 159; Eaton's Spring and Summer 1949 Catalogue, 158; Eaton's Fall and Winter 1951–52 Catalogue (Toronto: T. Eaton Company, 1951), 198.

73 In a sample of fifty-six Junior Boys' suit descriptions, the words *finish/finishes/finished* appeared seventeen times (a 30 percent rate of occurrence); *smart* appeared sixteen times (29 percent); *young* was used thirteen times (23 percent); *value, best, quality,* and *neat* each appeared eleven times (20 percent); *sturdily/sturdy/sturdiness* appeared ten times (18 percent), and *serviceable* was used nine times (16 percent). Words such as *serviceable, price,* and *sturdy* were each used to describe only 6 percent of the larger-sized suits. In forty-nine Senior and Grad suit descriptions, the word *smart* was used sixteen times (a 33 percent rate of occurrence); *tailored* and *sporty* both appeared ten times (20 percent); and *quality* was used nine times and *popular* appeared eight times, each occurring in approximately 18 percent of the sample. The word *sporty* was never used to describe suits for younger boys, and words such as *popular* occurred with less frequency than in descriptions of suits for older boys.

74 "Two-Way Nylon Strengthened," Eaton's Spring and Summer 1955 Catalogue, 237.

— Notes to pages 124–26 —

75 Eaton's Fall and Winter 1956–57 Catalogue, 306; Eaton's Spring and Summer 1957 Catalogue (Toronto: T. Eaton Company, 1957), 192, 194.

76 "Pleated Pants with Zipper Fly," Eaton's Spring and Summer 1940 Catalogue, 122.

77 "Single Breasted Suit – Rayon Twist with Duraleen Finish," Eaton's Spring and Summer 1957 Catalogue, 192.

78 Luis Alvarez, *The Power of the Zoot: Youth Culture and Resistance during World War II* (Berkeley: University of California Press, 2008); Jon Savage, *Teenage: The Creation of Youth, 1875–1945* (London: Chatto and Windus, 2007), 397–401.

79 Eaton's Fall and Winter 1951–52 Catalogue, 198.

80 "Grads Extra-Quality Suit," Eaton's Spring and Summer 1949 Catalogue, 158. In 1948, draped trousers were also offered in a suit that promised "Lots of Colour – Lots of Style!" Eaton's Fall and Winter 1948–49 Catalogue, 197.

81 Eaton's Fall and Winter 1951–52 Catalogue, 198.

82 Suits in green offered to older boys included "Here's a Sporty Style in All-Wool Check Tweed" and "Striped Tweed! Pleats! Zipper!" Eaton's Spring and Summer 1940 Catalogue, 122; "All-Wool Tweed Two-Trouser Suits" and "Reinforced for Extra Wear," Eaton's Spring and Summer 1940 Catalogue, 123; "Durable Check Tweeds," Eaton's Fall and Winter 1940–41 Catalogue, 159; "3-Piece Tweed," Eaton's Fall and Winter 1942–43 Catalogue (Toronto: T. Eaton Company, 1942), 189; "Smart Striped Worsted Suit," Eaton's Fall and Winter 1942–43 Catalogue, 191; and "Student's Suit," Eaton's Spring and Summer 1945 Catalogue, 106.

83 "Smart Striped Worsted Suit," Eaton's Fall and Winter 1942–43 Catalogue, 191; "All-Wool Tweed," Eaton's Spring and Summer 1945 Catalogue, 108; "Eatonia 'Grad' All-Wool Worsted," Eaton's Spring and Summer 1951 Catalogue, 152.

84 "Grads Extra-Quality Suit," Eaton's Spring and Summer 1949 Catalogue, 158.

85 Seven of the nineteen Teen-sized dresses in the catalogue sample were sold in fashion colours.

86 The Misses' dress offered in lime was described as a "peppy young fashion" because of its bright colour. See Eaton's Spring and Summer 1940 Catalogue, 8. The Girls' dress "Bewitchingly Be-bibbed," Eaton's Spring and Summer 1949 Catalogue, 145, was also offered in lime.

87 See Valerie Steele, "Dressing for Work," in *Men and Women*, ed. Kidwell and Steele, 75.

88 Valerie Mendes and Amy De La Haye, *20th Century Fashion* (London: Thames and Hudson, 1999), 72.

89 See "Gay Print Dress," Eaton's Spring and Summer 1931 Catalogue, 102; "Choice of Real Silk or Celanese," Eaton's Fall and Winter 1933–34 Catalogue, 30; "Gibson Girl Striper," Eaton's Fall and Winter 1948–49 Catalogue, 176; "Bewitchingly Be-bibbed," Eaton's Spring and Summer 1949 Catalogue, 145; and "Schoolroom Classic," Eaton's Fall and Winter 1950–51 Catalogue, 182.

90 Lisa Jacobson, *Raising Consumers: Children and the American Mass Market in the Early Twentieth Century* (New York: Columbia University Press, 2004), 137.

— Notes to pages 127–33 —

91 Jacobson, *Raising Consumers*, 137.

92 A 2005 study of six thousand women found that only 8 percent had an hourglass figure. Far more common body shapes were rectangular (46 percent) and pear-shaped (20 percent). See Helen McCormack, "The Shape of Things to Wear: Scientists Identify How Women's Bodies Have Changed in 50 Years," *Independent*, November 21, 2005, http://www.independent.co.uk/news/uk/this-britain/the-shape-of-things-to-wear-scientists-identify-how-womens-figures-have-changed-in-50-years-516259.html.

Chapter 5: Eaton's Goes to School

1 Staples Canada ULC, "Superpower Your School Contest Is Back to Reward Sustainable Schools with $20,000 in New Tech from Staples Canada," *Newswire*, January 9, 2020, https://www.newswire.ca/news-releases/superpower-your-school-contest-is-back-to-reward-sustainable-schools-with-20-000-in-new-tech-from-staples-canada-830945627.html.

2 See Catherine Gidney, *Captive Audience: How Corporations Invaded Our Schools* (Toronto: Between the Lines, 2019); Brian O. Brent, "Much Ado about Very Little: The Benefits and Costs of School-Based Commercial Activities," *Leadership and Policy in Schools* 8, 3 (2009): 307–36; Alex Molnar, *School Commercialism: From Democratic Ideal to Market Commodity* (New York: Routledge, 2005); and Larry Kuehn, *Beyond the Bake Sale: Exposing Schoolhouse Commercialism* (Ottawa: Canadian Centre for Policy Alternatives, 2006).

3 Gidney, *Captive Audience*, 156.

4 R.D. Gidney and Catherine Gidney, "Branding the Classroom: Commercialism in Canadian Schools, 1920–1960," *Histoire sociale/Social History* 41, 83 (2008): 345–79, https://doi.org/10.1353/his.0.0041.

5 Donica Belisle, *Retail Nation: Department Stores and the Making of Modern Canada* (Vancouver: UBC Press, 2011), ch. 4.

6 Malcolm Gladwell, "The Coolhunt," *New Yorker*, March 10, 1997, https://www.newyorker.com/magazine/1997/03/17/the-coolhunt-malcolm-gladwell. Gladwell later developed these ideas in his book, *The Tipping Point: How Little Things Can Make a Big Difference* (New York: Little, Brown and Company, 2000), ch. 2.

7 Klaus-Peter Wiedmann, Nadine Hennigs, and Sascha Langner, "Spreading the Word of Fashion: Identifying Social Influencers in Fashion Marketing," *Journal of Global Fashion Marketing* 1, 3 (2010): 142–53.

8 Mary Louise Adams, *The Trouble with Normal: Postwar Youth and the Making of Heterosexuality* (Toronto: University of Toronto Press, 1997), 43.

9 Report from Junior Executive meeting, Montreal, March 15, 1947, *Junior Executive Bulletin*, Archives of Ontario, T. Eaton Company fonds, T.H. Miller's

(183)

— Notes to pages 134–41 —

files relating to the Winnipeg Junior Council and Executive (hereafter AO F 229-198), box 1, file 21 – Junior Executive Bulletin, Spring 1947.

10 "Minutes of the Meeting of the Junior Council and Junior Executive Advisers held at Toronto, May 30, 31, and June 1, 1950," AO F 229-198, box 1, file 27.

11 W. Lloyd Wornell, Montreal store, copy of letter to school officials, March 21, 1947, AO F 229-198, box 1, file 28 – Miscellaneous Printed Matter.

12 "Junior Executives Chosen, 1951/52," AO F 229-198, box 1, file 23.

13 "Not Chosen," AO F 229-198, box 1, file 31; "Rejects," F 229-198, box 1, file 44. Only one of the twenty-five successful applicants listed a single official position; eleven listed two; four listed three. Thirty of the forty-three unsuccessful applicants listed between one and three official school positions on their applications; eight listed four or more.

14 Application form for David Williamson, AO F 229-198, box 1, file 4 – Executive Alternates.

15 Report from Junior Council meeting, Toronto, 1 May 1948, Archives of Ontario, T. Eaton Company fonds, J.A. Brockie files (hereafter AO F 229-151), box 2, file 88 – Junior Council.

16 Report from Junior Executive meeting, Montreal, February 15, 1947, *Junior Executive Bulletin*.

17 Report from joint meeting of the Junior Council and Executive, Hamilton, January 16, 1947, *Junior Executive Bulletin*.

18 Jack Brockie, Merchandise Display Department, memo to Mr. W Park, Merchandise Office, Toronto, December 8 1943, AO F 229-151, file 83 – Merchandise Office 1943.

19 Report from Junior Council meeting, Toronto, February 21, 1948, AO F 229-151, box 2, file 88 – Junior Council.

20 T.M. Miller, letter to W.J. McKeag, Merchandise Office, August 25, 1952, AO F 229-198, box 1, file 2 – Advertising file.

21 "Youth Unlimited: The Story of Eaton's Junior Council and Executive," *Contacts*, July 1950, 6–7.

22 I classified the listed occupations into the following: none; retired; not given; not specified; labourers (skilled and unskilled); foremen/supervisors; retail employees, salespeople, and clerks; professional and civil service; business; farmers. This broad system was appropriate given the scant information provided on most application forms and the categories are, as much as possible, mutually exclusive. The business code was applied only to proprietors and merchants, for example, not to people who worked *for* a particular company.

23 "Junior Executives Chosen, 1951/52."

24 M. Wisenthal, "Section W: Education," in *Historical Statistics of Canada*, ed. F.H. Leacy (Ottawa: Statistics Canada, 1983), https://publications.gc.ca/site/eng/9.692518/publication.html.

25 W. Lloyd Wornell, Montreal store, copy of letter to school officials, March 21, 1947.

— Notes to pages 141–46 —

26 "Minutes of the Meeting of the Junior Council and Junior Executive Advisers Held at Toronto, May 30, 31, and June 1, 1950," 9.

27 "Donations – Regular," 1936–1965, Archives of Ontario, T. Eaton Company fonds, Eaton's Public Relations Office donation lists (hereafter AO F 229-128), box 7.

28 "Minutes of the Meeting of the Junior Council and Junior Executive Advisers Held at Toronto, May 30, 31, and June 1, 1950," 10–11.

29 "Minutes of the Meeting of the Junior Council and Junior Executive Advisers, Held at Toronto, May 30, 31, and June 1, 1950," 10.

30 Gidney, *Captive Audience*, 10–23.

31 W.J. Bundy, Public Relations Department, memo to J.A. Brockie, 1953, re: Prep Shop at College Street Store, AO F 229-151, box 3, file 103 – Merchandise Display 1952–1956.

32 "Minutes of the Meeting of the Junior Council and Junior Executive Advisers Held at Toronto, May 1948," AO F 229-151, box 3, file 94 – Junior Council and Executive Conference Minutes.

33 "Minutes of Junior Executive Conference, August 14, 15, 16, 1946," AO F 229-198, box 1, file 21 – Junior Executive Bulletin, Spring 1947. While the file name suggests materials created in 1947, the contents were created from 1946 to 1948.

34 "Minutes of the Meeting of the Junior Council and Junior Executive Advisers Held at Toronto, May 30, 31, and June 1, 1950," 9.

35 C.W. Robb, Superintendent of Secondary Schools, letter to J.A. Brockie, Merchandise Display Department, September 4, 1947, AO F 229-151, box 3, file 96 – Junior Promotions.

36 "Minutes from the Junior Executive Advisers' Meeting, February 1947," AO F 229-151, box 3, file 92 – Jr. Exec. Conference.

37 "Minutes of Junior Executive Conference, August 14, 15, 16, 1946."

38 "Recommendations for Approval from Minutes of Junior Council and Junior Executive Advisers, May 19–21, 1947," AO F 229-151, box 3, file 93 – Jr. Exec. & Jr. Council Meeting.

39 "Students and a Store," 5.

40 George Buri, *Between Education and Catastrophe: The Battle over Public Schooling in Postwar Manitoba* (Montreal and Kingston: McGill-Queen's University Press, 2016), 153–58.

41 Jeffrey Keshen, *Saints, Sinners, and Soldiers: Canada's Second World War* (Vancouver: UBC Press, 2004), 219–21; R.D. Gidney, *From Hope to Harris: The Reshaping of Ontario's Schools* (Toronto: University of Toronto Press, 1999), 23–24; Cynthia Comacchio, *The Dominion of Youth: Adolescence and the Making of Modern Canada, 1920–1950* (Waterloo, ON: Wilfrid Laurier University Press, 2006), 189–209.

42 Katharine Rollwagen, "Classrooms for Consumer Society: Practical Education and Secondary School Reform in Post-Second World War Canada," *Historical Studies in Education* 28, 1 (2016): 46.

— Notes to pages 146–49 —

43 "Too Many Kids in Dead End Jobs? Industry Fosters a Plan to Pep Up Career Training," *Financial Times*, February 14, 1948, copy included in Library and Archives Canada (hereafter LAC), Canadian Education Association fonds (hereafter MG 28), vol. 13, file 2-1-3 – P.E. Comm. Miscellaneous.

44 "The Canadian Research Committee on Practical Education – Contributors, 1947–1951," June 22, 1951, LAC, MG 28, vol. 13, file 2-1-2 – P.E. Comm. Minutes of Special and General Meetings.

45 "Questionnaire to Employers on the Secondary School Requirements of Distributive Business," May 4, 1949, LAC, MG 28, vol. 7, file 126a.

46 The Canadian Youth Commission reported that many community organizations shared these beliefs about part-time work. See Rebecca Prigert Coulter, "Schooling, Work, and Life: Reflections of the Young in the 1940s," in *Rethinking Vocationalism: Whose Work/Life Is It?* ed. Rebecca Priegert Coulter and Ivor F. Goodson (Toronto: Our Schools/Ourselves Education Foundation, 1992), 71.

47 Angelo Patri, "Teach Youngsters Art of Handling Money," *Globe and Mail*, November 26, 1946. For an example of criticisms, see Samuel Henry Prince, "The Canadian Family in Wartime," *Marriage and Family Living* 4, 2 (1942): 27.

48 W.A. Osbourne, "Opportunities for Young Men and Women in Canada," *Canadian Education* 3, 1 (1947): 91.

49 "Minutes of the Alberta Advisory Committee of the Canadian Research Committee on Practical Education," September 26, 1950, 4, LAC, MG 28, vol. 7, file 126a.

50 Only sixteen of the forty-three rejected and alternate applicants (37 percent) listed jobs outside of school. See "Executive Alternates," "Not Chosen," and "Rejects."

51 Canadian Research Committee on Practical Education, "Two Years after School," *Canadian Education* 6, 1 (1951), 63–64.

52 Canadian Research Committee on Practical Education, "Better Schooling for Canadian Youth," *Canadian Education* 6, 4 (1951): 14.

53 Canadian Youth Commission, *Youth Challenges the Educators* (Toronto: Ryerson Press, 1946), 10–11.

54 "Teenagers Club," *Mayfair*, August 1945, 95.

55 M.H. Jewell, Assistant Principal at Malvern Collegiate Institute, memorandum to Jack Brockie, Head of Merchandise Display Department, undated, AO, 229-151, file 89 – Junior Exec. and Council 1942–1945.

56 Junior Executive and Council advisors' meeting minutes, Toronto, November 1947, AO F 229-151, box 3, file 93 – Jr. Exec. & Jr. Council Meeting.

57 "Budget Notes," 4 July 1944, AO F 229-151, file 105 – Merchandise Office 1944.

58 "Students and a Store," 2.

59 The sample includes minutes from most of the Junior Executive meetings at stores in Toronto, Montreal, Hamilton, Winnipeg, Calgary, and Edmonton between December 1946 and April 1947. Each group's advisor sent notes to the

— Notes to pages 150–54 —

national secretary at the Toronto store, where they were collated into a single document, the *Junior Executive Bulletin*, and shared with all advisors. The sample also includes minutes from Toronto Junior Council meetings between January and May 1948, kept in Jack Brockie's files (AO F 229-151, box 2, file 88 – Junior Council), and minutes from both groups at all the stores from January 1950 to January 1951 kept in Brockie and Miller's files.

60 Report from Junior Executive meeting, Edmonton, January 4, 1947, *Junior Executive Bulletin.*

61 Report from Junior Executive meeting, Montreal, February 18, 1950, AO F 229-198, Box 1, File 51 – Executive Meeting Minutes.

62 Report from Junior Executive Meeting, Winnipeg, March 8, 1947, *Junior Executive Bulletin.*

63 Donica Belisle, *Purchasing Power: Women and the Rise of Consumer Culture* (Toronto: University of Toronto Press, 2020), 97.

64 For more on the connections between postsecondary home economics programs, manufacturers, and retailers, illustrated during Home Economics Week in Edmonton in 1932, see Belisle, *Purchasing Power,* 78–96.

65 Report from Junior Council meeting, Toronto, February 28, 1948, AO F 229-151, box 2, file 88 – Junior Council; Report from Junior Council meeting, Calgary, January 14, 1950 and Junior Council meeting, Calgary March 25, 1950, AO F 229-198, box 1, file 20 – Junior Council Minutes.

66 Report from Junior Council meeting, Toronto, January 11 1950, AO F 229-198, box 1, file 20 – Junior Council Minutes.

67 Report from Junior Council meeting, Toronto, May 1, 1948, AO F 229-151, box 2, file 88 – Junior Council.

68 Report from Junior Council meeting, Calgary, January 14 1950, AO F 229-198, box 1, file 20 – Junior Council Minutes.

69 Report from Junior Council meeting, Winnipeg, December 2, 1950, AO F 229-198, box 1, file 20 – Junior Council Minutes.

70 Reports from Junior Council meetings, Toronto, February 14, 1948; April 3 1948; and October 5 1948, AO F 229-151, box 2, file 88 – Junior Council.

71 Advertising and Display Conference, June 14–17, 1965, Archives of Ontario, T. Eaton Company fonds, D.H. Morrison Public Relations Office, F 229-146, box 1.

Conclusion

1 Ellen Neuborne, "Generation Y," *Business Week,* 15 February 1999, 83.

2 Issie Lapowsky, "Why Teens Are the Most Elusive and Valuable Customers in Tech," March 3, 2014, https://www.inc.com/issie-lapowsky/inside-massive -tech-land-grab-teenagers.html#:~:text=Teenagers%20have%20always%20 been%20important,are%20telling%20them%20is%20cool.

(187)

— Notes to pages 155–58 —

3 "Youth Unlimited: The Story of Eaton's Junior Council and Executive," *Contacts*, July 1950, 6.

4 Katja Jezkova Isaksen and Stuart Roper, "The Commodification of Self-Esteem: Branding and British Teenagers," *Psychology and Marketing* 29, 3 (2012): 117–35; Matthew J. Easterbrook, Mark L. Wright, Helga Dittmar, and Robin Banerjee, "Consumer Culture Ideals, Extrinsic Motivations, and Well-Being in Children," *European Journal of Social Psychology* 44, 4 (2014): 349–59.

5 Claire Penhorwood, "Canada's Youth Face Job Crunch," *CBC News*, March 26, 2012, http://www.cbc.ca/news/canada/story/2012/03/19/f-canada-youth-unemployment.html. For an examination of the challenges facing many American youth, see Stephen Marche, "The War against Youth," *Esquire*, March 26, 2012, https://www.esquire.com/news-politics/a13226/young-people-in-the-recession-0412; Statistics Canada, "Rising Prices are Affecting the Ability to Meet Day-to-Day Expenses for Most Canadians," *The Daily*, June 9, 2022, https://www150.statcan.gc.ca/n1/daily-quotidien/220609/dq220609a-eng.htm.

6 Owen Mulhearn, "The 10 Essential Fast Fashion Statistics," *Earth.org*, July 24, 2022, https://earth.org/fast-fashion-statistics/.

7 Jon Savage, "Time Up for the Teenager?" *RSA Journal* 160, 5557 (2014): 19.

8 See Paul Stortz and Lisa Panayotidis, "Visual Interpretations, Cartoons, and Caricatures of Student Youth Cultures in University Yearbooks, 1898–1930," *Journal of the Canadian Historical Association* 19, 1 (2008): 195–227; Megan Blair, "Fraternity for Frustrated Females: The Gender Dynamics of 1970s Feminist Organizing at the University of Waterloo, Canada," *Gender and History* (2023): 1–17, https://doi.org/ 10.1111/1468-0424.12725.

9 Linda Mahood, *Thumbing a Ride: Hitchhikers, Hostels, and Counterculture in Canada* (Vancouver: UBC Press, 2019).

10 Paul Willis, *Learning to Labour: How Working-Class Kids Get Working-Class Jobs* (Farnborough, UK: Saxon House, 1977); Linda McDowell, *Redundant Masculinities? Employment, Change, and White Working-Class Youth* (Malden, MA: Blackwell, 2003).

Selected Bibliography

Archival Sources

Archives of Ontario
Canadian Education Association Fonds, MG 28
Canadian Museum of History, Library and Archives
Library and Archives Canada
Mail-order catalogues research project, History Records, H-164
T. Eaton Company Fonds, F-229

Magazines and Newspapers

Canadian Home Journal (Toronto)
Chatelaine (Toronto)
Contacts (Winnipeg)
Globe and Mail (Toronto)
Independent (London)
Ladies' Home Journal (New York)
Maclean's (Toronto)
Mayfair (Toronto)
Parents' Magazine (Des Moines)
Toronto Daily Star

Other Sources

Adams, Mary Louise. *The Trouble with Normal: Postwar Youth and the Making of Heterosexuality.* Toronto: University of Toronto Press, 1997.
Alexander, Kristine. "Childhood and Colonialism in Canadian History." *History Compass* 14, 9 (2016): 397–406.
Alexander, Rachel. *Imagining Gender, Nation and Consumerism in Magazines of the 1920s.* New York: Anthem Press, 2022.

— Selected Bibliography —

Alvarez, Luis. *The Power of the Zoot: Youth Culture and Resistance during World War II.* Berkeley: University of California Press, 2008.

Ambrose, Linda M. "The Canadian Youth Commission: Planning for Youth and Social Welfare in the Postwar Era." PhD diss., University of Waterloo, 1992.

–. "Collecting Youth Opinion: The Research of the Canadian Youth Commission, 1943–1945." In *Dimensions of Childhood: Essays on the History of Children and Youth in Canada*, ed. Russell Smandych, Gordon Dodds, and Alvin Esau, 63–83. Winnipeg: Legal Research Institute, University of Manitoba, 1991.

Axelrod, Paul. *Making a Middle Class: Student Life in English Canada during the Thirties.* Montreal and Kingston: McGill-Queen's University Press, 1990.

Baillargeon, Denyse. *Making Do: Women, Family and Home in Montreal during the Great Depression.* Translated by Yvonne Klein. Waterloo, ON: Wilfrid Laurier University Press, 1999.

Baxter, Kent. *The Modern Age: Turn-of-the-Century American Culture and the Invention of Adolescence.* Tuscaloosa: University of Alabama Press, 2008.

Belisle, Donica. "Crazy for Bargains: Inventing the Irrational Female Shopper in Modernizing English Canada." *Canadian Historical Review* 92, 4 (2011): 581–606.

–. "Eating Clean: Anti-Chinese Sugar Advertising and the Making of White Racial Purity in the Canadian Pacific." *Global Food History* 6, 1 (2020): 41–59.

–. *Purchasing Power: Women and the Rise of Canadian Consumer Culture.* Toronto: University of Toronto Press, 2020.

–. *Retail Nation: Department Stores and the Making of Modern Canada.* Vancouver: UBC Press, 2011.

–. "Sexual Spectacles: Saleswomen in Canadian Department Store Magazines between 1920 and 1950." In *Feminist History in Canada: New Essays on Women, Gender, Work, and Nation*, ed. Catherine Carstairs and Nancy Janovicek, 139–58. Vancouver: UBC Press, 2013.

–. "Toward a Canadian Consumer History." *Labour/Le Travail* 52 (Fall 2003): 181–206.

Bell, Katherine. "Teenagers." In *The Sage Encyclopedia of Children and Childhood Studies*, ed. Katherine Bell, 1551–54. Thousand Oaks, CA: Sage, 2020. https://doi.org/10.4135/9781529714388.

Benson, Susan Porter. *Counter Cultures: Saleswomen, Managers, and Customers in American Department Stores, 1890–1940.* Urbana and Chicago: University of Illinois Press, 1988.

Bertram, Laurie K. *The Viking Immigrants: Icelandic North Americans.* Toronto: University of Toronto Press, 2020.

Blair, Megan. "Fraternity for Frustrated Females: The Gender Dynamics of 1970s Feminist Organizing at the University of Waterloo, Canada." *Gender and History* (2023): 1–17. https://doi.org/10.1111/1468-0424.12725.

Brent, Brian O. "Much Ado about Very Little: The Benefits and Costs of School-Based Commercial Activities." *Leadership and Policy in Schools* 8, 3 (2009): 307–36.

— Selected Bibliography —

Broad, Graham. *A Small Price to Pay: Consumer Culture on the Canadian Home Front, 1939–1945*. Vancouver: UBC Press, 2013.

Brumberg, Joan Jacobs. *The Body Project: An Intimate History of American Girls*. New York: Random House, 1997.

Bullen, John. "Child Labour and the Family Economy in Late Nineteenth-Century Urban Ontario." *Labour/Le Travail* 18 (1986): 163–87.

Buri, George. *Between Education and Catastrophe: The Battle over Public Schooling in Postwar Manitoba*. Montreal and Kingston: McGill-Queen's University Press, 2016.

Canada, Wartime Prices and Trade Board. *Canadian War Orders and Regulations, 1942*. Ottawa: King's Printer, 1942.

Canadian Youth Commission. *Youth and Jobs in Canada*. Toronto: Ryerson Press, 1945.

Chenier, Elise. "Class, Gender, and the Social Standard: The Montreal Junior League, 1912–1939." *Canadian Historical Review* 90, 4 (2009): 671–710.

Chudacoff, Howard. *How Old Are You? Age Consciousness in American Culture*. Princeton, NJ: Princeton University Press, 1989.

Clemente, Deirdre. *Dress Casual: How College Students Redefined American Style*. Chapel Hill: University of North Carolina Press, 2014.

Cohen, Lizabeth. *A Consumer's Republic: The Politics of Mass Consumption in Postwar America*. New York: Alfred A. Knopf, 2003.

Collard, Constance Eileen McCarthy. *From Toddlers to Teens: An Outline of Children's Clothing circa 1780–1930*. Burlington, ON: N.p., 1973.

Colpitts, George. "The Domesticated Body and the Industrialized Imitation Fur Coat in Canada, 1919–1939." In *Contesting Bodies and Nation in Canadian History*, ed. Patrizia Gentile and Jane Nicholas, 134–54. Toronto: University of Toronto Press, 2013.

Comacchio, Cynthia. "Dancing to Perdition: Adolescence and Leisure in Interwar English Canada." *Journal of Canadian Studies* 32, 3 (1997): 5–35.

–. *The Dominion of Youth: Adolescence and the Making of Modern Canada, 1920–1950*. Waterloo, ON: Wilfrid Laurier University Press, 2006.

Connell, R.W. *Masculinities*. Berkeley: University of California Press, 1995.

Conor, Liz. *The Spectacular Modern Woman: Feminine Visibility in the 1920s*. Bloomington and Indianapolis: Indiana University Press, 2004.

Cook, Daniel T. *The Commodification of Childhood: The Children's Clothing Industry and the Rise of the Child Consumer*. Durham, NC: Duke University Press, 2004.

–. "The Dichotomous Child in and of Commercial Culture." *Childhood* 12, 2 (2005): 155–59.

–. "Introduction: Beyond Either/Or." *Journal of Consumer Culture* 4, 2 (2004): 147–53.

–. "Kiddie Capitalism: The History of the Child Consumer." *PopPolitics.com*, December 5, 2001.

–. "The Other 'Child Study': Figuring Children as Consumers in Market Research, 1910s–1990s." *Sociological Quarterly* 41, 3 (2000): 487–507.

— Selected Bibliography —

–. "Spatial Biographies of Children's Consumption," *Journal of Consumer Culture* 3, 2 (2003): 147–69.

Cook, Sharon. *Sex, Lies, and Cigarettes: Canadian Women, Smoking, and Visual Culture, 1880–2000.* Montreal and Kingston: McGill-Queen's University Press, 2012.

Coulter, Rebecca Priegert. "Schooling, Work, and Life: Reflections of the Young in the 1940s." In *Rethinking Vocationalism: Whose Work/Life Is It?* ed. Rebecca Priegert Coulter and Ivor F. Goodson, 69–86. Toronto: Our Schools/Ourselves Education Foundation, 1992.

Craig, Beatrice. *Backwoods Consumers and Homespun Capitalists: The Rise of a Market Culture in Eastern Canada.* Toronto: University of Toronto Press, 2009.

Cross, Gary. *The Cute and the Cool: Wondrous Innocence in Modern American Children's Culture.* Oxford: Oxford University Press, 2004.

–. *Kids' Stuff: Toys and the Changing World of American Childhood.* Cambridge, MA: Harvard University Press, 1997.

–. *Men to Boys: The Making of Modern Immaturity.* New York: Columbia University Press, 2008.

Davis, Simone Weil. *Living Up to the Ads: Gender Fictions of the 1920s.* Durham, NC: Duke University Press, 2000.

Dawson, Michael. *Selling Out or Buying In? Debating Consumerism in Vancouver and Victoria, 1945–1985.* Toronto: University of Toronto Press, 2018.

Demos, John. *Past, Present, and Personal: The Family and the Life Course in American History.* New York: Oxford University Press, 1986.

Dempsey, Lotta. *No Life for a Lady.* Don Mills, ON: Musson Book Company, 1976.

Doucette, Jeff. "Back to School Shopping in Canada, 2019." *Field Agent*, August 1, 2019. https://www.fieldagentcanada.com/blog/back-to-school-2019.

Durflinger, Serge. *Fighting from Home: The Second World War in Verdun, Quebec.* Vancouver: UBC Press, 2006.

Easterbrook, Matthew J., Mark L. Wright, Helga Dittmar, and Robin Banerjee. "Consumer Culture Ideals, Extrinsic Motivations, and Well-Being in Children." *European Journal of Social Psychology* 44, 4 (2014): 349–59.

Enstad, Nan. *Ladies of Labor, Girls of Adventure: Working Women, Popular Culture, and Labor Politics at the Turn of the Twentieth Century.* New York: Columbia University Press, 1999.

Entwistle, Joanne. *The Fashioned Body: Fashion, Dress and Modern Social Theory.* 2nd ed. Cambridge: Polity Press, 2015.

Evans, Caroline. "The Enchanted Spectacle." *Journal of Dress, Body and Culture* 5, 3 (2001): 271–310.

Ewen, Stuart, and Elizabeth Ewen. *Channels of Desire: Mass Images and the Shaping of American Consciousness.* New York: McGraw-Hill, 1982.

Fahrni, Magda. *Household Politics: Montreal Families and Postwar Reconstruction.* Toronto: University of Toronto Press, 2005.

— Selected Bibliography —

Fass, Paula. *The Damned and the Beautiful: American Youth in the 1920s.* Oxford: Oxford University Press, 1977.

Featherstone, Mike. "The Body in Consumer Culture." In *The Body: Social Process and Cultural Theory,* ed. Mike Featherstone, Mike Hepworth, and Bryan S. Turner, 170–96. London: Sage, 1991.

Fowler, David. *The First Teenagers: The Lifestyles of Young Wage-Earners in Interwar Britain.* London: Woburn Press, 1995.

–. *Youth Culture in Modern Britain, c. 1920–1970.* Houndmills, UK: Palgrave Macmillan, 2008.

Francis, Daniel. *The Imaginary Indian: The Image of the Indian in Canadian Culture.* Vancouver: Arsenal Pulp Press, 1992.

Francois, Samantha Yates. "Girls with Influence: Selling Consumerism to Teenage Girls, 1945–1960." PhD diss., University of California Davis, 2003.

Frank, Thomas. *The Conquest of Cool: Business Culture, Counterculture, and the Rise of Hip Consumerism.* Chicago: University of Chicago Press, 1997.

Garvey, Ellen Gruber. *The Adman in the Parlour: Magazines and the Gendering of Consumer Culture, 1880s–1910s.* Oxford: Oxford University Press, 1996.

Gauvreau, Michael. "The Protracted Birth of the Canadian 'Teenager': Work, Citizenship, and the Canadian Youth Commission, 1943–1955." In *Cultures of Citizenship in Post-war Canada, 1940–1955,* ed. Nancy Christie and Michael Gauvreau, 201–38. Montreal and Kingston: McGill-Queen's University Press, 2003.

Gentile, Patrizia. *Queen of the Maple Leaf: Beauty Contests and Settler Femininity.* Vancouver: UBC Press, 2020.

Gidney, Catherine. *Captive Audience: How Corporations Invaded Our Schools.* Toronto: Between the Lines, 2019.

–. "From a 'Disciplined Intelligence' to a 'Culture of Care': Shifting Understandings of Emotions and Citizenship in Twentieth-Century Educational Discourses." *Canadian Historical Review* 103, 4 (2022): 538–62.

Gidney, R.D. *From Hope to Harris: The Reshaping of Ontario Schools.* Toronto: University of Toronto Press, 1999.

Gidney, R.D., and Catherine Gidney. "Branding the Classroom: Commercialism in Canadian Schools, 1920–1960." *Histoire Sociale/Social History* 41, 83 (2008): 345–79. https://doi.org/10.1353/his.0.0041.

Gidney, R.D., and W.P.J. Millar. *How Schools Worked: Public Education in English in Canada, 1800–1940.* Montreal and Kingston: McGill-Queen's University Press, 2012.

Gillis, John R. *Youth and History: Tradition in Change in European Age Relations, 1770–Present.* New York: Academic Press, 1981.

Gladwell, Malcolm. *The Tipping Point: How Little Things Can Make a Big Difference.* New York: Little, Brown and Company, 2000.

Glassford, Sarah, and Amy Shaw, eds. *Making the Best of It: Women and Girls of Canada and Newfoundland during the Second World War.* Vancouver: UBC Press, 2020.

— Selected Bibliography —

Glazebrook, George Parkin de Twenebroker, Katharine B. Brett, and Judith McErvel. *A Shopper's View of Canada's Past: Pages from Eaton's Catalogues, 1886–1930.* Toronto: University of Toronto Press, 1969.

Gleason, Mona. "Children Obviously Don't Make History: Historical Significance and Children's Modalities of Power." *Journal of the History of Childhood and Youth* 16, 3 (2023): 343–60.

–. "Disciplining the Student Body: Schooling and the Construction of Canadian Children's Bodies, 1930 to 1960." *History of Education Quarterly* 41, 2 (2001): 189–215.

–. *Normalizing the Ideal: Psychology, Schooling, and the Family in Postwar Canada.* Toronto: University of Toronto Press, 1999.

–. "'They Have a Bad Effect': Crime Comics, Parliament, and the Hegemony of the Middle Class in Postwar Canada, 1948–1960." In *Pulp Demons: International Dimensions of the Postwar Anticomics Campaign,* ed. John A. Lent, 129–54. Vancouver: Fairleigh Dickinson University Press, 1999.

Gordon, Sarah A. *"Make It Yourself": Home Sewing, Gender, and Culture, 1890–1930.* New York: Columbia University Press, 2009.

Gouda, Frances. "From Emasculated Subjects to Virile Citizens: Nationalism and Modern Dress in Indonesia, 1900–1949." In *Representing Masculinity: Male Citizenship in Modern Western Culture,* ed. Stefan Dudink, Karen Hagemann, and Anna Clark, 235–57. Houndmills, UK: Palgrave Macmillian, 2007.

Gourluck, Russ. *A Store Like No Other: Eaton's of Winnipeg.* Winnipeg: Great Plains Productions, 2004.

Gutman, Marta, and Ning de Coninck-Smith, eds. *Designing Modern Childhoods: History, Space, and the Material Culture of Children.* New Brunswick, NJ: Rutgers University Press, 2008.

Hall, Stuart. "Culture, the Media, and the 'Ideological Effect.'" In *Mass Communication and Society,* ed. James Curran, Michael Gurevitch, and Janet Wollacott, 315–48. London: Edward Arnold, 1977.

–, ed. *Representation: Cultural Representation and Signifying Practices.* London: Sage/ Open University, 1977.

Heron, Craig. "The High School and the Household Economy in Working-Class Hamilton, 1890–1940." *Historical Studies in Education/Revue d'histoire de l'éducation* 7, 2 (1995): 217–59.

Hollander, Anne. *Sex and Suits.* New York: Alfred A. Knopf, 1994.

Hollander, Stanley C. *Was There a Pepsi Generation before Pepsi Discovered It? Youth-Based Segmentation in Marketing.* Chicago: American Marketing Association, 1992.

Hurl, Lorna F. "Restricting Child Labour in Late-Nineteenth-Century Ontario Factories." *Labour/Le Travail* 21 (Spring 1988): 87–121.

Isaksen, Katja Jezkova, and Stuart Roper. "The Commodification of Self-Esteem: Branding and British Teenagers." *Psychology and Marketing* 29, 3 (2012): 117–35.

— Selected Bibliography —

Ishiguro, Laura. "'Growing Up and Grown Up ... in Our Future City': Discourses of Childhood and Settler Futurity in Colonial British Columbia." *BC Studies* 190 (Summer 2016): 15–19.

Jacobson, Lisa. *Children and Consumer Culture in American Society: A Historical Handbook and Guide.* New York: Bloomsbury, 2007.

–. *Raising Consumers: Children in the American Mass Market in the Early Twentieth Century.* New York: Columbia University Press, 2004.

Johansson, Barbro. "Subjectivities of the Child Consumer: Beings and Becomings." In *Childhood and Consumer Culture,* ed. David Buckingham and Vebjorg Tingstad, 80–93. London: Palgrave Macmillan, 2010.

Joselit, Jenna Weissman. *A Perfect Fit: Clothes, Character, and the Promise of America.* New York: Henry Holt, 2001.

Kasser, Tim, and Susan Linn. "Growing Up under Corporate Capitalism: The Problem of Marketing to Children, with Suggestions for Policy Solutions." *Social Issues and Policy Review* 10, 1 (2016): 112–50. https://doi.org/10.1111/sipr.12020.

Keshen, Jeff. *Saints, Sinners, and Soldiers: Canada's Second World War.* Vancouver: UBC Press, 2004.

Kett, Joseph F. *Rites of Passage: Adolescence in America, 1790 to the Present.* New York: Basic Books, 1977.

Korinek, Valerie. *Roughing It in the Suburbs: Reading* Chatelaine *Magazine in the Fifties and Sixties.* Toronto: University of Toronto Press, 2006.

Kidwell, Claudia Brush, and Valerie Steele, eds. *Men and Women: Dressing the Part.* Washington: Smithsonian Institution Press, 1989.

Kuehn, Larry. *Beyond the Bake Sale: Exposing Schoolhouse Commercialism.* Ottawa: Canadian Centre for Policy Alternatives, 2006.

Kutcha, David. *The Three-Piece Suit and Modern Masculinity.* Berkeley: University of California Press, 2002.

La Fleur, Louise Beatrice. "A Comparative Study of Body Measurements of a Selected Group of College Women, with Certain Commercial Patterns." MSc thesis, Department of Textiles and Clothing, Kansas State College of Agricultural and Applied Science, 1931.

Lampland, Martha, and Susan Leigh Star, eds. *Standards and Their Stories: How Quantifying, Classifying, and Formalizing Practices Shape Everyday Life.* Ithaca, NY: Cornell University Press, 2009.

Leach, William. *Land of Desire: Merchants, Power, and the Rise of a New American Culture.* New York: Vintage Books, 1993.

Leacy, F.H., ed., *Historical Statistics of Canada,* 2nd ed. Ottawa: Statistics Canada, 1983. https://www150.statcan.gc.ca/n1/en/catalogue/11-516-X.

Lears, T.J. Jackson, and Richard Wightman Fox, eds. *The Culture of Consumption: Critical Essays in American History, 1880–1980.* New York: Pantheon Books, 1983.

Legget, Robert F. *Standards in Canada.* Ottawa: Information Canada, 1971.

— Selected Bibliography —

Linn, Susan. *Consuming Kids: Protecting Our Children from the Onslaught of Marketing and Advertising.* New York: Anchor Books, 2005.

Liverant, Bettina. *Buying Happiness: The Emergence of Consumer Consciousness in English Canada.* Vancouver: UBC Press, 2018.

–. "From Budgeting to Buying: Canadian Consumerism in the Post War Era." *Past Imperfect* 8 (1999–2000): 62–92.

MacDonald, Heidi. "'Being in Your Twenties, in the Thirties': Liminality and Masculinity during the Great Depression." In *Bringing Children and Youth into Canadian History: The Difference Kids Make,* ed. Mona Gleason and Tamara Myers, 156–67. Toronto: Oxford University Press, 2017.

MacDonald, Sara Z. *University Women: A History of Women and Higher Education in Canada.* Montreal and Kingston: McGill-Queen's University Press, 2021.

MacPherson, Mary-Etta. *Shopkeepers to a Nation: The Eatons.* Toronto: McClelland and Stewart, 1963.

Mahood, Linda. *Thumbing a Ride: Hitchhikers, Hostels, and Counterculture in Canada.* Vancouver: UBC Press, 2019.

Massoni, Kelly. *Fashioning Teenagers: A Cultural History of* Seventeen *Magazine.* Walnut Creek, CA: Left Coast Press, 2010.

–. "'Teena Goes to Market': *Seventeen* Magazine and the Early Construction of the Teen Girl (As) Consumer." *Journal of American Culture* 29, 1 (2006): 31–42.

Maza, Sarah. "The Kids Aren't All Right: Historians and the Problem of Childhood." *American Historical Review* 125, 4 (2020): 1261–85.

McCalla, Douglas. *Consumers in the Bush: Shopping in Rural Upper Canada.* Montreal and Kingston: McGill-Queen's University Press, 2015.

McCutcheon, J.M. "Clothing Children in English Canada, 1880–1930." PhD diss., University of Ottawa, 2002.

McDowell, Linda. *Redundant Masculinities? Employment, Change, and White Working Class Youth.* Malden, MA: Blackwell, 2003.

McIntosh, Robert. "Constructing the Child: New Approaches to the History of Childhood in Canada." *Acadiensis* 28, 2 (1999): 126–40.

McQueen, Rod. *The Eatons: The Rise and Fall of Canada's Royal Family.* Toronto: Stoddart, 1999.

Mendes, Valerie, and Amy De La Haye. *20th Century Fashion.* London: Thames and Hudson, 1999.

Mintz, Steven. *Huck's Raft: A History of American Childhood.* Cambridge, MA: Belknap Press/Harvard University Press, 2004.

Mitchinson, Wendy. *Fighting Fat: Canada, 1920–1980.* Toronto: University of Toronto Press, 2018.

Molnar, Alex. *School Commercialism: From Democratic Ideal to Market Commodity.* New York: Routledge, 2005.

Molyneaux, Heather Ann. "The Representation of Women in 'Chatelaine' Magazine Advertisements: 1928–1970." MA thesis, University of New Brunswick, 2002.

— Selected Bibliography —

Nayak, Anoop, and Mary Jane Kehily. *Gender, Youth and Culture: Young Masculinities and Femininities*. Houndmills, UK: Palgrave Macmillan, 2008.

Neuborne, Ellen. "We Are Going to Own This Generation." *Business Week*, February 15, 1999, 80–88.

Nicholas, Jane. *The Modern Girl: Feminine Modernities, the Body, and Commodities in the 1920s*. Toronto: University of Toronto Press, 2015.

–. "On Display: Bodies and Consumption in the 'New' Canadian Cultural History." *History Compass* 17, 2 (2019). https://doi.org/10.1111/hic3.12519.

O'Donnell, Lorraine. "Visualizing the History of Women at Eaton's, 1869 to 1976." PhD diss., McGill University, 2002.

Olsen, Stephanie, Kristine Alexander, Susan Miller, Ville Vuolanto, Simon Sleight, Mischa Honeck, Sarah Emily Duff, and Karen Vallgårda. "A Critical Conversation on Agency." *Journal of the History of Childhood and Youth* 17, 2 (2024): 169–87.

Onusko, James. *Boom Kids: Growing Up in the Calgary Suburbs, 1950–1970*. Waterloo, ON: Wilfrid Laurier University Press, 2021.

Osbourne, W.A. "Opportunities for Young Men and Women in Canada." *Canadian Education* 3, 1 (1947): 91.

Owram, Doug. *Born at the Right Time: A History of the Baby Boom Generation*. Toronto: University of Toronto Press, 1996.

Packard, Vance. *The Hidden Persuaders*. New York: Pocket Books, 1981.

Palladino, Grace. *Teenagers: An American History*. New York: Basic Books, 1996.

Parr, Joy. *Domestic Goods: The Material, the Moral, and the Economic in the Postwar Years*. Toronto: University of Toronto Press, 1999.

Peate, Mary. *Girl in a Sloppy Joe Sweater: Life on the Canadian Home Front during World War II*. Montreal: Optimum Publishing International, 1988.

Peiss, Kathy. *Hope in a Jar: The Making of America's Beauty Culture*. Philadelphia: University of Pennsylvania Press, 1998.

–. *Zoot Suit: The Enigmatic Career of an Extreme Style*. Philadelphia: University of Pennsylvania Press, 2011.

Penfold, Steve. *A Mile of Make-Believe: A History of the Eaton's Santa Claus Parade*. Toronto: University of Toronto Press, 2016.

Peril, Lynn. *College Girls: Bluestockings, Sex Kittens, and Coeds, Then and Now*. New York: W.W. Norton, 2006.

Phenix, Patricia. *Eatonians: The Story of the Family behind the Family*. Toronto: McClelland and Stewart, 2002.

Prince, Samuel Henry. "The Canadian Family in Wartime." *Marriage and Family Living* 4, 2 (1942): 25–28.

Robbins, J.E. *Dependency of Youth: A Study Based on the Census of 1931 and Supplementary Data*. Census Monograph no. 9. Ottawa: Dominion Bureau of Statistics, 1937.

Robinson, Daniel. *Cigarette Nation: Business, Health, and Canadian Smokers, 1930–1975*. Montreal and Kingston: McGill-Queen's University Press, 2021.

— Selected Bibliography —

Rollwagen, Katharine. "Classrooms for Consumer Society: Practical Education and Secondary School Reform in Post-Second World War Canada." *Historical Studies in Education* 28, 1 (2016): 21–41.

–. "The Young Medium: Regulating Television in the Name of Canadian Childhood." *Canadian Historical Review* 101, 1 (2020): 27–48.

Rudy, Jared. *The Freedom to Smoke: Tobacco Consumption and Identity.* Montreal and Kingston: McGill-Queen's University Press, 2005.

Ryan, Patrick. "How 'New' Is the New Social Study of Childhood? The Myth of a Paradigm Shift." *Journal of Interdisciplinary History* 38, 4 (2008): 553–76.

Santink, Joy. *Timothy Eaton and the Rise of His Department Store.* Toronto: University of Toronto Press, 1990.

Savage, Jon. *Teenage: The Creation of Youth, 1875–1945.* London: Chatto and Windus, 2007.

–. "Time Up for the Teenager?" *RSA Journal* 160, 5557 (2014): 19.

Scanlon, Jennifer. *Inarticulate Longings: The* Ladies' Home Journal, *Gender, and the Promises of Consumer Culture.* New York: Routledge, 1995.

Schor, Juliet. *Born to Buy: The Commericialized Child and the New Consumer Culture.* New York: Scribner, 2004.

Schrum, Kelly. *Some Wore Bobby Sox: The Emergence of Teenage Girls' Culture, 1920–1945.* New York: Palgrave Macmillan, 2004.

Schwartz Cohen, Ruth. *More Work for Mother: The Ironies of Household Technology from the Open Hearth to the Microwave.* New York: Basic Books, 1983.

Seiter, Ellen. *Sold Separately: Parents and Children in Consumer Culture.* New Brunswick, NJ: Rutgers University Press, 1993.

Smith, Michelle J., and Jane Nicholas. "Soft Rejuvenation: Cosmetics, Idealized White Femininity, and Young Women's Bodies, 1880–1930." *Journal of Social History* 53, 4 (2020): 906–21.

Snell, James G., and Cynthia Comacchio Abeele. "Regulating Nuptiality: Restricting Access to Marriage in Early Twentieth-Century English-Speaking Canada." *Canadian Historical Review* 69, 4 (1988): 466–89. https://doi.org/10.3138/CHR-069-04-02.

Snyder, Thomas D., ed. *120 Years of American Education: A Statistical Portrait.* Washington: National Office of Education Statistics, 1993.

Sparrman, Anna, Bengt Sandin, and Johanna Sjöberg, eds. *Situating Child Consumption: Rethinking Values and Notions of Children, Childhood and Consumption.* Lund, Sweden: Nordic Academic Press, 2012.

Spencer, Erin. *Lipstick and High Heels: War, Gender, and Popular Culture.* Kingston, ON: Canadian Defence Academy Press, 2007.

Spring, Joel. *Educating the Consumer-Citizen: A History of the Marriage of Schools, Advertising, and Media.* Mahwah, NJ: Lawrence Erlbaum Associates, 2003.

Springhall, John. *Coming of Age: Adolescence in Britain, 1860–1960.* Dublin: Gill and Macmillan, 1986.

— Selected Bibliography —

–. *Youth, Popular Culture and Moral Panics: Penny Gaffs to Gansta-Rap, 1830–1996.* New York: St. Martin's Press, 1998.

Srigley, Katrina. *Breadwinning Daughters: Single Working Women in a Depression-Era City, 1929–1939.* Toronto: University of Toronto Press, 2010.

–. "Clothing Stories: Consumption, Identity, and Desire in Depression-Era Toronto." *Journal of Women's History* 19, 1 (2007): 82–104.

Stanger-Ross, Jordan, Christina Collins, and Mark J. Stern. "Falling Far from the Tree: Transitions to Adulthood and the Social History of Twentieth-Century America." *Social Science History* 29, 4 (2005): 625–48.

Statistics Canada. *Canadian Demographics at a Glance.* Catalogue number 91-003-XWE. Ottawa: Statistics Canada, 2007. https://www150.statcan.gc.ca/n1/pub/91-003-x/91-003-x2007001-eng.pdf.

–. *Historical Compendium of Education Statistics from Confederation to 1975.* Ottawa: Statistics Canada, 1978.

Stearns, Peter N. *Childhood in World History.* New York: Routledge, 2006.

Stephens, Jennifer. *Pick One Intelligent Girl: Employability, Domesticity, and the Gendering of Canada's Welfare State, 1939–1947.* Toronto: University of Toronto Press, 2007.

Stortz, Paul, and Lisa Panayotidis. "Visual Interpretations, Cartoons, and Caricatures of Student Youth Cultures in University Yearbooks, 1898–1930." *Journal of the Canadian Historical Association* 19, 1 (2008): 195–227.

Sutherland, Fraser. *The Monthly Epic: A History of Canadian Magazines, 1789–1989.* Markham, ON: Fitzhenry and Whiteside, 1989.

Sutherland, Neil. *Children in English-Canadian Society: Framing the Twentieth-Century Consensus.* Toronto: University of Toronto Press, 1976.

–. *Growing Up: Childhood in English Canada from the Great War to the Age of Television.* Toronto: University of Toronto Press, 1997.

–. "Popular Media in the Culture of English-Canadian Children in the Twentieth Century." *Historical Studies in Education* 14, 1 (2002): 1–33.

T. Eaton Company. *The Story of a Store: The History of Eaton's from 1869.* Toronto: T. Eaton Company, 1947.

Tebbutt, Melanie. *Making Youth: A History of Youth in Modern Britain.* London: Palgrave, 2016.

Thompson, Cheryl. *Beauty in a Box: Detangling the Roots of Canada's Black Beauty Culture.* Waterloo, ON: Wilfrid Laurier University Press, 2019.

–. "'I'se in Town, Honey': Reading Aunt Jemima Advertising in Canadian Print Media, 1919 to 1962." *Journal of Canadian Studies* 49, 1 (2015): 205–37.

Tillotson, Shirley. *The Public at Play: Gender and the Politics of Recreation in Post-war Ontario.* Toronto: University of Toronto Press, 2000.

Tinkler, Penny. *Constructing Girlhood: Popular Magazines for Girls Growing Up in England, 1920–1950.* London: Taylor and Francis, 1995.

— Selected Bibliography —

–. "*Miss Modern*: Youthful Feminine Modernity and the Nascent Teenager, 1930–1940." In *Women's Periodicals and Print Culture in Britain, 1918–1939: The Interwar Period,* ed. Catherine Clay, Maria DiCenzo, Barbara Green, and Fiona Hackney, 153–69. Edinburgh: Edinburgh University Press, 2018.

Trentmann, Frank. "Beyond Consumerism: New Historical Perspectives on Consumption." *Journal of Contemporary History* 39, 3 (2003): 373–401.

Ulrich, Martha Jane. "A Comparison of the Body Measurements of Girls from 6 to 14 with the Measurements of Dresses of Corresponding Size." MSc thesis, Department of Textiles and Clothing, Kansas State College of Agricultural and Applied Science, 1938.

Valverde, Mariana. "Building Anti-delinquent Communities: Morality, Gender, and Generation in the City." In *A Diversity of Women: Women in Ontario since 1945,* ed. Joy Parr, 46–72. Toronto: University of Toronto Press, 1995.

Vancouver Centennial Museum. *The Shopping Guide of the West: Woodward's Catalogues, 1898–1953.* Vancouver: J.J. Douglas, 1977.

Wailoo, Keith. *Pushing Cool: Big Tobacco, Racial Marketing, and the Untold Story of the Menthol Cigarette.* Chicago: University of Chicago Press, 2021.

Walker, Nancy A. *Shaping Our Mothers' World: American Women's Magazines.* Jackson: University Press of Mississippi, 2000.

Wall, Sharon. *The Nurture of Nature: Childhood, Antimodernism, and Ontario Summer Camps, 1920–1955.* Vancouver: UBC Press, 2009.

Warsh, Cheryl Krasnick, and Dan Malleck, eds. *Consuming Modernity: Gendered Behaviour and Consumerism before the Baby Boom.* Vancouver: UBC Press, 2013.

Weinbaum, Alys Eve, Lynn M. Thomas, Priti Ramamurthy, Uta G. Poiger, Madeleine Yue Dong, and Tani Barlow, eds. *The Modern Girl around the World: Consumption, Modernity, and Globalization.* Durham, NC: Duke University Press, 2008.

Wiedmann, Klaus-Peter, Nadine Hennigs, and Sascha Langner. "Spreading the Word of Fashion: Identifying Social Influencers in Fashion Marketing." *Journal of Global Fashion Marketing* 1, 3 (2010): 142–53.

Willis, Paul. *Learning to Labour: How Working-Class Kids Get Working-Class Jobs.* Farnborough, UK: Saxon House, 1977.

Wright, Cynthia. "Feminine Trifles of Vast Importance: Writing Gender into the History of Consumption." In *Gender Conflicts: New Essays in Women's History,* ed. Franca Iacovetta and Mariana Valverde, 229–60. Toronto: University of Toronto Press, 1992.

–. "'The Most Prominent Rendezvous of the Feminine Toronto': Eaton's College Street and the Organization of Shopping in Toronto, 1920–1950." PhD diss., University of Toronto, 1992.

Zelizer, Viviana A. *Pricing the Priceless Child: The Changing Social Value of Childhood.* New York: Basic Books, 1985.

Zukin, Sharon. *Point of Purchase: How Shopping Changed American Culture.* New York: Routledge, 2004.

Image Credits

1.1 Reprinted with the permission of the Kimberly-Clark Corporation. National Library Collection, Library and Archives Canada, 1081127940.

1.2 National Library Collection, Library and Archives Canada, 1080359730.

1.3 Archives of Ontario, F 229-308-0-2239, T. Eaton Company fonds, Eaton's Archives photographic and documentary art subject files, Promotions – Man. – Winnipeg – Youth – Eaton's Jr. Councillors and Jr. Executives.

2.1 Reprinted with the permission of the Archives de la Ville de Montreal, P500-Y-1_068-004.

3.1 Archives of Ontario, F 229-308-0-2239, T. Eaton Company fonds, Eaton's Archives photographic and documentary art subject files, Promotions – Man. – Winnipeg – Youth – Eaton's Jr. Councillors and Jr. Executives.

3.2 Reprinted with the permission of the Archives de la Ville de Montreal, P500-Y-1_068-017.

3.3 Archives of Ontario, F 229-308-0-2239, T. Eaton Company fonds, Eaton's Archives photographic and documentary art subject files, Promotions – Man. – Winnipeg – Youth – Eaton's Jr. Councillors and Jr. Executives.

3.4 Archives of Ontario, F 229-153-0-3, T. Eaton Company fonds, Eaton Auditorium programmes and handbills, Eaton Auditorium Programmes – Miscellaneous.

3.5 Archives of Ontario, F 229-308-0-1899, T. Eaton Company fonds, Eaton's Archives photographic and documentary art subject files, Merchandise – Ont. – Toronto – Dresses – includes Business Girl's shop – 4th floor, Queen St. store.

3.6 Archives of Ontario, F 229-308-0-1899, T. Eaton Company fonds, Eaton's Archives photographic and documentary art subject files, Merchandise – Ont. – Toronto – Dresses – includes Business Girl's shop – 4th floor, Queen St. store.

4.1 Archives of Ontario, F 229-1-0-115, T. Eaton Company fonds, T. Eaton Toronto catalogues, Fall/Winter 1935–36.

4.2 Archives of Ontario, F 229-1-0-139, T. Eaton Company fonds, T. Eaton Toronto catalogues, Spring/Summer 1941.

4.3 Archives of Ontario, F 229-1-0-169, T. Eaton Company fonds, T. Eaton Toronto catalogues, Spring/Summer 1948.

4.4 Archives of Ontario, F 229-1-0-172, T. Eaton Company fonds, T. Eaton Toronto catalogues, Fall/Winter 1948–49.

— Image Credits —

5.1 Reprinted with the permission of the Archives de la Ville de Montreal, P500-Y-1_068-003.

5.2 Reprinted with the permission of the Archives de la Ville de Montreal, P500-Y-1_068-016.

5.3 Reprinted with the permission of the Archives de la Ville de Montreal, P500-Y-1_068-015.

5.4 Archives of Ontario, F 229-308-0-2251, T. Eaton Company fonds, Eaton's Archives photographic and documentary art subject files, Research Bureau – Ont. – Toronto – Mr. E.J. Tyrrell.

Index

Note: "(f)" after a page number indicates a figure. *CHJ* stands for *Canadian Home Journal.*

Abercrombie & Fitch, 103
Acton, James, 25
Adams, Mary Louise, 53, 74, 133
adolescence, 5, 7–8; changing meaning due to Baby Boom generation, 4; defined by puberty, 8, 51, 174n91; importance of physical and social success during, 75–76
adolescents, 5, 13, 21, 39; and awkward body shapes, 111, 115–16, 123, 129; cultural influence of, 4; as distinct from teenagers or youths, 9; and propensity to adopt fads, 73–76; skin care advice for, 42. *See also* adolescence; teenagers; youth
advertising: and child psychology, 74; coolhunting, 132–33; critique of, 18–19; of fur coats, 35–36; and mass-market magazines, 25–26, 33; part of the "beauty industrial complex," 46; and racialized stereotypes of Black women, 28–29; in schools, 130–31, 141–44; to teenagers, 9, 31, 155; to women, 6
advisory groups, 55–64. *See also* Eaton's Junior Council and Executive; Teen Session (*CHJ*); 'Teen-Age Specials (*Chatelaine*)
Alexander, Jean, 42

Alexander, Kristine, 17
allowance, 4, 18, 35, 147. *See also* budgeting; spending money
appearance: and age-appropriate dress, 110–13; and beauty advice, 40–44; of Eaton's staff, 84; feminine, 25, 32, 36–40, 51, 58, 77–78, 128–29; masculine, 9, 58, 67, 69, 113, 128–29; as reflection of personality, 74–77; teenaged, 14, 32, 47–49, 53, 69–71, 85, 120–21, 124; on university campuses, 36–40. *See also* co-ed; sloppy joe sweater; zoot suit
Aunt Jemima, 29

back-to-school shopping, 31, 35–37, 166n32
Band Box, 94, 136–38
Beauprie, Don, 60(f)
beauty pageants. *See* pageants
Belisle, Donica, 151
Boys' (size range): adjectives used to describe, 124–25, 181n73; changing physique of boys wearing, 120; colours offered in catalogue, 125; correlation between size and age, 108–9, 179n35; distinguishing between smaller and larger boys, 113–15; vs Grad suits, 120; lack of sizing standards, 108. *See also* Grad (size range); suits; zoot suit
Brockie, J.A. (Jack): creator of the Junior Council and Executive, 56–57,

— Index —

82–83; effectiveness of teen advisory councils, 63–64; plans to connect store promotions to high school clubs, 138; relationships with school administrators, 142–44; request for extra funds for fashion shows, 90; role at Eaton's, 11–12

Brown, Audrey, 102

Brown, Tom, 67

budgeting: to pay for fads, 78; to pay for new clothing, 35–36, 56; as a valuable skill for teenaged girls, 78

Buri, George, 73

Calling All Girls (magazine), 27

Canadian Council on Child Welfare, 15

Canadian Education (journal), 146

Canadian Education Association, 145–49

Canadian High News, 59, 95, 138

Canadian Home Journal (CHJ), 14, 20; audience, 26–27, 30, 41; and back-to-school issues, 31, 41; and beauty advice, 41–42; and budgeting, 78–79; circulation, 26, 165n9; and columns for teenaged readers, 30, 32, 53; and Cover Girl competition, 44–50, 91, 99; and shaping the co-ed identity, 25, 29–30; and teen advisory groups, 56, 62–63; and teenage fads, 65, 70, 76–80. *See also* Garner, Grace; Kirk, Helen; Teen Session *(CHJ)*; Teenager's Datebook *(CHJ)*; 'Teens and Twenties *(CHJ)*

Canadian Manufacturers' Association, 146

Canadian Research Committee on Practical Education, 145–48

Canadian Retail Federation, 146

Canadian Youth Commission, 17, 148

casual clothing: on college campuses, 38–39, 61; criticisms of, 70–72; rise of

sportswear in Canadian wardrobes, 106. *See also* sloppy joe sweater

Chanel, Coco, 126

Chatelaine, 14, 20, 24(f), 25; audience, 27; and back-to-school content, 31, 166n32; and beauty advice, 36–40, 41–43; circulation, 26, 165n9; and columns for teenaged readers, 31–33; and constructions of whiteness, 29; and shaping the co-ed identity, 25, 29–30; and teen advisory groups, 56, 61–62; and teenage fads, 70–71, 77, 79–80. *See also* Damon, Carolyn; Dempsey, Lotta; Teen Tempo *(Chatelaine)*; 'Teen-Age Specials *(Chatelaine)*

childhood: commercialization of, 83–84; and consumer culture, 18–20, 156; growing distinction from adulthood in the twentieth century, 15–16, 18, 52–55; loss of childhood innocence during wartime, 57; role in establishing settler state, 16–18

Clare, John, 3–4, 22, 154

class. *See* middle class

clothing. *See* Boys' (size range); casual clothing; dresses; fur coats; Girls' (size range); Grad (size range); Senior Girls' (size range); suits; Women's (size range); zoot suit

co-ed: and affluence, 34–36; as audience for magazine content, 29–30; and beauty advice, 40–44; definition of, 20–21; figure on college campuses, 36–40; as a growing segment of the American retail market, 30; representation in magazines, 24–25, 27, 31; variation of the modern girl, 29; and whiteness, 49–50

College Toggery (Eaton's), 97, 99, 100(f)

Collegiate Club (Simpson's), 13, 56–57, 59

Collins, Cora Sue, 97, 98(f)

(204)

— Index —

Comacchio, Cynthia, 5, 7
Combe, Vivien, 152
Commercial High School, 143(f)
commercial persona, 9–10, 13, 20–21, 155, 158
commercial-sartorial hierarchy, 95–102
Coninck-Smith, Ning de, 16
Conor, Liz, 28, 47–48
consumer education, 149–53
consumerism, 4–6, 10, 18; and environmental degradation, 156; feminist debates about, 19; key to national development, 28; more limited expansion in postwar Canada, 55; and psychological consequences for young people, 156–57
Consumers' Association of Canada, 108
Cook, Daniel Thomas, 9–10, 20, 95–96
Cook, Pat, 152
coolhunting, 132–33
Cover Girl competition, 44–50, 91, 99; display of winner in Eaton's College Toggery, 100(f)

Damon, Carolyn, 71, 77–78
Dawson, Michael, 14
Dempsey, Lotta, 61–62, 70–71
department stores: as agents of modernization, 5; and distinct retail spaces defined by gender, 83; and fashion shows, 91, 93; and financial support for the Canadian Research Committee on Practical Education, 146; as part of an expanding consumer society, 5, 8; paternalism, 84–85, 102; and services for middle-class women, 83–84; shared marketing techniques, 13–14; and teenage shops, 95; and youth advisory groups, 55–57, 63–64. See also Dupuis Frères (department

store); Eaton's; Holman's (department store); Hudson's Bay Company (department store); John Northway & Sons (department store); Macy's (department store); Marshall Fields (department store); Montgomery Ward (department store); Ogilvy's (department store); Powers (department store); Sears Roebuck (department store); Simpson's (department store); Spencer's (department store)
Desmond, Viola, 29
Dick, David, 66
dresses: formal, 94; as part of the "college trousseau," 37; use in sample, 106. See also Girls' (size range); Juniors' and Misses' (size range); Senior Girls' (size range); Teenster (size range); Women's (size range)
Dupuis Frères (department store), 13, 105, 146
Durbin, Deanna, 115–16
Durflinger, Serge, 68

Eaton, R.Y., 84
Eaton, Timothy, 84
Eaton's: agent of modernization, 5; commodification of female employees, 131; Contacts (newsletter), 57, 85, 93; market share, 10; paternalism 84–85, 102; relationship with school boards and schools, 140–44. See also Brockie, J.A. (Jack); College Toggery (Eaton's); Eaton's Junior Council and Executive; Eaton's mail-order catalogue; Hi-Spot (Eaton's); Miller, T.M. (Tom); Santa Claus Parade; Young Canada Shops; Young Moderns' Shop, Young Toronto Shop (Eaton's)

— Index —

Eaton's College Street, 12, 152; Junior Council and Executive activities at, 86, 87(f), 88; location of the Young Canada Shops, 101

Eaton's Junior Council and Executive: application process, 133–35, 139, 184n22; contests, 46, 49–50, 88, 148–49; and Eaton's advertising, 59, 60(f), 98, 135, 138; field trips, 150–52; gendered activities of, 91–95, 149–53; as influencers, 132–34; meeting locations, 86–88; meeting minutes sampled, 186n59; and merchandise approval tags, 59; program description, 11, 85, 131; program origins, 56–57, 83; as a public relations exercise, 22, 138, 144; publicity about 85, 144; and surveys, 58–59; uniform, 85; volunteering in the stores, 90. *See also* advisory groups; Cover Girl competition; fashion shows; part-time jobs

Eaton's mail-order catalogue, 5, 9, 103–6; illustrations, 109, 126–28. *See also* Boys' (size range); Girls' (size range); Grad (size range); Juniors' and Misses' (size range); Senior Girls' (size range); Teenster (size range); Women's (size range)

education: attainment, 33–34; practical, 22, 145–49. *See also* consumer education; high school

fads: commodification of, 65, 79, 124; definition of, 64; and do-it-yourself projects, 78–79; as a form of self-expression for teens, 55, 73–78; and juvenile delinquency, 72–73; symbolizing immaturity during Second World War, 64–73; using advisory groups to identify, 56–57. *See also* sloppy joe sweater; zoot suit

fashion shows, 90–95, 135, 138, 148

Featherstone, Mike, 50

Fellows, Rusty, 87(f)

femininity: association with passive consumption, 9; and beauty contests, 44–50; and clothing styles, 104; and fads, 76–78; and fashion shows, 91–94; and heteronormativity, 121–23; performed in department stores, 86; and purchasing power, 5; taught to girls in magazines, 31–32; threatened by sloppy dress, 69–73; threatened by waged work in wartime, 69–70; and whiteness, 5, 20–21, 28–29, 49–50. *See also* appearance; Cover Girl competition; gender

Financial Times, 146

Fleming, Dot, 93–94

Forever 21, 103

Foster, L., 93

fur coats, 35–36

Garner, Grace, 30–31, 34, 39, 76

Garvey, Ellen Gruber, 25

gender: and consumer education, 132, 149–53; and fads, 64–65; and fashion shows, 90–95; and growth, 115–16, 119–20, 129; and retail employment, 149; and retail space, 82, 84; and selling clothing in mail-order catalogues, 103, 104, 107, 118, 121, 123

Gentile, Patrizia, 45–46, 48

Gidney, Catherine, 130–31

Girls' (size range): colours offered in catalogue, 113, 126; correlation between size and age, 107–8; lack of sizing standards, 108; vs Senior Girls' (size range), 112(f); vs Teenster (size range), 118–20; typical style features of dresses in, 111, 113, 117(f), 123. *See also* Senior Girls' (size range); Teenster (size range)

(206)

— Index —

Girls' Own Paper, 27
Gladwell, Malcolm, 132
Gleason, Mona, 74
Globe and Mail, 14, 58, 59, 65, 94
Grad (size range): colours, 125; comparison to Boys' and Men's sizes, 120–21, 181*n*73; connecting suits to social status and masculinity, 121, 123–24, 127–29; cost savings, 120; description, 120; first use in catalogue, 118. *See also* Boys' (size range); suits; zoot suit
Gutman, Marta, 16

Hall, G. Stanley, 8
Hall, Stuart, 14, 27
Hardy, Joy, 49–50
Heffernan, J.P., 63–64
high school: and age grading, 162*n*39; Eaton's employees' relationship with administrators, 140–44; enrolment, 33, 54, 139; suggestions to reform the curriculum, 146–48. *See also* education; high school students
high school students: as consumers, 8, 13, 44; as cover girls, 44–50; labelled an ideal teenager, 4, 30–32, 54–55; members of advisory groups, 55–63; target of magazine content and advertising, 20–21, 24–25
Hi-Spot (Eaton's), 95–102
Hollister, 103
Holman's (department store), 10
home economics, 151–53
Hudson's Bay Company (department store), 13, 146
Hunt, Marjorie, 152

Ishiguro, Laura, 16

Jacobson, Lisa, 116
Jewell, Milton, 142

John Northway & Sons (department store), 56
Junior Boys' (size range). *See* Boys' (size range)
Junior councillors. *See* Eaton's Junior Council and Executive
"Junior Deb": to describe Eaton's Hi-Spot customer, 97
Junior Executives. *See* Eaton's Junior Council and Executive
Junior Fashion Council, 56–57
Junior League, 26, 167*n*46
Juniors' and Misses' (size range), 107–8; associated with body shape rather than age, 109; available in black, 126; as mature styles that created an hourglass shape, 119–20; sold in the Young Moderns' Shop and College Toggery, 97; worn by older teens, 100, 101. *See also* Women's (size range)
juvenile delinquency, 54, 62, 73, 75, 145, 147. *See also* fads

Kelly, Evelyn, 36, 61
Kirk, Helen, 63
Knapman, C., 138
Kotex sanitary napkins, 24, 24(f), 43–44

Ladies' Home Journal, 25, 30
Langston, Corinne, 76–77
Laycock, Samuel, 75–76
Lister, Eve, 78
Liverant, Bettina, 5, 6, 55

MacDonald, Heidi, 53
Mackie, Ellen, 71
Maclean, J.B., 25
Maclean Hunter, 26–27, 33, 165*n*9
Maclean's, 3, 4, 75, 155
Macy's (department store), 13
magazines. *See* women's magazines
Mahood, Linda, 157

(207)

— Index —

mail-order catalogues. *See* Eaton's mail-order catalogue

Malvern Collegiate Institute, 142

market actors, 14, 17, 18, 53; definition of, 4, 8; legitimizing young people's participation in consumer marketplace, 19–21, 55, 74; and repeated discovery of teenaged consumer, 155; use of terms to describe younger customers, 9

market research, 154–56. *See also* advisory groups; Eaton's Junior Council and Executive

Marshall Fields (department store), 13

masculinity, 129; and boys' participation in fashion shows, 93–95; and dress, 104; and heterosexuality, 128; military uniform vs zoot suit, 66, 69; and pant length, 113; and shopping priorities, 86, 123; and style consciousness, 121, 124. *See also* suits; zoot suit

Mayfair, 14, 20; audience, 26–27, 30, 41; and back-to-school content, 31, 41, 166n32; and beauty advice, 41–42; and budgeting, 35; circulation, 26; and shaping the co-ed identity, 25, 29–31, 37–39; and teen advisory groups, 61; and teenage fads, 70–72. *See also* fur coats; Mackie, Ellen; Stayner, Gertrude

McCall's Magazine, 25

McDowell, Linda, 157–58

McMaster University, 61

measuring: for mail-order catalogues, 107–8, 119(t)

menstruation, 41–44

middle class: association with consumer culture, 7, 10; and department stores, 83, 104; mothers, 10; parents, 18; and postwar childhoods, 55; racialized as white, 10, 44, 46; reformers, 15; as targeted

teenaged customer, 7, 13, 24, 34, 50, 64–65, 95, 140; and women's magazines, 26, 27, 30

Miller, T.M. (Tom), 11, 133–34, 138, 140

Miss Chatelaine, 15, 27, 33

Miss Modern, 27

Misses' (size range), 107–8; association with youth, 109; colours, 112–13, 182n86; compared to Teenster sizes, 119–20, 126; description, 109; preferred by junior councillors, 97, 100

Mitchinson, Wendy, 12, 178n9

modelling: in advertisements, 59, 60(f); by Eaton's junior councillors, 46, 60(f), 93–94. *See also* Cover Girl competition; fashion shows

modern girl, 6, 25, 28–29, 40, 42

Montgomery Ward (department store), 13

Mooney, John, 150

mothers: as audience for consumer magazines, 30; and breeching, 113; as consumers, 9–10, 12, 82–84, 114, 118; disagreements with daughters while shopping, 82–83, 96; as responsible for cultivating good taste in daughters, 74–75, 77–78

National Selective Service, 70–71

Nicholas, Jane, 28, 40

Nurick, Irving, 24

Ogilvy's (department store), 13

Ontario Farm Service Force, 67

Onusko, James, 4

Osbourne, W.A., 147

Owram, Doug, 4

Packard, Vance, 18–19, 142

pageants, 45–46, 48; and similarities to fashion shows, 91; and visual culture, 28. *See also* Cover Girl competition; fashion shows

(208)

— Index —

Parents (magazine), 74–75
part-time jobs, 134, 139; and connection to completing high school, 148; at Eaton's, 89–90, 148–49; as part of the high school curriculum, 146–48
Peate, Mary, 23–25, 34
Penfold, Steve, 10, 11
Powers (department store), 95
practical education. *See* education
puberty, 24; and changing styles of dress, 96, 107, 115; linked to adolescence, 8; linked to girls' desires for fads, 77, 174*n*91; as period of social adjustment, 75; threatening an ideal appearance, 41–44. *See also* adolescence; adolescents; teenagers

Queen's University, 61

retailers. *See* department stores; Eaton's
Rice, Rosemary, 97, 98(f)
Robb, C.W., 143
Robert Simpson Company, 13, 56, 146. *See also* Simpson's (department store)
Runnymede Collegiate, 141

sanitary napkins, 24(f), 31, 42–44
Santa Claus Parade, 10, 11, 13; and child consumers, 83–84; Jack Brockie's organization of, 56; Junior councillors' and executives' participation in, 89
Saturday Night (magazine), 25
Saunders, Leslie, 73
Savage, Jon, 157
Schrum, Kelly, 78
Sears Roebuck (department store), 13
Second World War: as an event that shaped adults' views of children and growing up, 17, 54, 57; and patriotic consumption, 21; and per capita consumption, 6; and regulation of

suit styles, 65–66; remake clinics, 66; and women's employment, 69
secondary school. *See* high school
Senior Boys' (size range). *See* Boys' (size range)
Senior Girls' (size range), 110–13
Seventeen (magazine), 15, 27, 31
sewing: advertisements for patterns and sewing machines, 30, 31, 105; altering or making clothing to keep up with fads, 78–79; replicating clothing in mail-order catalogues, 105
shopping: in the children's wear department, 99; as a feminine activity, 58, 83, 86, 96, 123; and loyalty, 84; to prepare for the beginning of school, 32, 35; as a skill, 78; teenagers shopping without mothers, 97; and understanding girls' clothing preferences, 56, 99; window shopping, 105
Simpson's (department store), 13, 57, 59
skin care, 42–43
Skinner, Patricia, 49
sloppy joe sweater, 64–65, 69–73
Smith, J., 98
Spencer's (department store), 10
spending money, 7, 36. *See also* allowance
Srigley, Katrina, 105
St. Andrew's College (Toronto), 142
standard sizing for ready-made clothing, 108
Staples Canada, 131
Stayner, Gertrude, 35, 36, 76
"Store for Young Canada" (Eaton's slogan), 11, 88, 90
students. *See* co-ed; high school students; university
suits, 88, 106, 110; and heteronormative masculinity, 123; wartime regulation

(209)

of, 65–66. *See also* Boys' (size range); Grad (size range); zoot suit

Sutherland, Neil, 15–16

teen clothing. *See* Grad (size range); Teenster (size range)

Teen Session (*CHJ*), 32, 62–63, 166n32

Teen Tempo (*Chatelaine*), 32, 78–80, 166n32

'Teen-Age Specials (*Chatelaine*), 31, 62

teenagers: as capable consumers, 3–4, 20, 53, 57, 80, 149, 156; as a market segment, 5, 9, 11, 15, 33; racialized as white, 17–18, 49–50; symbols of a national future, 17, use of the term to describe young people, 8–9, 160n16

Teenager's Datebook (*CHJ*), 32, 78, 166n32

'Teens and Twenties (*CHJ*), 30–31

Teenster (size range), 118–23, 125–27; sold in fashion colours, 182n85

Thompson, Cheryl, 28–29

Thornton, Margaret, 37

Tinkler, Penny, 31

toddler, 9, 16; as a distinct market and clothing size, 74, 108

Toronto Board of Education, 143

Toronto Daily Star, 67, 118

tween, 16

university: as an aspiration of Junior Executive applicants, 139–40; enrolment in Canada compared to United States, 33–34; location of the co-ed, 25, 29, 34, 36–40

University College (University of Toronto), 61

Valverde, Mariana, 73

Verdun, QC, 68–69

Victoria's Secret, 103

visual culture, 28

Warner, B., 97, 101

Wartime Prices and Trade Board (WPTB), 65–66

White, Adele, 42, 76

Wilcox, Vivian, 43

Williams, Cynthia, 79

Williamson, Dave, 67

Willis, Paul, 157

Wolf, Eva Nagel, 41–43, 49

women: and clothing sizes in mail-order catalogues, 107–9, 178n9; and feminist debates about consumption, 19; as home economists, 151; increasing purchasing power of, 5, 25, 40; as irrational consumers, 64, 84, 123; and pageants, 48; and university enrolment before 1960, 33–34; white, settler women as ideal, 28–29, 40–41, 109–10; working outside the home, 30, 34, 53, 153, 162n38. *See also* co-ed; femininity; modern girl; mothers

Women's (size range), 107–8; described as youthful, 111; inconsistency of, 178n9; overlap with Juniors' and Misses' sizes, 109; sold in fashion colours, 113, 125–26; styled for adult women, 110–11. *See also* dresses

women's magazines: audience, 23, 26–27, 41; excluding representations of Indigenous, Black, and other racialized women, 28–29; and origins in trade publications, 25–26; read by teenaged girls, 23–24. See also *Canadian Home Journal* (*CHJ*); *Chatelaine*; *Mayfair*

Wornell, W. Lloyd, 88, 134, 141

Young Canada Shops, 101–2

Young Moderns' Shop, Young Toronto Shop (Eaton's), 97, 99, 101

— Index —

youth: anxieties about, 5; category shaped by age, class, and race, 9; commodification of, 41; and prolonged dependency during Depression, 17, 53–54; shared culture of prolonged schooling, 5, 50; synonymous with beauty, 40–43

Zelizer, Viviana, 18
zoot suit, 64–69, 72–73, 80, 124. *See also* Boys' (size range); Grad (size range); suits

Printed and bound in Canada

Set in Dante MT Pro with HooliganJF, TamarilloJF, P22 Underground,
and TT Norms by Lara Minja, Lime Design
Copyeditor: Camilla Blakeley
Proofreader: Kristy Lynn Hankewitz
Cover designer: Lara Minja, Lime Design
Cover images: Archives of Ontario, T. Eaton Company fonds,
T. Eaton Toronto catalogues: F 229-1-0-169, Spring/Summer 1948 (top);
F 229-1-0-139, Spring/Summer 1941 (bottom left and right).
Authorized Representative: Easy Access System Europe – Mustamäe tee 50,
10621 Tallinn, Estonia, gpsr.requests@easproject.com